9371173

Organizational Behavior and Public Management

PUBLIC ADMINISTRATION AND PUBLIC POLICY

A Comprehensive Publication Program

Executive Editor

JACK RABIN
Graduate Program for Administrators
Rider College
Lawrenceville, New Jersey

Other volumes in preparation

Organizational Behavior and Public Management

Debra W. Stewart
G. David Garson

*Department of Political Science
and Public Administration
North Carolina State University
Raleigh, North Carolina*

MARCEL DEKKER, INC.   New York and Basel

Library of Congress Cataloging in Publication Data

Stewart, Debra W.
  Organizational behavior and public management.

  (Public administration and public policy ; 17)
  Includes bibliographies and index.
  1. Organizational behavior. 2. Public administration.
I. Garson,G. David. II. Title. III. Series.
HD58.7.S745 1983   350   83-5145
ISBN 0-8247-7008-0

MARCEL DEKKER, INC.
270 Madison Avenue, New York, New York 10016

Current printing (last digit):
10 9 8 7 6 5 4 3 2 1

PRINTED IN THE UNITED STATES OF AMERICA

PREFACE

DEFINING OUR TERMS

Organizational behavior is a field of study which focuses on the behaviors, attitudes, and performances of people within an organization. It is especially concerned with the influence of both formal organization and informal group structure on employees, the effect of employees on the organization, and the work environment's effect on both the organization and on the people working within it. (Szilagyi and Wallace, 1980.) Students of organizational behavior want to know all about what people *do* in organizations. Because of this broad focus, the field is necessarily interdisciplinary, drawing heavily from the behavioral sciences, particularly the core disciplines of anthropology, psychology, and sociology. The purpose of behavioral science research is to improve the manager's ability to predict the behavior of people, so knowledge generated by Organizational Behavior research speaks to questions posed by managers. For the most part, practitioners set the research agenda for the organizational behavior field.

Because of its focus on the behavior of people, psychology has contributed heavily to the concepts and theories of organizational behavior. Most research is conducted on three levels: analysis of the individual, the group, and the organization. Also of special interest to us is how organizations change.

Since so little work has been done on public management, there is no conceptual framework in this area (Allison, 1979) on which we may smugly hang our hat. We must rely on plain English to explain what public management is.

Management is simply the organization and direction of resources to achieve a desired result, so public management must be the organization and direction of such resources in the public or governmental sector. General management functions can be broken down into: planning, organizing, staffing, directing, coordinating, reporting, and budgeting. (Gulick, 1937.) These functions are common to both public and private sector management. But we cannot overemphasize the great difference that a public setting makes in how these activities are carried out. This is what our book is about.

In the public sector, diffusion of power and political accountability make the critical difference. While in private business general management functions are concentrated in the Chief Executive Officer, these functions are, by constitutional design, spread in the public sector among a number of competing institutions. Thus, they are shared by a number of individuals whose ambitions are set against one another. (Allison, 1979.) The three branches of government and the three levels of government—a design rooted in balance of power and federalist principles—join to produce this unique management environment.

The public setting creates a different context for management on a number of specific dimensions. Four important differences are:

- Time Horizon—government managers have short horizons for implementing programs, a product of the election cycle.
- Performance Measurement—little agreement exists on standards and measurement of performance. The private sector's bottom line of profit has no counterpart in the public sector.
- Personnel Constraints—the existence of two layers of management, civil service and political appointees, each with a measure of autonomy vis à vis the other, frustrates the capacity for control possible in private management.
- Press and Media Relations—the public has a "right to know" about public management activities while the private manager freely denies media access to management decision making.

ON THE INTERSECTION: FOCUS OF THIS TEXT

The first teaching of "public administration" took place in departments of political science, but as the domain of "public service" grew through the 20th century, and the range of activities demanding management expertise expanded, students of public management pressed beyond the boundaries of the parent discipline. Driven by an environment oblivious to disciplinary limits, contemporary public management study is marked by the convergence of several disciplines.

This book is on the intersection of organizational behavior and public management studies. It centers on the human behavior issues public managers confront in organizing and directing resources to advance the programs and policies of their agencies. Figure 1 displays four qualities guiding inquiry on the intersection.

Studying organizational behavior in a public management context is necessarily interdisciplinary, drawing on the traditional behavioral sciences of psychology,

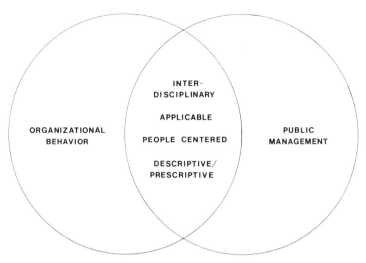

Figure 1. The intersection of organizational behavior and public management.

sociology and anthropology, as well as the more normatively oriented disciplines of political science and economics. But theory as it emerges in these disciplines doesn't always present itself in a useful form. Harlan Cleveland has noted: "The tightest bottleneck in modern civilization just now is relevant theory." (Cleveland, 1979.) This means our theories must be applicable to everyday management experience to be useful to anyone. Literature at the intersection of organizational behavior and public management needs to meet this standard of applicability. Modern study of organizational behavior from a public management perspective thus becomes an exercise in theory application. The success of our theories and their applications is measured by our capacity to illuminate the feelings, attitudes and behaviors of real people, the human resources of the public organization. The analytical skills generated and/or sharpened by the study of organizational behavior in a public sector context must be both descriptive and prescriptive in kind. Study at the intersection will equip public managers to analyze both critical cause and effect relationships in organizations and will raise questions about how human interaction should proceed in modern organizations. In summary, this book focuses on the intersection of organizational behavior and public management. As an area of study that intersection is *interdisciplinary, applicable, people centered,* and both *descriptive* and *prescriptive.*

Study centering on this intersection of organizational behavior and public management may be more important today than ever before. In recent years public confidence in government has dipped to an all-time low. In 1964, 69 percent of Americans acknowledge their government leaders, ". . .know what they are doing," but by 1978 that figure dropped to 40 percent. In the late 1950's, 56 percent of Americans polled believed, "You can trust the government in Washington to do what is right most of the time." By the late 70's the figure dropped to 29 percent. (Cleveland, 1979.) In fairness we should stress that the drop in confidence is a realistic reflection of a more complex world. Nonetheless the public demand for performance and efficiency from government is intense. A study of organizational behavior premised on the need for self-conscious development of a public management approach to managing people in organizations is one way to help meet this demand.

CONTENT AND STRUCTURE

Our book moves from a micro- to a macro-analysis in two respects: first, from individual to group to organization; and second, from isolated instances of applied theoretical concerns to organizational challenges stimulating concerted managerial response. Figure 2 illustrates the progression of the chapters.

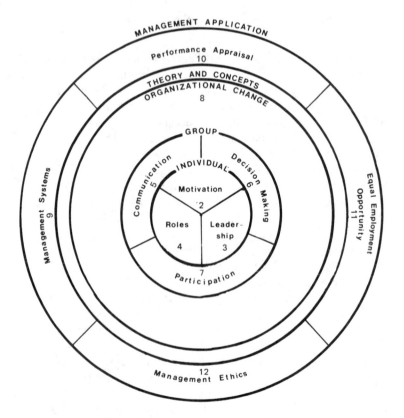

Figure 2. Content and structure of the book.

The first analytical cut takes the *individual* as the unit of analysis. Three bodies of literature consider individual actors in organizational life: motivation theory, role theory, and leadership theory. Following the introduction the first three chapters draw on these literatures to show how individual predispositions and situational characteristics join to produce particular attitudes and behaviors of people at work. The *group* provides the second subject for analysis. Three aspects of group interaction central to organizational performance, communication, decision making, and participation, are discussed in the next three chapters. To achieve its mission an organization must be able to modify its own patterns and practices, so we discuss the *organization* and its capacity for change in Chapter 8.

Literature dealing with individual, group, and organizational variables provides insight into organizational life in public agencies by providing concepts and propositions generated through decades of research on organizational behavior. But each of these homes in on a single aspect of human activity while freezing for analytical purposes other dimensions of life in the organization. The fourth concentric circle in Figure 2, labeled *management applications*, signifies the four chapters exploring applied management problems. Drawing on implicit or explicit models of how individuals and groups function and how organizations change, these chapters provide opportunity for integrated analysis of all dimensions of organizational behavior. This holistic thrust is accomplished by examining four specific management challenges: performance appraisal, equal employment opportunity, management information systems, and management ethics.

REFERENCES

Allison, Graham T., Jr. (1979), Public and Private Management: Are They Fundamentally Alike in All Unimportant Respects? *Setting Public Management Research Agendas*, Proceedings for the Public Management Research Conference, U.S.O.P.M., November 19-20, Washington, D.C.

Cleveland, Harlan (1979), Public Management Research: The Theory of Practice and Vice Versa, *Setting Public Management Research Agendas*, Proceedings for the Public Management Research Conference, U.S.O.P.M., November 19-20, Washington, D.C.

Gulick, Luther and Lyndall Urwick, Eds. (1937), *Papers on the Science of Administration*, New York: Institute of Public Administration.

Szilagyi, Andrew D., Jr. and Marc J. Wallace, Jr. (1980), *Organizational Behavior and Performance*, 2nd Ed., Santa Monica, Ca.: Goodyear Publishing Company.

Debra W. Stewart
G. David Garson

CONTENTS

PART II - MANAGEMENT APPLICATIONS

Organizational Behavior and Public Management

INTRODUCTION

This book is structured analytically and centers on issues public managers face in organizations. While learning is facilitated by freezing all dimensions of organizational life save that which one is studying at a particular point in time, the theories and concepts, the tools of organizational analysis, were born in a holistic context. Thinking about the total nature of work led theorists to generate propositions and concepts to help managers better understand organizational behavior and foster the achievement of organizational objectives. Thus, for example, when we focus on the individual in the early chapters of the text we introduce theories and concepts which reappear in later analysis of group behavior. A brief historical overview of the theoretical development which generated the blocks for building a theory of public management and organizational behavior provides a kind of mental anchoring for the concepts and constructs as they are introduced and reappear in the chapters.

Organizations are human groupings deliberately constructed and reconstructed to seek specific goals (Parsons, 1960). As such they exhibit certain ideal type features which Max Weber described in his observation of the Prussian civil service. Weber saw bureaucracy as inevitably associated with industrial development. The dominant trait of bureaucracy, a new form of organization in the late 1800's, was its impersonality. As a neutral structure, able to function under very different personalities, bureaucracy was an apparatus characterized by technical competence, predictability of action, precision, and stability. In a sense 20th century organizational studies can be viewed as continuing Weber's effort to understand the bureaucratic institutions, but the specific aspects of organizations studied and the values motivating such works vary greatly. The major streams of thought contributing to public management studies can be subsumed under five distinct approaches: classical, human relations, decision making, neohuman relations, and systems models.

THE CLASSICAL APPROACH

The classical approach to organizational studies grew from the desire to reach organizational goals more effectively and efficiently. At the shop level it was expressed in terms of a theory of work design and motivation known as Scientific Management. Frederick W. Taylor, a turn of the century industrial consultant, fathered Scientific Management in America. Taylor's approach was to study operations, analyze all relevant facets of the work situation and derive from this observation principles to ensure efficiency in operation. Four general principles of scientific management formed the framework for managerial action: 1) workers should be scientifically selected, trained, and placed in jobs for which they are mentally and physically suited; 2) the job to be done should be analyzed scientifically; 3) close cooperation between supervisor and worker is necessary to ensure deviations from scientific methods of work are minimal; 4) management and workers should share responsibility—each for their own part in the overall production effort (Taylor, 1911). Scientific management focused on micro-issues of employer-employee dynamics.

A second theme in the classical approach addressed the macro level issues of administering the organization as a whole and debated the relative worth of alternative administrative structures. The underlying assumption of this school was that management was a universal process, the same across kinds of organizations and cultures. Accordingly, this literature spelled out the "rules" or principles associated with the five central managerial functions of planning, organizing, staffing, directing, and controlling. In the late 1930's, Luther Gulick and Lyndall Urwick summarized the major tenets of this administrative theory in their *Papers on The Science of Administration* (Gulick and Urwick, 1937).

Authors in the classic approach are linked by their focus on the organization or bureau as the unit of analysis and by their concern with issues of hierarchy, authority, chain of command, efficiency, and effectiveness.

THE HUMAN RELATIONS APPROACH

The human relations approach to management studies stemmed from empirical research which found workers and their interpersonal relations to significantly affect what happens in an organization. The central tenets of this approach emerged from a series of studies known as the Hawthorne Studies conducted by Elton Mayo at Western Electric Company's Hawthorne Works from 1927 to 1932. The results of the Hawthorne studies were popularized by Roethlisberger and Dickson in their volume, *Management and the Worker*. The thinking of the Human Relations School can be summarized in three points: 1) "The level of production is set by social norms, not by physiological capacity. . .; 2) noneconomic rewards and sanctions significantly affect the behavior of workers and largely limit the effect of economic incentives and plans. . .; 3) often workers do not act or react as individuals but as members of groups" (Etzioni, 1964). Significant implications accompanied this shift from a focus on the organization (the classical approach) to a focus on the individual and the work group. With inquiry centered on inter-personal and intergroup relations, communications, and motivation, the value to be achieved became worker satisfaction.

THE DECISION MAKING APPROACH

In many ways the classical approach and the human relations approach are diamet-rically opposed in both focus and goals for analysis. A third model, often called the decision making approach, stands apart from but draws on each tradition. The unit of analysis in this approach is the decision a manager makes.

This approach traces its ancestry to Chester Barnard, who wrote in the late 1930's. His work, *The Functions of the Executive* (1938) called attention to the individual decision to participate in an organization. Barnard saw the manager's job as allocating satisfactions or rewards in exchange for an employee's acquiesence to the prescribed behavior. But it was Herbert Simon, writing in the 1950's, who described organizational behavior explicitly in terms of the decision processes in-volved. In his classic book, *Administrative Behavior* (1957), Simon portrays or-ganizational decision making as a kind of compromise between rational, goal-oriented behavior and nonrational behavior. An organization provides the frame-work for a decision making process in which people characteristically look for a course of action which is not perfect, but rather is good enough in a given situation. In other words, organizational actors will select the "satisfactory" alternative rather than relentlessly pursue the optimal solution to problems (Simon, 1957). Building on this model of organizational actors as decision makers, Cyert and March (1963) went on to describe organizations as decision making systems with special focus on the degree of rationality decision making systems can develop. Generally, the values endorsed by the decision making approach are those of rationality, efficiency, and productivity.

Two additional approaches offer interpretations of organizational behavior. Each traces its roots to an earlier approach. While there are marked differences between these two approaches their points of view are complimentary on some dimensions of analysis.

THE NEOHUMAN RELATIONS APPROACH

The neohuman relations approach is an expression of contemporary organizational psychology. It traces its ancestry to the Harvard group of Mayo, Roethlisberger, and Dickson and it shares with that tradition a concern for intergroup and interpersonal relations. However, it criticizes traditional human relations for seeking easy answers or techniques instead of questioning organizational structures and philosophies (Silverman, 1977).

Abraham Maslow's work on motivation forms the basis for much subsequent writing in this school. According to Maslow human needs can be considered in terms of a hierarchy. The lowest level or physiological needs for food, shelter, and the like motivate behavior until they are satisfied. Next come safety needs and so on up the hierarchy with each need becoming operative only when the next lower level need has been satisfied. The need to self-actualize holds top place in the need hierarchy.

The neohuman relations scholars adopt this hierarchy of needs model and derive from it specific recommendations about managerial action. Douglas McGregor distinguishes between Theory X and Theory Y management. Theory X management assumes employees are motivated by lower level needs while Theory Y rejects that assumption. Believing people to be growth oriented, Theory Y management encourages people to assume responsibility and actively participate in organizational decision making. Renis Likert describes work designs which would foster that possibility (Likert, 1961). The values promoted by this approach are those of personal growth, individual dignity and organizational effectiveness.

THE SYSTEMS APPROACH

The systems approach to organizational studies traces its ancestry to the decision making approach with its strong emphasis on process and rich description. But the purposes of the systems approach are different: rather than striving for efficiency, rationality, and productivity the scholars in this tradition try to understand existing structures. The basic assumptions underlying the notion of organization as a system are: 1) organizations are made up of independent parts; 2) organizations take actions. The classic description of an organization as a system appears in Katz and Kahn, *The Social Psychology of Organizations* (1966). The authors present a process model for describing organizations in terms system "inputs," "throughputs," and "outputs." They argue that organizations are open systems which interact with their environment and are shaped by their environment.

The neohuman relations approach and the systems approach come together in a very applied expression—organization development. Organization development (OD) refers to the intervening of external or internal behavioral science consultants in organizations to improve an organization's problem-solving capabilities and its capacity to cope with its external environment. OD is based on assumptions and values similar to those of Theory Y but includes assumptions about total systems and the values of an organization's relationship to its environment (French, 1973). Its basic method typically includes five phases: data collection, diagnosis, action planning, intervention, and evaluation.

CONCLUSION

The five basic approaches to organizational behavior outlined above are offered as background for our discussion of theory, concepts and their application to public sector management. A public manager uses the knowledge of human behavior to build an environment conducive to achieving goals mandated by the people through their representatives. We turn now to the most basic question managers face in trying to create that environment—how do we motivate employees?

REFERENCES

Barnard, C. (1938), *The Functions of the Executive*. Boston: Harvard University Press.

Cyert, R. M. and J. G. March (1963), *A Behavioral Theory of the Firm*. New York: Wiley.

Etzioni, Amitai (1964), *Modern Organizations*. Englewood Cliffs, New Jersey: Prentice-Hall.

French, Wendell (1973), Organizational Development: Objectives, Assumptions, and Strategies, in Jong S. Jun and William B. Storm (eds.) *Tomorrow's Organization*. Glenview, Illinois: Scott, Foresman and Company.

Gulick, L. and L. Urwick, eds. (1937), Papers on the Science of Administration. New York: Institute of Public Administration, Columbia University.

Katz, D. and R. Kahn (1966), *The Social Psychology of Organizations*. New York: Wiley.

Likert, Renis (1961), *New Patterns of Management*. New York: McGraw Hill.

Parsons, Talcott (1960), Structure and Process in Modern Societies, Glencoe, Illinois: The Free Press.

Raethlisberger, F. J., W. J. Dickson (1939), *Management and the Worker*.

Silverman, David (1971), *The Theory of Organizations*. New York: Basic Books.

Simon, Herbert (1957), Administrative Behavior (2nd ed.). New York: The Macmillan Company.

Taylor, Fredrick W. (1911), *The Principles of Scientific Management*. New York: Harper and Bros.

PART I
THEORY AND CONCEPTS

MOTIVATION

Every organization needs people. In the public sector people may be the most important resource. Stimulating employees' decisions to participate and to produce at work is the hallmark of an effective organization. (March and Simon, 1958.) To be sure, in studying motivation we look at only one aspect of the human factor in organizational performance. But from the vantage point of public managers at all levels, wedding human action to achieving organizational objectives begins with an understanding of motivation.

The importance of motivation as a starting point for studying behavior is confirmed by the extensive and sustained interest of the research community in this topic. This chapter introduces the fundamentals of motivation literature, outlining both motivation and work setting theories and how they stimulate each other. Next, we consider motivational models applying the basic principles to the work setting, and stress the limitations of these models in public sector application. Finally, the critical issue of the relationship between job satisfaction and performance is addressed. We propose to highlight and compare rather than to advocate any single theory.

BASIC MOTIVATION THEORY

Why do human beings behave as they do? For many students of organizations this is the fundamental question in the study of human motivation. Yet, by the way this question is posed, it posits a certain assumption. It presupposes a *cognitive* approach to the study of human behavior. This approach is best understood by reference to a simple model (Fig. 3).

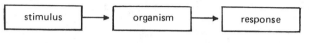

Figure 3.

As the model indicates, this approach is guided by a single question: what takes place in the organism to produce a specific response to a given stimulus? Questioning changes in or experiences of the organism assumes that what counts as an explanation for behavior is an understanding or an elaboration of those antecedent events in the person. Conscious thoughts or decisions are presumed to intervene between the stimulus from the person's environment and the behavior that follows. Understanding behavior demands understanding these experiences that trigger conscious thoughts or decisions.

Some theorists shun cognitive approaches in favor of acognitive approaches to studying human behavior. Denying the importance of changes in the human organism, proponents of the *acognitive* approach focus on the influence of the environment to account for human behavior. Faithful to the tradition of B. F. Skinner, acognitive theorists consider the type of reinforcement for behavior as critical. Both cognitive and acognitive approaches hold important lessons for students of organizational behavior.

THE COGNITIVE APPROACH

The general assumption of the cognitive approach is that understanding how and why human behavior occurs is possible. The organism is perceived to be an active link in the stimulus → organism → response chain. But theorists disagree on what transpires within the organism to produce that behavior.

The philosophy of hedonism sums up our very earliest understanding of why humans behave as they do. Articulated by the early Greek philosophers and advanced in the 19th century social philosophies of Adam Smith, Jeremy Bentham, and John Stuart Mill, hedonism explains behavior in terms of the pain/pleasure principle—organisms try to maximize pleasure and minimize pain. Thorndike, the early empirical psychologist, buttressed hedonism as an explanation by pointing out how animals, when confronted with puzzle boxes, would learn to master them when the solution led to pleasurable outcome.

> *Of several responses made to the same situation, those which are accompanied or closely followed by satisfaction. . .will, other things being equal, be more firmly connected to the situation, so that, when it recurs, they will be more likely to recur; those which are accompanied or closely followed by discomfort. . .will, other things being equal, have their connections with that situation weakened, so that, when it recurs, they will be less likely to occur. The greater the satisfaction or discomfort the greater the strengthening or weakening of the bond. (Thorndike, 1911).*

William James, in his seminal work, *Principles of Psychology*, stressed two additional concepts which shaped psychological analysis at that time: the instinct and the unconscious. These two concepts formed the core of one of three major approaches to understanding motivation, the tension reduction approach. In this discussion of cognitive approaches to motivation we will first look at the evolution of this *tension reduction approach* and then turn to a discussion of two additional approaches to understanding motivation, the *expectancy value approach,* and the *human growth and development approach.*

Drive or Tension Reduction Theory

The concept of instinct, acknowledged by James, found full-blown defense and elaboration in Darwin's *Origin of the Species* published in 1859. Seeing human beings as different from animals only in terms of a continuous biological evolution, Darwin turned to "instinct" to explain human and animal action. The term "instinct" was defined for psychologists by William McDougall in his 1908 work, *Introduction to Social Psychology*.

> *"We may then define an instinct as an inherited or innate psycho-physical disposition which determines its possessor to perceive, and to pay attention to, objects of a certain kind, and to experience an emotional excitement of a particular quality upon perceiving such an object, and to act in regard to it in a particular manner, or at least, to experience an impulse to such action."*

Explaining behavior in terms of instinct was favored by psychologists in this earlier period, but with the growth of instinct theory and the proliferation of "instincts" (McDougall proposed a list of eighteen), disagreement among psychologists became apparent. By the 1930's this proliferation of instincts, accompanied by disagreement among the researchers as to what was or wasn't an instinct, led to a general abandoning of the instinct concept as "unscientific."

The concept of "drive" soon came to replace instinct as the explanation for action. Woodsworth had introduced the notion of drive as early as 1819 in his work *Dynamic Psychology*. Another psychologist, Edward Tolman, contributed to the development of the drive concept in his work, *Purposive Behavior in Animals and Men* (1932). Clark Hull fully developed the drive concept. His model was simple: Behavior = Drive x Habit. In controlled laboratory settings Hull tested hypotheses derived from mathematical models. The ultimate decline in these highly scientific and empirically based drive theories is attributed to their gradual neglect of the cognitive process and their assumption that human beings were analogous to machines. (Weiner, 1980.) Today the instinct or drive concept is alive among ethologists, who study instinctive behavior among animals and use these findings to theorize about aspects of human behavior.

Freudian psychoanalytic theories constitute a second type of drive—need reduction explanations for human action. Individuals act in order to meet personal needs. Needs are met by some form of adapting to the world. Two core concepts in Freudian thinking are homeostasis, the tendency toward the maintenance of a relatively stable environment, and hedonis, the seeking of pleasure and happiness. Pleasure results from being in a state of equilibrium with all one's goals satisfied. Critical to this tension reduction process are the components of the personality: the *id*, which is responsible for all psychological energy, the *ego*, with its power to delay gratification, and the *super ego*, the conscience of the personality. While the pleasure principle governs the id, the ego is regulated by the reality principle. It is the conflict generated in the interaction between the id and the ego that is the core of the Freudian view of motivation.

> *"The ego, driven by the id, confined by the super ego, repulsed by reality, struggles to master its economic task of bringing about harmony among the forces and influences working in and on it." (Freud, 1933, cited in Weiner, 1980.)*

According to Freud, all behavior is ultimately drive-determined, an unconscious process. The tendency toward drive reduction is omnipresent because it yields pleasure.

Theorists in this tradition, whether psychoanalytic or more empirical, see behavior as determined by psychological energy (in Freud, the id; in Hull, habits). They also share the belief that actions are taken to satisfy unmet needs (homeostasis) and that fulfillment of these needs is satisfying (hedonism). The major difference is the much more highly scientific and empirical approach taken by the drive reductionists.

Expectancy Value Theories

Kurt Lewin is truly a bridge theorist between earlier drive theorists and contemporary expectancy value theorists. Like Freud and Hull, Lewin makes both hedonistic and homeostasis assumptions about human behavior. New in Lewin, and central to all expectancy value theories, is the assumption that human behavior is determined by how the world is perceived. Lewin's conceptual framework of "field theory" sees behavior as a function of the person and the environment $[B = F (P, E)]$. People have needs which create tensions. Tension can be dissipated only by attaining goals in the environment. The amount of valence (value to a person) an object in the environment holds is related to the intensity of the need in the person. In addition to the intensity of the need and properties of the object in the environment (valence), the relative distance of a person from his goal comes into play to influence the amount of force on a person to act. The formula Lewin proposed saw force as a function of the value of the goal and the psychological distance between the person and the goal.

$$\text{force} = F \; \frac{Va(G)}{e}$$

When the goal is obtained the need is met and the tension relieved because the object loses its positive value, thus the "force field" is removed. (Weiner, 1980).

Building on the perception dimension introduced by Kurt Lewin, David McClelland articulated an expectation—determined conception of motivation. Focusing specifically on the notion of achievement, McClelland and his close associate Atkinson, postulated that striving for achievement depends on a combination of expectancy of success and value of success. They used the projective Thematic Apperception Test (TAT) developed by Murray (Weiner, 1980) to measure achievement. In the TAT individuals were asked to write stories about ambiguous pictures. Their motivational differences are measured by their responses. The full-blown theory of motivation advanced by Atkinson based on work conducted with McClelland suggests that achievement related behavior is a function of a conflict between hope for success (labeled approach motivation) and fear of failure (called avoidance motivation) (Atkinson, 1962). The approach and avoidance tendencies in any situation result from:

1. the need for achievement and anxiety about failure;
2. the expectancy of success and failure;
3. the incentive value of success or failure.

The third expectancy value motivation theory with implications for organizational behavior is identified with the psychologist Julian Rotter. Rotter, a social learning theorist, stressed the importance of the external situation as a determinant of behavior. As with all expectancy value theorists, behavior in his view is a function of the expectancy of goal attainment and the value of the goal. However, the expectancy variable is formulated by Rotter in a different way. Expectancy in Rotter's work is a "product of the prior reinforcement history in a specific stimulus situation and a generalized belief about reinforcers learned from behavior in similar situations." (Weiner, 1980.) An important development in Rotter's research concerns the differences in perceptions of environment as personally or externally controlled. Persons with "internal locus of control" display more information seeking and make better use of information than do persons with external locus of control.

Human Growth and Development Theory

The third major approach to understanding human motivation finds its most popular expression in the works of Abraham Maslow. Common to the group of humanistic psychologists including Maslow, Carl Rogers, and Gordon Alport is the thesis that people are fundamentally motivated to grow and to enhance themselves. Acceptance of a tendency towards self actualization is a basic tenet of this humanistic psychology. Such a tendency is not itself subject to testing.

Abraham Maslow, organizer and first president of the Association of Humanistic Psychology, dominated the study of motivation within humanistic psychology with his conceptualization of a hierarchy of needs. Maslow saw human beings as motivated by a hierarchal system of basic, "instinctoid" needs. These hierarchically arranged needs include, from lowest to highest level, physiological needs, safety needs, affiliative needs, esteemed needs and, finally, the need to self actualize. A later development in Maslow's work included creativity, knowledge, understanding, and aesthetic fulfillment as needs critical to understanding motivation. Lower level needs, according to Maslow, will dominate the next higher level need until the lower level need is met. For example, the need for friendship (affiliative) would not be felt until one is fed, clothed, and sheltered. (Maslow, 1943.) Only unsatisfied needs are motivators. When a need is satisfied, a higher level need emerges to motivate behavior.

Looking back into the work discussed earlier in the drive reduction focus of Freud and Hull, Maslow characterizes lower level needs as deficient values: "attainment of their desired goal produced tension reduction and returning the organism to a state of equilibrium." (Weiner, 1980.) But Maslow also describes a different set of values. *Being* values are those values associated with growth motivation. These values are sought in self actualization. This focus on growth and development is the hallmark of this approach.

The Examination of Specific Motives

In the discussion of three major approaches to understanding human motivation, a number of specific motives have been mentioned. Motives have been categorized in the literature, as the foregoing review suggests, in a variety of ways. One typology common to several approaches dicotomizes needs into primary and secondary motives. Primary motives are innate and biogenic, while secondary motives are acquired and psychogenic. Primary motives typically include hunger, thirst, sex, pain avoidance, rest, and sleep. The secondary list typically includes security, affiliation, achievement, and competence. These latter four motivators have been the subject of considerable research. They are particularly important factors in the study of organizational behavior.

Security

Security motives should be understood as an extension of biogenic needs to an expanded time frame. (Behling, 1976.) In post-industrial societies, security is defined as economic in nature. Morgan and King see security motives as the feeling involved in holding on to what one has, in being sure that the future will treat one as well as the past. Insecurity by contrast means fearing that " 'things may not last,' that one may lose what one now has." (Morgan and King, 1966.) Saul Gellerman refines the notion of security motive to distinguish between conscious security motives, as discussed above, and unconscious security motives. A person guided by this unconscious security motive is burdened by a vague feeling that the environment is threatening. (Gellerman, 1963.)

> *"All conscious security motives, . . . result from early experiences which portray life as either too uncontrollable to make initiative worthwhile or too benevolent to make initiative necessary. The individual therefore, places himself. . .at the mercy of the environment, with either a sense of futility or sense of subligned assurance." (Gellerman, 1963.)*

The unconscious security motive leads the individual to seek out a safe and protective environment.

Affiliation

Affiliation is often thought to be a second major source of motivation in our society. Where the achievement motive, discussed next, is directed largely to task, affiliation refers to the social context necessary to support action. Elton Mayo, theorizing from the work of the French sociologist Emiel Durkheim, saw the need for affiliation as a central part of work. Work groups assume such great importance because people seek out stable social relationships not available to them elsewhere in industrial society (Mayo, 1945.)

Research rich in potential for management application focuses on conditions eliciting expression of need for affiliation. Relying on anecdotal and autobiographical sources, Stanley Schachter (1959) reports that people who are imprisoned, lost or in some sense prevented from social contact report anxiety and discomfort. In an experimental setting, affiliation with others has been shown to be a way of reducing anxiety. In Schachter's famous "misery loves company" experiment, one group of women were told they would receive painful shock and a second group were told they would receive mild shock. While waiting for the study to begin each group was given the opportunity to choose whether they would wait alone or with other women who were waiting for the study to begin. Twice as many women who were "high anxiety" (in the group anticipating painful shock) chose to wait with other women rather than to wait alone. However, in a second study, Schachter found that women anticipating shock if given a choice of waiting alone or with other women not involved in the experiment, all preferred to wait alone. The summary conclusion from these studies is that misery does love company, but it must be company in the same boat. While in general threatening situations producing anxiety can enhance the need for affiliation, not all kinds of adverse situations produce that effect. Sarnoff and Zimbardo (1961) found that when male subjects had to suck a pacifier instead of receiving a shock as the experiment "treatment" they prefer to wait alone. Shame or embarassment as an adverse condition doesn't lead to the need for affiliation.

Approval

The need for comfort is not the only driving force behind affiliation. Sometimes we seek the company of others simply to gain social approval. While substantial variation exists in the need for social approval, it does seem that there's an inter-action between affiliation and the approval need. Affiliation may be a consequence of a need for approval but continuation of affiliation may depend on whether ap-proval is forthcoming (Jung, 1978.) Research on variation in approval needs has produced a number of interesting findings for students of organizations. People high in approval motivation are found to be more likely to conform to group standards. Individuals with a strong drive for approval seem to learn more rapidly when the experimenter approves of correct responses than when he remains silent. Finally need for approval may influence choice of task. In one study—a dart throw-ing situation—where subjects were permitted to stand at any distance from the target, individuals high on approval motive chose intermediate distances. The mid-dle ground was viewed as the most socially desirable place to stand. (Lindsey, et al., 1967.)

Achievement

The achievement motive is the desire to be successful in a competition situation (Luthens, 1972.) Considerable research aims to describe the high achievers. The high achiever is a person who will take moderate risks and wants immediate feed-back. Such persons tend to rely on the satisfaction of accomplishing the task as the reward and often shun extrinsic rewards. High achievers tend to be very task-oriented (McClelland, 1961).

Of all the motives discussed, achievement has been the most thoroughly re-searched in the applied management literature. The question always asked is: how can need for achievement be enhanced? Though achievement-related dispositions are thought to be formed in childhood, the product of early independence train-ing, achievement theorists have initiated programs designed to improve the need to achieve. Such programs teach the advantage of intermediate risk taking and de-ferred gratification. McClelland and his associates have tried to increase partici-pants' need to achieve through such programming. Specifically, McClelland's achievement development training aims to increase the need for achievement by:

1. teaching people to think and talk and act like a person with high achievement;
2. stimulating people to set higher but carefully planned and real-istic work goals for themselves;
3. giving people knowledge about themselves;
4. creating a group espirit de corps though the group experience (McClelland, 1966).

However, at this point the effectiveness of achievement motivation change remains

uncertain. Positive results have been reported with under achievers (Kolb, 1965), school teachers (de Charms, 1972) and businessmen (McClelland and Winter, 1969). However the amount of research to date on expanding achievement needs remains small. (Weiner, 1980.)

Competence

Competence, sometimes called mastery, is a concept proposed by Robert White in 1959. It has seldom been the direct subject of psychological research, though its application as a motivator in organizational behavior is significant. Proponents of the competence concept suggest that a central motive underlying behavior is the person's ability to interact effectively with the environment.

One psychologist, Nutten (1973), has found that a "causality pleasure" results from a subject causing an event. In his research children were placed in an experimental room containing two "machines." Each machine was equipped with colored lights and movable handles. For machine A, lights went on according to preprogramming by the experimenter. The lights on machine B went on and off when the handle was moved beyond a certain point. Both machines provided perceptual stimulation, but the children caused the stimulation only with machine B. Researchers found that children preferred machine B over machine A. Other mastery experiments with children suggest that accomplishment augments a feeling of confidence, yielding a pleasurable feeling resulting from engaging in the action.

THE ACOGNITIVE APPROACH

One assumption guides the work of all motivation theories in the cognitive tradition. Transformations occurring in the organism explain behavior in the stimulus → organism → response process. In contrast, the acognitive approach to understanding behavior eschews any concern with events transpiring in the organism itself in favor of examining the relationship between the stimulus and the response. The seminal work in the acognitive tradition is that of B. F. Skinner.

The principle guiding Skinner's theory is that behavior is determined by its consequences. Behling elaborates on this basic principle by identifying three characteristics of Skinner's thought which set it apart from other approaches to motivation.

1. The organism is a passive mediating element in the stimulus → organism → response chain.
2. There is no need to postulate any internal or external need or purpose to explain behavior.
3. Operant conditioning explains most kind of behavior. (Behling, 1976.)

This last point requires some explanation. Behling describes operant conditioning as follows:

> "In simplest form, operant conditioning presupposes an organism emitting random behavior. It explores its environment and acts upon it in many ways. These behaviors are followed by a variety of environmental consequences - some favorable to the organism, some neutral, some noxious . . . these consequences determine the likelihood that a given operant behavior will be emitted in the future, and to change behavior one must change the consequences of the behavior and/or rearrange contingencies (the way in which the consequences are related to the behavior)."

Environmental consequences come in four basic types: positive reinforcement, omission, punishment, and negative reinforcement (see Table 1). They are defined by whether a pleasant or a noxious consequence is present or absent. Each of these processes can be understood in a classroom example provided by Hampton, et al.

> ". . .an instructor may provide students with positive reinforcement in the form of high grades for writing good essay examinations. The examination system may provide students with negative reinforcement in the form of anxiety about examinations; the anxiety is removed by completing the examinations. The instructor may not reinforce. . .class participation by omitting credit for it. The instructor may punish class participation by providing sarcastic and humiliating critiques of ideas voiced by participating students." (Hampton, et al., 1978, p. 545.)

These consequences yield two strategies for controlling human behavior. Affirmative strategies strengthen behavior by producing pleasant consequences or diminish behavior by removing existing reinforcing consequences, and are more appropriate in the managerial context. The adversive control strategies of punishment, in particular, often backfire on managers and may even worsen a situation by affecting general morale (Brown and Presbie, 1976.)

TABLE 1. Operant Conditioning Control Strategies

	Consequences Presented	Consequences Removed	
Pleasant Consequences	Positive Reinforcement	Omission	Affirmative Control Strategies
Noxious Consequences	Punishment	Negative Reinforcement	Adversive Control Strategies

Source: From *Introduction to Modern Behaviorism* by Howard Rachlin. W. H. Freeman and Company. 2nd Bd. Copyright 1976, p. 77.

A key concept in the organizational application of Skinner's theory is the reinforcement schedule, which concerns the quantitative relationship between environmental consequences and response. Different schedules are linked to different effects on behavior. (Fessler and Skinner, 1957; Skinner, 1969.) The key distinction comes between intermittent schedules, where the reinforcement does not follow every response, and continuous schedules, where the reinforcer does follow every response.

Most of the applications of operant conditioning principles have been in highly-controlled settings, such as mental hospitals (Allyon and Azrin, 1965), or prisons, or have been designed to effect only narrowly defined changes, such as in programmed learning situations (Petrock and Gamboa, 1976). Generalizing from such findings to organizational settings requires substantial caution. Still, as early as 1969 Nord argued that the work of B. F. Skinner had not been recognized in the administrative and management literature to the extent that it deserved. Serious application of this approach was advocated for organizations in the areas of personnel development, job design, compensation and alternative rewards, and organizational design. (Nord, 1969.) Work by Campbell (1971) and Jablonsky and DeVries (1972) made similar arguments.

MOTIVATION IN THE WORK PLACE

The preceding review of basic motivation theory provides the conceptual building blocks for models predicting and analyzing motivation on the job. Like the theories of motivation put forth above, research on employee motivation falls into two broad categories: 1) research focusing on how changes occurring in the worker yield changes in behavior (rooted in cognitive theory); and 2) research asking how reinforcement of behavior itself yields changed behavior (rooted in acognitive theory). Each of the three approaches in the cognitive tradition give rise to distinctive prescriptive models for motivating employees.

Applications Deriving from the Cognitive Tradition

The first model stemming from the human growth development approach is advanced by Douglas McGregor in his Theory X, Theory Y analysis of motivation. The second model, rooted in the drive reduction tradition, finds practical expression in Herzberg's two-factor theory of motivation. The third model stems from the expectancy-value approach to motivation and is put forth in the work of Victor Vroom and Porter and Lawler.

Douglas McGregor, in his classic work *The Human Side of Enterprise* (1957), builds a theory of work motivation premised on the humanistic psychology of Abraham Maslow. Two of Maslow's concepts are central:

1. There are at least five sets of goals which we may call basic
   needs. . .
2. These basic goals are related to each other, being arranged in a
   hierarchy of prepotency. .when a need is fairly well satisfied,
   the next prepotent ("higher") need emerges, in turn to dominate the conscious life and to serve as the center of organization of behavior, since gratified needs are not active motivators."
   (A. H. Maslow, 1943.)

Accepting this analysis of human nature with needs arranged from psysio-
logical, to safety, to social, to ego, to self fulfillment in ascending order of potency,
McGregor criticizes conventional managerial theory for making incorrect assumptions about the management process. According to McGregor conventional management theory, or Theory X, believes that without active intervention by management, people would be passive, even resistant, to organizational needs. Theory X
sees the average person as indolent by nature lacking ambition, disliking responsibility, and preferring to be led. The typical employee is inherently self-centered,
indifferent to organizational needs and by nature resistant to change. (McGregor,
1957.)

McGregor argues that the Theory X philosophy confuses cause and effect in
its analysis of human nature. If the employee in the modern organization is the
passive indifferent actor described above, it is in response to existing management
philosophy, policy and practice. She is "sick" because of deprivation of a higher
level need. This sickness has behavioral consequences outlined above. While the
contemporary organization meets the psychological and safety needs of most employees, social needs, ". . .for belonging, for acceptance by his fellows, for giving
and receiving friendship and love" are viewed by management as a threat to the
organization. Since a tendency to groupiness is natural in human beings, when
thwarted by a threatened management the employees may become "resistant, an-
tagonistic, uncooperative." But even if these social needs are met by management
the very structure of the contemporary organization would frustrate the fulfillment of the next two higher level needs: ego needs (needs for self-confidence, independence, achievement, status, and recognition), and self-fulfillment needs. The
outcome of this frustration is the worker depicted in the Theory X model.

As an alternative approach McGregor proposes a theory of management which
fits the real motivational structure of human beings. Theory Y management makes
these assumptions:

- "People are not by nature passive or resistant to organizational
  needs. They have become so as the result of experience in organizations.
- The motivation potential for development, the capacity for assuming responsibility, a readiness to direct behavior toward organizational goals are all present in people. . .It is a responsibility

of management to make it possible for people to develop these human characteristics for themselves.

- The essential task of management is to arrange organizational conditions and methods of operation so that people can achieve their own goals best by directing their own efforts toward organizational objectives." [McGregor (1957) in Natemeyer (1978).]

The level of motivation evident in any organization will be a function of the set of assumptions selected. According to McGregor, management is capable of constructing a climate that either opposes or enhances the motives people bring to the organization.

Though McGregor has enjoyed such popularity that Theory X - Theory Y analysis has become virtually conventional wisdom in organizational behavior, his work has not gone uncriticized. His principal critics allege that his application of Maslowian humanistic psychology to the work setting is simplistic. Indeed, we should point out that Maslow himself was too uncertain of the empirical validity of his own notions to feel fully comfortable with the applications that he saw in popular management literature. This uneasiness found clear expression in 1965 when Maslow wrote:

> "After all, if we take the whole thing from McGregor's point of view, a contrast between theory x view of human nature, a good deal of evidence upon which he bases his conclusions comes from my researches and my papers on motivation, self actualization, et. cetera. But I of all people should know just how shaky this foundation is as a final foundation. . .I am a little worried about this stuff which I consider to be tentative being swallowed whole by all sorts of enthusiastic people, who really should be a little more tentative in the way that I am" (Maslow, 1965.)

Notwithstanding this tenuous theoretical foundation, Theory X - Theory Y analysis has had a profound effect on management theory and practice. In the chapter on performance appraisal we discuss Management By Objectives (MBO) as one of the most significant practical developments founded in large part upon McGregor's work. The Theory X, Theory model has indeed been criticized on the grounds that it is simplistic, yet it seems to provide significant insight to managers. In particular it focuses attention on one very important question for the manager: "Do you make one set of assumptions about the motivation of your employees and another set of assumptions about your own motivations?" (Boshear and Albrecht, 1977.) Theory Y warns against applying a double standard and stresses the commonality of needs and therefore motivation among all human beings.

Motivational models coming out of the humanistic psychology tradition see human motivation as a function of the need level at which a particular employee is operating. Frederick Herzberg, in his "Two Factor Theory of Motivation," departs from this pure growth and development model. He asks a simple question:

"How do you install a generator in an employee?" Fitting comfortably into the tradition which explains behavior in terms of drive reduction, Herzberg argues that organizational factors leading to job satisfaction are different from those which lead to job dissatisfaction. The key to understanding the difference resides in the pleasure-pain principle. One set of needs stems from the person's animal disposition and centers on the avoidance of loss of life, hunger, pain, sexual deprivation, and so on. The second dimension of human nature is pleasure-seeking oriented or motivating. According to Herzberg human beings have a compelling urge to reach their own potentiality by continuous psychological growth. (Herzberg, 1966.) Those aspects of work which are motivators include classic growth factors. Included among these are:

1. recognition;
2. achievement;
3. advancement;
4. responsibility;
5. nature of work itself; and
6. opportunity for growth.

Aspects of work which cause dissatisfaction sometimes called maintenance factors or hygiene factors are related more to a need to avoid unpleasantness. Included among these factors are:

1. working conditions;
2. interpersonal relationships;
3. salary;
4. supervisory skill;
5. company policy;
6. administration.

The implication of this theory is that a management which insists on stressing extrinsic or hygiene awards will fail to harness the full energy of its employees, for these rewards will only make the work situation more tolerable. No matter how positive the hygiene factors are, motivation will not be affected. To motivate an employee the work itself must be made valuable. Only intrinsic rewards can engage those higher level needs.

This theory of motivation leads to a focus on job enrichment as the entry point for motivating employees. Herzberg acknowledges that many job enrichment efforts have failed. However, he attributes their failure to the fact that managers confuse horizontal with vertical job loading. Horizontal job loading simply enlarges already meaningless work. Only vertical job loading, a form of job enrichment which directly taps motivators, will produce motivated action. The principles of such job enrichment should include:

1. removing some control while retaining accountability;
2. increasing the accountability of individuals for own work;
3. giving a person a complete natural unit of work (module, division, area, and so on);
4. granting additional authority to an employee in his activity;
5. making periodic reports directly available to the worker himself rather than to the supervisor;
6. introducing new and more difficult tasks not previously handled;
7. assigning individuals specific or specialized tasks, enabling them to become experts.

Herzberg and his associates report extensive research on this two-factor theory. Studies conducted on over 1600 employees, including lower level supervisors, agricultural administrators, foremen, military officers, engineers, scientists, and accountants, lend support to the Herzberg model. Also, Schwartz, Jerusaitis, and Stark (1963), claimed support for the two-factor theory in study of public utility workers, and Dysinger (1965) found support in his study of scientists and engineers. However, Herzberg's proposition seems to hold only when essentially the same methodology is used, i.e., when respondents are asked to relate critical incidents about "satisfying" and "dissatisfying" events (Behling, et al. 1968). In general, studies employing different ways of measuring factors leading to satisfaction support the notion that any factor can produce effects ranging from satisfaction to dissatisfaction. (Graen, 1968.) Wernimont and Dunnette (1964), using a forced-choice questionnaire to identify causative factors found items labeled by Herzberg as "motivators" accounted for the greatest variance in satisfaction and dissatisfaction. Frielander (1964) reported similar findings.

The expectancy-value approach to human motivation has enjoyed broad application to work behavior over the last twenty years. Georgopolos, Mahoney and Jones (1957) made the first application of this motivational model to the work setting. Georgopoulos, et al. saw worker productivity as a function of individual needs, perceptions of the instrumentality of high production, and worker freedom. A worker was thought to be motivated to produce when he is activated by desiring a goal (need engaged) and when he perceives that high productivity is a path toward this goal. But for the relationship between worker need and high expectation to hold the worker must be free from limiting considerations. The principal limiting consideration is informal group pressure.

The first fully-developed expectancy model was put forward by Victor Vroom. Vroom's theory was based on three concepts: valence (value of an outcome or anticipated satisfaction resulting from an outcome), expectancy (subjective probability of achieving an outcome), and force (expected value of an act). The resulting model is:

Force (motivation = Σ Valence X Expectancy

The model asserts that "the probability of a person performing an act is a direct function of the algebraic sum of the products of the valence of outcomes and expectancies that they will occur given the act." (Vroom, 1964.)

Motivation in this context is understood in terms of a model which sees behavior as "subjectively rational and as directed toward the attainment of desired outcomes and away from adverse outcomes." (Vroom, 1964.)

Vroom's work, focusing on "process" rather than content, has been well received by those desiring a more explicit examination of the relationship between motivation and achieving organizational goals. (Luthens, 1972.) In Galbraith and Cumming's (1967) application of Vroom's model to predict productivity, workers were found to be motivated to produce when production led to desired goals. Graen (1969) stresses that explicit recognition of organizational clarity is necessary as a prerequisite to employee motivation. Henneman and Schaw (1970) argue that the empirical research done on Vroom's theory, completed in the work setting, disallows standardization of measurement or research design. Thus they warn against generalization. Hunt and Hill (1969) criticize the Vroom model on a much more basic level by suggesting that it is not a behavioral theory, but simply one of motivation. Its weakness is that it ignores key intervening factors between motivation and performance.

Building on Victor Vroom's theoretical work, Porter and Lawler advance a well-received and comprehensive expectancy model. The model as originally promulgated is represented in Figure 4.

The basic building blocks of this model are derived from the Vroom constructs: value of reward (valence), perceived effort → reward possibility (expectancy), and effort (motivational force). To see effort as a product of the interaction between value of reward and perceived effort → reward probability is to adopt the basic Vroom proposition. But as the figure above suggests, the Porter-Lawler model further elaborates the factors that intervene between motivation and performance and satisfaction. The relationship between motivation or effort and performance is modified by 1) abilities and traits, (relatively stable characteristics of individuals); and 2) role perceptions, (the individual's subjective definition of the job). The wavy line on the model above suggests that while there is a relationship between rewards and performance, it may often be a tenuous one, e.g., when promotions are made on the basis of seniority while ignoring performance. The next variable considered in the model is satisfaction, seen here as a product of reward. But, again, the relationship is modified by subjective equity judgment of the recipient, labeled perceived equitable reward. Perceived equitable rewards has to do with the input-output discrepancies an employee perceives in comparing him/her self with another person. An employee who perceives he/she commits more to the organization and receives less than colleague will suffer a decline in satisfaction. Five field studies support the evidence of equity as a norm in the workforce (Schesler

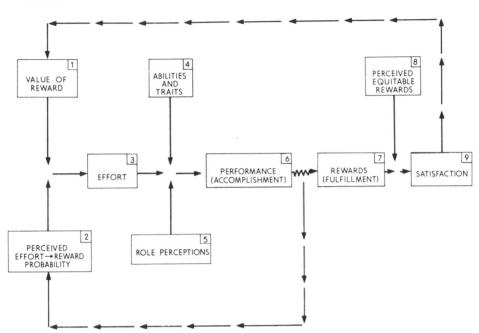

Figure 4. The original Porter-Lawler Model. Source: L. W. Porter and E. E. Lawler, III, *Managerial Attitudes and Performance,* (Homewood, Ill.: Richard D. Irwin, Inc., 1968 c), p. 17.

and Clark, 1970; Zeddek and Smith, 1968; Henricks, 1969; Finn and Lee, 1972; Correle, 1978). Other studies have found the causal link between equity, satisfaction, and absence of turnover (Klein, 1973; Telley, French, and Scott, 1971; and Dittrick and Carrell, 1979).

After testing this model on a group of 568 administrators in seven different organizations, Porter and Lawler concluded that two modifications were in order. First, a direct causal link between performance and perceived equitable reward was added. Managers perceiving themselves as high performers established a higher standard for equitable reward than did those who saw themselves as low performers. Second, rewards had to be refined to distinguish intrinsic and extrinsic rewards. Intrinsic rewards (relating to higher level needs) related more closely to performance than extrinsic rewards (fulfilling lower level needs). (Porter and Lawler, 1968.) The revised model is represented in Figure 5.

Research testing this model is modest, and its results would have to be dedefined as mixed.

The limitations of the expectancy theory in general are several. First, expectancies are difficult to assess accurately. In fact, rather than what we do being determined by what we want, as expectancy theory would suggest, the opposite may be true. Our values and wants may develop to conform with our behavior. Many critics suggest that expectancy theory defers too much to the nineteenth century

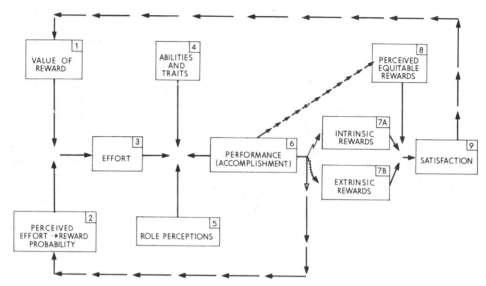

Figure 5. The revised Porter-Lawler model. Source: L. W. Porter and E. E. Lawler, *Managerial Attitudes and Performance*, Homewood, Ill.: Richard D. Irwin, Inc., 1968, c, p. 165.

ideal of the economic man. Secondly, when used in a prescriptive fashion, expectancy theory assumes that employees are reasonably informed and knowledgeable about outcomes. In fact, given the high degree of interdependency among and between units in complex organizations, employees cannot be as knowledgeable about outcomes as the model assumes.

Implications for Public Sector Organizations

For the manager in a public agency this review of motivation models stemming from the cognitive tradition stimulates a practical concern. Do findings from the private sector apply in a straightforward fashion to the public sector, or is there something unique in a public work force or work setting that calls for a most cautious application of such organizational behavior findings?

The literature on human resource management in the public sector presents two points of view on this issue. One view, implicit in O. Glenn Stahl's discussion of motivation in his standard text, *Public Personnel Administration*, (1976) is that differences across settings create no serious problem in applying motivation theory. In Stahl's treatment of motivation, for example (pp. 183-192), findings from the broader literature are reviewed without ever raising the question of appropriateness of public sector application. Robert Lee's text in *Public Personnel Management* (1979) starts from a different presumption. Lee sees that legal constraints in particular impede easy application of common private sector motivational principles. According to Lee, "rigid civil service systems hinder removing unproductive workers and providing financial incentives to productive ones." (p. 360.) Budget and personnel ceilings may force managers into assigning work to unqualified employees (p. 360.) And the heavy demands on the time of public managers leave few opportunities ". . .to contemplate how best to help each employee self-actualize." (p. 360.)

Our review of the literature on motivation suggests that the differences between the public and the private sector is not well documented. But it does appear that most of the motivational analysis that is available tends to come out of a "drive" or a "growth" tradition. Many analyses of public employees see motivated action as differing depending upon the nature of the need producing the behavior. Since these theories of motivation see human beings as sharing the same basic set of needs and/or growth patterns, theories are applicable across organizational settings.

According to Stahl (1971), higher level needs are strongly tapped in public sector work. He indicates that most public programs have a built-in advantage regarding their intrinsic value, for their very purpose is to serve the entire population. Stahl argues: "the compelling demands, the imponderables in most public issues, the sheer complexity of serving the public interest, create challenges that are seldom equaled in other pursuits. . . In other words, there is much job satisfaction to be derived from governmental activities simply because they are what they are—provided unwise organization and controls do not deprive work of all that may be gained from this natural advantage." (Stahl, 1971.)

Research finding governmental service less prestigious in both the eyes of the public (Gortner, 1977) and the judgment of higher federal civil servants themselves (Stanley, 1964; Kilpatrick, Cummings, Jennings, 1964) suggests a limited opportunity to gain motivation from the esteem of others in the public sector. Nevertheless, the inherent meaningfulness of work may enhance self-esteem. Kilpatrick et al., in their classic study of 948 federal civil servants, found that "significant numbers find factors such as autonomy, variety, opportunity for self expression and creativity, challenging work, a sense of doing something that is worthwhile and constructive, interesting work—all these, and more in their job as a federal employee." (Kilpatrick et al.)

Guyot (1961) found, comparing middle managers in government and business on their own need for achievement, affiliation, and power, that government managers had a higher need for achievement, lower need for affiliation, and similar power needs to private sector managers. A more recent study of students about to enter management careers found no significant difference between nonprofit (mostly governmental) entrants and private sector entrants regarding a need for power and need for security. (Rawls and Nelson, 1975; Rawls, Ullich, Nelson, 1975.) The most current evidence lends support to the assumption that higher level needs are met for many public servants. In 1978 the national center for productivity and quality of working life study found a solid majority of employees, responding to a series of attitude surveys, gave their jobs high marks. Eighty-four percent of managers and 64 percent of non managers rated the content of their jobs as good, and only 14 percent of managers and 23 percent of nonmanagers failed to see that their jobs made good use of their skills and abilities. (National Productive and Quality of Work Life, 1978.)

Thus, the issue at stake here is not whether or not specific theories are applicable. Both drive and growth-based models have been applied in the public sector context. The question, rather, is: do the findings using these theories hold across public and private sectors? In other words, could one take the finding from one setting and apply it to another? Regarding drive and growth-based theories of motivation, the answer is probably yes. Gortner is right in concluding that ". . .in spite of the stereotypes about civil servants, there is really little difference between the attitudes and values of public and private employees. . .since there is little difference between public and private employees, there should be little or no difference in the application of motivation theories to the various work groups." (Gortner, 1977.)

When one shifts from drive/growth theories of motivation (Maslow, Herzberg, etc.) to expectancy-value theories of motivation (Vroom, Porter - Lawler, etc.), the ease of applying findings across the private and public sector diminishes. The Vroom and Porter - Lawler motivational models are classic examples. Making no assumption about the universality of activated needs, these models simply posit that needs exist, but are triggered as motivators only in relation to expectancy.

You will recall the basic formula from the early discussion of expectancy models: motivation $= F (E \times V)$. The difficulty of a straightforward application of private sector findings to the public sector is that critical aspects of the work and work environment differ regarding both expectancy (subjective probability of achieving outcome) and valence (value of an outcome) from conditions found in the private sector.

Buchanan (1974) sets forth several characteristics of public sector employment which affect motivation. Three of these characteristics especially impact the straightforward application of expectancy model findings. He sees the public sector setting as different from the private sector in that it lacks:

1. goal crispness;
2. personal significance reinforcement;
3. stability of expectations.

Where private sector employers can make goals sharp, clear, or crisp, public sector managers are systematically confronted with diffuse and conflicting goals. Models which posit a necessary link between goal crispness and personal significance reinforcement (or the gaining of personal satisfaction from a job accomplished) may be of limited utility in the public sector. In many public programs, it is difficult for an employee to see the link between her contribution and organizational success.

Legislative and executive conflicts often saddle agencies with conflicting goals, radically reducing worker's ability to recognize any clear goals. Yet clarity of job goals does seem to be a necessary first step in any prescriptive use of expectancy models. Graen (1969) has stressed the importance of organizational goal clarity as a necessary prerequisite to employee motivation in this model. The stability of expectations issue is related as well. Public sector employees often feel that there is no stable commitment to the objectives they pursue. A change in administration at the top, guaranteed periodically, could and often does produce a major shift in the goals toward which employees are working. In other words, goals are not only unclear and conflicting, but also subjected to significant changes.

All of these aspects of the public sector work environment militate against a simplistic transfer of private sector expectancy model findings to the public sector scene. While drive and growth models focus more on people, who doubtless are more alike than different, whether in the public sector or in the private sector, expectancy models focus more on the work and the work environment. All this indicates that significant differences do emerge when attention is focused on the public sector.

Application From The Acognitive Tradition

Though full-fledged operant conditioning programs are rare in the real world of organizations, principles of operant conditioning are applied everyday by managers and employees alike. Advocates of behavior modification in organizations argue for a more conscious and therefore effective strategy of behavior management. Their definition of management means changing behavior to increase employee effectiveness, using five basic steps:

1. *pinpoint* the behavior critical to employee effectiveness;
2. *measure* and *chart* the behavior;
3. *change* the behavior by changing antecedents, consequences, or both;
4. *evaluate* your behavior improvement project;
5. *change* the program as necessary.

A number of private sector firms such as Bell Telephone, Emory Air Freight, B. F. Goodrich, General Motors, Allied Foods, and Questor Corporation have applied operant conditioning principles to their operations for as long as 10 years. For the most part these efforts follow the model designed by Emory Freight, the private sector pioneer in behavior modification in organizations, whose methods aim to let employees know how well they are achieving specific goals, while rewards of praise and recognition are forthcoming for improvement. (Business Week, 1972, December 2.)

One prominent public sector application of operant conditioning is the Orange

County, California Police Department program to decrease crime rates through use of a performance reinforcement program. After a number of critical behaviors were pinpointed (checking for unlocked cars, assisting merchants to electrically mark sold items, conducting underground surveillance, etc.) local government agreed to across-the-board wage increases if the total number of specific crimes decreased by specified amounts during an eight month period. A decrease of 3 to 6 percent would lead to a 1 percent salary increase. If there was a 6 to 8 percent decrease, salaries would rise by 2 percent; and so on. To achieve these increases the Police Department initiated a number of programs designed to strengthen the pinpointed behavior. Table 2 shows the results.

Another example of applying operant conditioning principles to the public sector is the City of Detroit Garbage Collector productivity improvement program. Here the reinforcements of bonuses and praise were provided on a quarterly and daily basis in an effort to strengthen productivity and weaken unproductive behaviors in garbage collection. As a result of the program citizen complaints declined significantly, the City saved money after the bonuses were paid (Brown and Presbie, 1976).

Critics of the application of behavior modification to the organization see it as ethically repulsive, as manipulative, involuntary, and patently exploitative. Inferring from the capacity of researchers to control subject behavior in experimental settings, critics raise the specter of employee enslavement to these scientific control methods. Proponents of operant conditioning respond that productivity is in everyone's interest, employer and employee alike, that employees typically help identify the critical behaviors in the program design phase and often actively participate in the program development, and that employees, often backed by unions, are far from powerless in negotiating program issues with employers.

TABLE 2. Performance Reinforcement in Orange County

	Baseline		After New procedures applied	
	Number	Dollar loss	Number	Dollar loss
RAPE	17	–	6	–
ROBBERY	37	22,264	45	17,383
BURGLARY	1,023	250,828	779	265,145
LARCENY	–	1,068,862	–	266,462
AUTO THEFT	196	196,795	200	179,805
TOTAL	1,273	1,538,749	1,028	728,795
Percent of change from baseline	–	–	-19.1%	53.0%

Source: McAdams (1976).

Motivation and Productivity

From the vantage point of a practicing public manager the most important question about motivation is: how does it affect performance? Applied research speaks to this question by exploring both job satisfaction and rewards in relation to performance.

The early managerial theories regarding employee performance paid scant attention to how employees felt about their jobs. The dominant model of the scientific management era directed the manager's attention to "rewards" and painted the employee as a mere robot, predictably responsive to properly structured payment. Performance was a function of carefully constructed jobs and reward systems. To the first theoretician of scientific management, Frederick W. Taylor (1911), employee and employer shared an interest in high productivity and motivation was a matter of facilitating productive work. However, as a result of the pioneering research at the Hawthorne Works of Western Electric in the late 1920's and early 1930's (Roethlisberger and Dickson, 1939), worker satisfaction emerged as central to understanding job performance. Social interaction on the job and the expressed concern of supervisors came to the fore as significant factors in employee satisfaction. Satisfaction, in turn, was assumed to influence performance. Notwithstanding a reanalysis of the Hawthorne data which suggests that social context variables did not in fact explain the variation in worker performance or satisfaction (Hawthorne, 1975), the social context assumption exercised significant influence over organizational behavior research for decades.

Today the models for testing the relationship between satisfaction and performance on the job are more refined and empirical research on this relationship is more extensive. But researchers are far from a consensus on the affect of any one variable. Victor Vroom, after evaluating 20 empirical studies looking at satisfaction and performance, concluded: "there is no simple relationship between job satisfaction and performance. Correlations between these variables vary within an extremely large range. . . We do not know the conditions which affect the magnitude and direction of relationships between satisfaction and performance." (Vroom, 1964.) Other research reviews concur that findings are inconclusive (Brayfield and Crockett, 1955; Herzberg, Mausner, Peterson, and Capwell, 1957; Schwab and Cummings, 1970). For example, Locke (1970) focuses on the issue of whether satisfaction causes or results from performance and concludes that it is primarily the result of performance and only indirectly a cause. Cherrington, Reitz, and Scott (1971) conclude there is no inherent relationship between satisfaction and performance, though with proper enforcement one can produce a relationship between task performance and reports of satisfaction.

In the main there are two streams of research focusing on this satisfaction - performance issue. One stream sees satisfaction as an independent motivating variable, causally associated with performance (Herzberg, 1957) or with variables that seem to be otherwise connected to productivity, like absence and turnover (Porter and Steers, 1973). The other stream of research sees satisfaction as a dependent variable—a product of productivity and the reward system (Vroom, 1964, Lawler and Porter 1968). Wanous and Lawler (1972) suggest that the conflicting reports on the relationship between job satisfaction and performance derive from the different operational definitions of satisfaction in the empirical research. Their literature review has uncovered nine operational definitions of satisfaction.

In addition an array of factors influence an employee's satisfaction to further confound interpreting satisfaction—performance research. Bass (1979) lists among the salient factors: personality, sex, education, race, age, length of service, ability, and interest in work. In terms of *personality*, Weitz found that employees who are satisfied with their jobs seem to be satisfied with many other aspects of life: home, politics, etc., while employees who were dissatisfied with their jobs were dissatisfied with other aspects of life as well. *Gender* has traditionally been considered an important factor in job satisfaction; in the past women were generally more satisfied workers than men. (Bass and Ryterband, 1979). But since the 1960's and women workers increase in volume and expectations, the passivity of the American female worker is diminishing. In fact, one recent survey indicated considerably more dissatisfaction among women than men (Mills, 1979). *Race* enters as an important controlling factor in two senses. First, Black men may lack self-esteem and thus find satisfaction in competitive situations difficult to come by; second, white supervisors may be unwilling to take the same risks with blacks as white—though these risks are a potential source of job satisfaction for Blacks. *Age* and *length of service* go together to influence significantly employee satisfaction on the job. Younger workers are generally thought to be more restless and dissatisfied. National surveys find nearly 40 percent of younger workers "unhappy" in their jobs, while less than 20 percent of older workers express this dissatisfaction. (Robert P. Quinn, et al. 1973.) Younger workers have shorter tenure in jobs, they tend to change jobs and occupations more frequently, seeking more opportunity for development and advancement. (Saminer and Eck, 1977.) *Ability* seems to be key to job satisfaction in a fairly straightforward fashion. If an employee is too skilled, too highly educated, or too intelligent for a job, dissatisfaction results. At the same time an employee lacking the abilities to perform the job well may experience frustration leading to dissatisfaction. Finally *interest* in work itself is a central factor in any meaningful analysis of employee satisfaction or dissatisfaction. Several studies show that without intrinsic interest in work itself, satisfaction at least among higher level employees falters. (Herzberg, Mausner, Snyder, 1959.) The consensus of research on job satisfaction is that the intrinsic versus extrinsic sources of satisfaction merit special attention.

Intrinsic Versus Extrinsic Satisfaction

Edward Deci has defined the concepts for studying intrinsic and extrinsic motivation. According to Deci, ". . . a person is intrinsically motivated if he engages in an activity to feel competent and self-determining in relation to the activity. There is no external reward; the reward is internal to the person and takes the form of feelings he has about himself. Human beings are organisms in constant interaction with their surroundings; they need to feel effective or competent in relation to their environment. This basic need is the essence of intrinsic motivation." (Deci, 1975.) Extrinsic motivation, by contrast, comes through reward external to the job itself. It takes the form of some extrinsic drive reduction in hunder, thirst, material reward, or others. Intrinsic motivation is a motivational force ultimately tied to intrinsic outcomes, while extrinsic motivation is a motivational force ultimately tied to extrinsic outcomes (Mailer, 1980.) Typically public agencies offer employees a mixture of intrinsic and extrinsic rewards.

Deci (1975) and Straw (1975) have both reported studies showing that when extrinsic rewards are administered for performance of an intrinsically motivating activity, a decrease in the level of intrinsic motivation for performance may occur. Much research has focused on the conditions that must prevail regarding the extrinsic reward for the reduction to occur. One important aspect is whether or not the rewards are contingent on performance. In order for an external reward to be effective it must be continent on performance. This very fact, however, presents a dilemma, highlighted by Deci: "to use rewards as an extrinsic motivator of performance, one must take these rewards directly contingent upon performance. However, doing so decreases intrinsic motivation. Making rewards noncontingent on performance will not interfere with intrinsic motivation; but neither will it motivate extrinsically." (Deci, 1975.) However, at least one study suggests that Deci's findings may not hold under all conditions. Arnold (1976) reports that when intrinsic motivation is high enough, extrinsic rewards either do not affect or enhance intrinsic motivation. Whatever the impact on intrinsic motivation, Lache et al., review the literature concerning the monetary incentives and conclude that performance gains doubtless result from the use of the extrinsic rewards. (Lache, et. al., 1979.)

The general implication of these findings remains that the manager should be sensitive to the dampening effect rewards may potentially have on intrinsic motivation, except in those rare cases where very high intrinsic motivation is manifested. If jobs cannot be made intrinsically interesting managers have little to lose by heavy manipulation of extrinsic rewards. Finally, managers should remember that intrinsic motivation requires employee feedback and knowledge of results to work.

Whatever the precise relationship between performance and intrinsic/extrinsic motivation, it does seem clear that a positive relationship between satisfaction and performance is worth developing and preserving. Whether satisfaction causes performance (an intrinsically satisfying work motivates high performance) or performance causes satisfaction (high performers received extrinsic rewards and feel good as a result), it remains true that satisfied employees stay with their employment. If the satisfaction—performance linkage is strong, the most productive employees will also be those who remain to make careers in the agency.

Given this conclusion, that a strong relationship between satisfaction and performance is desirable, the question becomes how to produce it. Porter and Lawler suggest two methods for strengthening that relationship. First, construct a reward system so the very top performers receive proportionally higher extrinsic rewards. Second, modify the task so it yields intrinsic rewards for a performance. Reforms recently enacted in the federal civil service reflect strong commitment to the first method.

A common refrain among critics of public sector management is that civil service regulations impede effective use of extrinsic rewards to motivate employees. Though merit increases and even performance bonuses are a part of the reward structure for many public employees, public managers have been seldom empowered to hone financial rewards to levels of employee performances. But in a radical departure from past federal sector practices, key provisions of the Civil Service Reform Act of 1978 strongly endorsed monetary incentives in the Senior Executive Service and in the Merit Pay Provisions for middle managers. The monetary incentive provisions were motivated by President Carter's belief that the federal service suffered from inadequate motivation attributed in part to, ". . .too few rewards for excellence and too few penalties for unsatisfactory performance." (President's Speech, cited in Thayer, 1978.) Annual cash bonuses awarded or denied on the basis of performance were included to enhance the productivity of top civil servants. For the middle level manager an incentive pay system providing one half of the annual increase to be allocated according to stringent merit criteria, introduces a more modest version of the same principle covering civil servants in the G.S. 13 to 15 range.

The extent to which the second method for strengthening the satisfaction - performance linkage will be pursued through the reformed federal service remains unclear, since the capacity to redesign tasks to make them intrinsically motivating necessarily resides deep in the bureaucracy where individual tasks, or clusters of tasks, are accomplished. Whether and how intensively this method is used will vary from agency to agency much as it has in the past. With the ubiquitous threat of budget and program cuts, this second method of motivating employees is the one that public managers may need increasingly to attend to in the decade of the 1980's. Chapters on leadership, participation, and decision-making provide some strategies that will help.

REFERENCES

Arnold, Hugh J. (1976), Effects of Performance Feedback and Extrinsic Reward Upon High Intrinsic Motivation. *Organizational Behavior and Human Performance. Psychological Bulletin. 52*:pp. 396-424.

Atkinson, J. W. (1964), *An Introduction to Motivation*. Princeton, N.J.: Van Nostrand.

Ayllon, T. Azrin, N. H. (1965), The Measurement and Reinforcement of Behavior of Psychotis. *Journal of the Experimental Analysis of Behavior. 8*:pp. 357-383.

Bass, Bernard, M. and Edward C. Ryterband (1979), *Organizational Psychology*. Boston, Allyn and Bacon.

Behling, O., G. Labowitz, R. Kosmo (1968), The Herzberg Controversy: A Critical Reappraisal. *Academy of Management Journal*. 11(1):pp. 99-108.

Behling, Orlando, and Chester Schriesheim (1976), *Organizational Behavior*. Boston: Allyn and Bacon Co.

Boshear, Walton C. and Karl G. Albrecht (1977), *Understanding People, Models and Concepts*. La Jolla, California: University Associates, Inc.

Brown, Paul L. and Robert J. Presbie (1976), *Behavior Modification in Business, Industry and Government*. New Paltz, New York: Behavior Improvement Associates.

Buchanan, B., II. (1974), Government Managers, Business Executives, and Organizational Commitment. *Public Administration Review*. 35:pp. 339-347.

Business Week, (1972), December 2.

Campoell, J. P., M. D. Dunnette, E. E. Lawler and K. E. Weich (1970), *Managerial Behavior, Performance and Effectiveness*. New York: McGraw-Hill.

Carrell, M. R. (1978), A Longitudinal field assessment of employee perceptions of equitable treatment. *Organization Behavior and Human Performance*. 21:pp. 108-118.

Castore, Carl H., J. Keith Murnighan (1978), Determinants of Support for Group Decisions. *Organizational Behavior and Human Performance*. 22:pp. 75-92.

Cherrington, D. J., H. J. Reitz, and W. E. Scott (1971), Effects of Contingent And Noncontingent Reward on the Relationship Between Satisfaction and Task Performance. *Journal of Applied Psychology*. 55:pp. 531-536.

Clark, Kerr, and J. M. Rostow (1979), *Work in America: The Decade Ahead*. (ed.) New York: Van Nostrand.

Deci, E. L. (1976), Hidden Costs of Rewards. *Organization Dynamics*, 4(3):pp. 61-72.

Deci, Edward (1975), *Intrinsic Motivation*. New York: Plenum Press.

de Charms, R. (1972), Personal Causation Training in Schools. *Journal of Applied Social Psychology*. 2:pp. 95-113.

Dittrich, John E. and Michael R. Carrell (1979), Organizational Equity Perceptions, Employee Job Satisfaction, and Departmental Absence and Turnover Rates. *Organizational Behavior and Human Performance*. 24:pp. 29-40.

Dittrich, J. E. and Carrell, M. R. (1976), Dimensions of Organizational Fairness As Predictors of Job Satisfaction, Absence and Turnover. Academy of Management Proceedings. pp. 79-83.

Dubin, Robert, and Joseph E. Champaux (1977), Central Life Interests and Job Satisfaction. *Organizational Behavior and Human Performance*. 18:p. 376.

Dysinger, D. W. (1966), Motivational Factors Affecting Civilian Army Research and Development Personnel. *Report AIR*-D-95-5165-TR. (cited by Ewen, et al., 1966).

Evans, M. G. (1969), Conceptual and Operational Problems in the Measurement of Various Aspects of Job Satisfaction. *Journal of Applied Psychology. 53*: pp. 93-101.

Ewen, R. B., P. C. Smith, C. L. Hulin, and E. A. Lerh (1966), An Empirical Test of the Hertzberg Two-Factor Theory. *Journal of Applied Psychology*. 50:

Farr, James L. (1976), Task Characteristics, Reward Contingency, and Intrinsic Motivation. *Organizational Behavior and Human Performance. 16*:pp. 294-307.

Finn, R. H. and Lee, S. M. (1972), Salary Equity: Its determination, analysis and correlates. *Journal of Applied Psychology. 56*:pp. 283-292.

Fisher, Cynthia D. (1978), The Effects of Personal Control, Competence, and Extrinsic Reward Systems on Intrinsic Motivation. *Organizational Behavior and Human Performance. 21*:pp. 273-288.

Friedlander, F. (1964), "Job Characteristics as Satisfiers and Dissatisfiers". *Journal of Applied Psychology. 48*:

Galbraith, J., and Cummings, L. L. (1967), Empirical Investigation of Motivational Determinents of Task Performance-Interactive Effects between Instrumentality-Valence and Motivation-Ability. Organization Behavior and Human Performance 2(3):pp. 237-257.

Gellerman, Saul W. (1963), *Motivation and Productivity*. New York: American Management Association.

Georgopoulos, Basil S., Gerald M. Mahoney, and Nyle W. Jones (1957), A Path Goal Approach to Productivity. *Journal of Applied Psychology. 41*:pp. 345-353.

Gortner, Harold F. (1977), *Administration in the Public Sector*. New York: John Wiley and Sons.

Graen, G. (1969), Instrumentability Theory of Work-Motivation-Some Experimental Results and Suggested Modifications. *Journal of Applied Psychology*. 53:p. 1.

Graen, G. B., C. L. Hulin (1968), Addendum to an empirical investigation of the two-factor theory of job satisfaction. *Journal of Applied Psychology. 52*: pp. 341-342.

Guyot, James F. (1961), Government Bureaucrats Are Different. *Industrial and Labor Relations Review*, 22:pp. 195-202.

Hampton, D. R., C. E. Summer and R. A. Webber (1978), *Organizational Behavior and the Practice of Management. :Scott, Foreman.*

Hawthorne Revisited: The Legend and the Legacy (1975), *Organizational Dynamics*. Winter:pp. 66-80.

Heneman, Herbert G., III and Donald P. Schwab (1972), Evaluating Research on Expectancy Theory Predictions of Employee Performance. *Psychological Bulletin*. 78:pp. 1-9.

Henrichs, J. R. (1969), Correlates of Employee Evaluations of Pay Increases, *Journal of Applied Psychology*. 53:pp. 481-489.

Herzberg, F., B. Mausner, R. O. Peterson, and D. F. Campbell (1957), Job Attitudes: Review of Research and Opinions. *Psychological Services of Pittsburgh*, Pittsburgh, Pennsylvania.

Hulin, C. and P. Smith (1967), An Empirical Investigation of Two Implications of the Two-Factor Theory of Job Satisfaction. *Journal of Applied Psychology*. 51:pp. 396-402.

Hunt, J. G. and J. W. Hill (1969), The New Look in Motivation Theory in Organizational Research. *Human Organizations*. Summer: pp. 100-109.

Ivanevich, John (1978), The Performance to Satisfaction Relationship: A Causal Analysis of Stimulating and Non-Stimulating Jobs. *Organizational Behavior and Human Performance*. 22:pp. 350-365.

Ivanevich, John M. (1979), High and Low Task Stimulation Jobs: A Causal Analysis of Performance Satisfaction Relationships. *Academy of Management Journal*. 22:pp. 206-222.

Jablonsky, J. F. and D. L. DeVries (1972), Operant Conditioning Principles Extrapolated to the Theory of Management. *Organizational Behavior and Human Performance*. 7:pp. 340-358.

Jung, John (1978), *Understanding Human Motivation*. New York: Macmillan Publishing Co.

Kilpatrick, Franklin P., Milton C. Cummings, Jr., and M. Kent Jennings (1964), *The Image of the Federal Service*. The Brookings Institution, Washington, D.C.

Klein, S. M. (1973), Pay Factors as predictors to satisfaction. A comparison of reinforcement equity and expectancy. *Academy of Management Journal*. pp. 598-610.

Kolb, D. (1965), Achievement Motivation Training for Underachieving High School Boys. *Journal of Personality and Social Psychology*. 2:pp. 783-792.

Latham, G. P., and D. C. Dossett (1978), Designing Incentive Plans for Unionized Employees: A Comparison of Continuous and Variable Ration Reinforcement Schedule. *Personnel Psychology*. 31:pp. 47-61.

Lee, Robert (1979), *Public Personnel Systems*. Baltimore, Maryland: University Park Press.

Lindsay, C., E. Marks, and L. Gorlow (1967), The Herzberg Theory: A Critique and Reformation. *Journal of Applied Psychology*. 51:pp. 330-339.

Locke, E. A. (1973), Job Satisfaction and Job Performance: A Theoretical Analysis. *Organizational Behavior and Human Performance*. 9:pp. 482-503.

Locke, E. A. (1969), What is Job Satisfaction? *Organizational Behavior and Human Performance*. 4:pp. 309-336.

Locke, E. A., D. B. Feren, V. M. McCaleb, K. N. Shaw, and A. T. Denny (1970), The Relative Effectiveness of Four Methods of Motivating Employee Performance.

Luthans, F. (1972), *Contemporary Readings in Organizational Behavior*. New York: McGraw-Hill, 1972.

Maslow, A. H. (1943), Theory of Human Motivation. *Psychological Review*, Volume 50, pp. 370-396, cited in Natemeyer, *Classics of Organizational Behavior*. (1978). Oak Park, Ill.: Moore Publishing Co.: 55.

Maslow, A. H. (1971), *The Farther Reaches of Human Nature*. New York: Viking Press.

Mawhinney, Thomas C. (1979), Intrinsic X Extrinsic Work Motivation: Perspectives from Behaviorism. *Organizational Behavior and Human Performance*. 24:pp. 411-440.

Mayo, Elton (1945), *The Social Problems of an Industrial Civilization*. Cambridge: Howard University Graduate School of Business.

McAdams, J. (1976), Police are 'Busting' Out All Over in Orange County, California. *Work Performance*. 2. (January). pp. 14-17.

McClelland, David C. (1961), *The Achieving Society*. Princeton, N.J.: Van Nostrand.

McClelland, D. and D. G. Winter (1969), *Motivating Economic Achievement*. New York: Free Press.

McCurdy, H. E. (1973), Fiction, Phenomenology and Public Administration. *Public Administration Review*. 33:pp. 52-60.

McDougall, William (1923), *Outline of Psychology*. New York: Scribner.

McGregor, Douglas M. (1957), The Human Side of Enterprise, reproduced in Walter E. Natemeyer ed. *Classics of Organizational Behavior*. Oak Park, Ill.: Moore Publishing Co., 1978.

Mills, D. Quinn (1979), Human Resources in the 1980's. *Harvard Business Review*. (July, August):pp. 154-162.

Mindell, Mark G. and L. H. Jackson (1980), Motivating the New Breed. *Personnel*. 57:pp. 53-61.

Mitchell, Vance F. and Pravin Moredgill (1976), Measurement of Maslow's Need Hierarchy. *Organizational Behavior and Human Performance*. 16:pp. 334-349.

Morgan, Clifford and Richard King (1966), *Introduction to Psychology* (3rd ed.) New York: McGraw-Hill.

Moch, Michael K. (1980), Job Involvement, Internal Motivation, and Employees' Integration into Networks of Work Relationships. *Organizational Behavior and Human Performance*. 25:pp. 15-31.

National Commission on Productivity and Work Quality (1975), *Employee Incentives to Improve State and Local Government Productivity*. U.S. Government Printing Office, Washington, D.C.

National Center for Productivity and Quality of Working Life (1978), *Employee Attitudes and Productivity Differences Between the Public and Private Sector*. U.S. Civil Service Commission, Washington, D.C.

Nord, Walter R. (1969), Beyond the Teaching Machine: The Neglected Area of Operant Conditioning in the Theory and Practice of Management. *Organizational Behavior and Human Performance*. 4:pp. 375-401.

Nuttin, J. R. (1973), Pleasure and Reward in Motivation and Learning, in D. Berlyne (ed.) *Pleasure, Reward, Preference*. New York: Academic Press.

Petrock, F. and V. Gamboa (1976), Expectancy Theory and Operant Conditioning: A Conceptual Approach in *Concepts and Controversy in Organizational Behavior*, ed. W. R. Nord, Pacific Palisades, Ca.: Goodyear:pp. 175-187.

Porter, L. W. and R. M. Steers (1973), Organizational Work and Personal Factors in Employee Turnover and Absenteeism. *Psychological Bulletin*. 80:pp. 151-176.

Pritchard, Robert D., John Hollenbach, and Philip J. DeLeo (1980), The Effects of Continuous and Partial Schedules of Reinforcement on Effort, Performance, and Satisfaction. *Organizational Behavior and Human Performance*. 25:336-353.

Pritchard, Robert D., Dale W. Leonard, Clarence W. VonBergen, Jr., and Raymond J. Kirk (1976), The Effects of Varying Schedules of Reinforcement on Human Task Performance. *Organizational Behavior and Human Performance*. 16: pp. 205-230.

Quinn, Robert P., Thomas W. Mangione, Martha S. Baldi de Mandelovito (1973), Evaluating Working Conditions in America. *Monthly Labor Review*. (November) p. 32.

Rachlin, Howard (1976), *Introduction to Modern Behaviorisms*, 2nd edition. New York: W. H. Freeman, Co.

Rabinowitz, S. (1977), Organizational Research on Job Involvement. *Psychological Bulletin*. 84:pp. 265-288.

Rainey, H. G. (1979), Perceptions of Incentives in Business and Government: Implications for Civil Service Reform. *Public Administration Review*. 39: pp. 440-448.

Rainey, H. G. (1979), Reward Expectancies Role, Perceptions, and Job Satisfaction Among Government and Business Managers: Indications of Commonalities and Differences. *Proceedings of the Thirty-Ninth Annual Meeting of the Academy of Management*. pp. 357-361.

Rainey, H. G., Backoff, R. W., Levine, C. H. (1976), Comparing Public and Private Organizations. *Public Administration Review*. 36:pp. 223-244.

Rawls, J. K., Nelson, O. T., Jr. (1975), Characteristics Associated With Preferences For Certain Managerial Positions. *Psychological Reports*. 36:pp. 911-918.

Rawls, J. R., Ulrich, R. A., Nelson, O. T., Jr. (1975), A Comparison of Managers Entering or Reentering the Profit and Nonprofit Sectors. *Academy of Management Journal*. 18:pp. 616-662.

Rhinehart, J. B., Barrell, R. P., DeWolfe, A. S., Griffin, J. E., Spaner, F. E. (1969), Comparative Study of Need Satisfaction in Governmental and Business Hierarchies. *Journal of Applied Psychology*. 53:pp. 230-235.

Roethlisberger, F. J., Dickson, W. J. (1939), *Management and the Worker*. Harvard University Press, Cambridge, Massachusetts.

Ronen, S. (1978), Personal Values: A Basis for Work Motivational Set and Work Attitude. *Organizational Behavior and Human Performance*. 21:pp. 80-107.

Saminer, Dixie and Alan Eck (1977), Occupational Mobility in the American Labor Force. *Monthly Labor Review*. (January) 3.

Sarnoff, I. and P. O. Zimbardo (1961), Anxiety, Fear, and Social Affiliation. *Journal of Abnormal and Social Psychology*. 62:pp. 356-363.

Schachter, S. (1959), *The Psychology of Affiliation*. Stanford, Ca: Stanford, University Press.

Schuster, J. R. and Clark, B. (1970), Individual differences related to feelings toward pay. *Personnel Journal*. 1970. 23:pp. 591-604.

Schwab, D. P., Cummings, L. L. (1970), Employee Performance and Satisfaction with Work Roles: A Review and Interpretation of Theory. *Industrial Relations*. 9:pp. 408-430.

Schwartz, M. M., Jerusaitis, E. and Stark H. (1963), Motivational Factors Among Supervisors in the Utility Industry. *Personnel Psychology*. 16:pp. 45-63.

Skinner, B. F. (1969), Contingencies of Reinforcement: A Theoretical Analysis. New York: Appleton-Century-Crofts.

Stahl, O. Glenn (1971), The Personnel Job of Government Managers. *International Personnel Management Association*. Chicago, Illinois.

Stahl, O. Glenn (1976), *Public Personnel Administration*. 7th ed., Harper and Row Publishers, New York, N.Y.

Stanley, David T. (1964), The Higher Civil Service: An Evaluation of Federal Personnel Practices. *The Brookings Institution*. Washington, D.C.

Staw, B. M. (1975), Attribution of Causes of Performance. General Alternative Interpretation of Cross Sectional Research on Organizations. *Organizational Behavior and Human Performance*, 13(3):pp. 414-432.

Taylor, F. W. (1967), *The Principles of Scientific Management*. New York, Norton.

Telley, C. S., French, W. L. and Scott, W. G. (1971), The Relationship of inequity to turnover among hourly workers. *Administrative Science Quarterly*. 16:pp. 164-171.

Thayer, Frederick (1978), The Presidents Management "Reforms:" Theory X Triumphant. *Public Administration Review*. 38:. 4;pp. 309-314.

Thorndike, E. L. (1911), *Animal Intelligence*. New York: MacMillan.

Tolman, E. C. (1932), *Purposive Behavior in Animals and Men*. New York: Appleton-Century-Crofts.

Vroom, Victor H. (1964), *Work and Motivation*. New York: John Wiley & Sons.

Wanous, J. P. (1974), A Causal-Correlational Analysis of the Job Satisfaction and Performance Relationship. *Journal of Applied Psychology*. 59:pp. 139-144.

Wanous, John P., Lawler, Edward E., III (1972), Measurement and Meaning of Job Satisfaction. *Journal of Applied Psychology*. 57:pp. 95-105.

Weiner, Bernard (1980), *Human Motivation*. New York: Holt, Rinehart and Winston.

Wernimont, P. F. and M. D. Dunnette (1964), Intrinsic and Extrinsic Factors in Job Satisfaction. Paper read at Midwestern Psychological Association, St. Louis, 1964. (cited in Ewen, et al., 1966).

White, W. L., Becker, J. W. (1980), Increasing the Motivational Impact of Employee Benefits. *Personnel*. 57:pp. 32-37.

Woodworth, R. S. (1918), *Dynamic Psychology*. New York: Columbia University Press.

Work in America Institute (1978), *Productivity and the Quality of Work Life*. Scarsdale, New York.

Yukl, G. A., Latham, G. P. (1975), Consequences of Reinforcement Schedules and Incentive Magnitudes for Employee Performance: Problems Encountered in an Industrial Setting. *Journal of Applied Psychology*. 60:pp. 294-298.

Yukl, G. A., Latham, G. P., Pursell, E. D. (1976), The Effectiveness of Performance Incentives Under Continuous and Variable Ratio Schedules of Reinforcement. *Personnel Psychology*. 29:pp. 221-231.

Yukl, G., Wexley, K. N., Seymore, J. D. (1972), Effectiveness of Pay Incentives
Under Variable Ratio and Continuous Reinforcement Schedules. *Journal of
Applied Psychology*. 56:pp. 19-23.

Zedeck, S. and Smith, P. E. (1968), A Psychophysical Determination of Equitable
Payment: A Methodological Study. *Journal of Applied Psychology*. 52:
pp. 343-347.

LEADERSHIP

Because of the presumed importance of leadership in public administration, numerous leadership training or leadership selection approaches have arisen. Leadership training is now a common part of executive development programs at federal, state, and even local levels of government. Governments are faced routinely with a rapid turnover in upper management, geared to the electoral cycle. New managers entering government have frequently been trained in law or some other profession, but not in management. Leadership training seems almost essential in such situations.

In contrast to this common sense view, however, is a much more complex reality. Studies of the relationship of leadership to organization effectiveness frequently conclude there is little, if any, correlation. How can we reconcile these findings, to be discussed below, with the common sense view that leadership is critical? To answer this question we will review the three major approaches to the study of leadership: the trait approach, the behavioral approach, and the situational (contingency) approach.

In studying the three major approaches to leadership we will find a trend from simple, one-factor theories to complex, multi-factor theories. The earliest approaches, associated with *"trait theories"* of leadership, simply sought to identify outstanding leader qualities such as achievement orientation. Later *behavioral researchers* emphasized leadership behaviors, such as participative management (a single-factor theory) or combined social/task orientation (a dual factor theory). Because both trait and behavioral approaches found only slender evidence that the factors they studied led to organizational effectiveness, many contemporary scholars have rejected generalized theories of leadership in favor of *contingency theories*, which link particular leader behaviors to particular organizational settings. The transition from trait to behavioral to contingency theories is outlined below, followed by a conclusion which summarizes what practical lessons may be derived by the practicing public manager from leadership research.

THE TRAIT APPROACH TO LEADERSHIP

The trait approach to the study of leadership is the most direct. Effective leadership is defined in terms of the traits of leaders thought to exemplify good leadership. This circular method is sometimes labelled the "attitudinal approach to leadership" since most of the traits studied are attitudes and values, such as integrity or sociability. (Compare the discussion of drive theory in Chapter 1.) In addition, learned abilities, such as expertise, may be included. Through this method it is possible to compile a long list of desirable leadership characteristics. Agencies may then screen managerial candidates by these criteria (e.g., in psychological tests at entrance), train existing managers to be more in conformity with prescribed leadership traits, or provide role models to encourage the imitation of these traits.

Some of the leadership traits identified by researchers are these:

- achievement drive (Stogdill, 1974; Mills and Bohannon, 1980);
- ascendance/dominance (Stogdill, 1974; Mills and Bohannon, 1980);
- consistency (Straw and Ross, 1980);
- emotional balance (Stogdill, 1974);
- expectancy of high standards (Scanlon, 1979);
- fairness (Sank, 1974);
- independence (Hornaday and Bunker, 1970);
- inner direction (Zaleanik, 1977);
- integrity (Argyris, 1955);
- originality (Argyris, 1955);
- political awareness (Radin, 1980);
- self-confidence (Argyris, 1955; Motowidlo, 1980);
- sociability (Stogdill, 1974);
- understanding (Sank, 1974);

In addition, researchers have found correlations between leadership position and certain personal abilities and characteristics:

- verbal fluency (Stogdill, 1974);
- height (Stogdill, 1948);
- intelligence (Stogdill, 1974; Mills and Bohannon, 1980);
- expertise (Sank, 1974; Kabanoff and O'Brien, 1979; Knight and Weiss, 1980).

So many leadership traits have been identified that it is difficult to know which are critical. Which are the essential ones that make leaders different from other managers?

How Are Leaders Different?

Based on a study of American public and private sector leaders, Abraham Zaleznik (1977) concluded that among the many leadership traits the essential one differentiating top managers was inner direction. These individuals, Zaleznik noted, are apt to be subject as children to parental demands for self-reliant performance. They adopt an inner-world orientation. They feel separate from their environments, even from other people. Their sense of self-esteem is based on inner drives, not social roles or peer attitudes. Zaleznik found such individuals form deep attachments to one or two strong mentors. General Fox Connor was such a mentor to Dwight Eisenhower, as was banking financier David Rockefeller to Henry Kissinger, later Nixon's Secretary of State. Through inner drives for achievement combined with deep attachments to organizational mentors, Zaleznik concluded, inner-directed individuals rise to top leadership positions.

Zaleznik's research on leadership is reminiscent of Abraham Maslow's hierarchy of needs theory of motivation (Maslow, 1956) discussed in Chapter 1. Maslow held that human values expressed in organizational life would center first on basic human needs (e.g., food, shelter). Only when these were fulfilled would people be able to give priority to the next higher need—social needs for affiliation and friendship. Next would come ego needs for esteem and power. Finally, needs for self-actualization would emerge as the priority of a mature society. Inner-directed achievement in Zaleznik's research corresponds to Maslow's self-actualization stage.

Other leadership researchers have also found self-actualization to be a key leadership trait. Michael Maccoby's study of 250 executives uncovered four types of leadership (Maccoby, 1976), each exhibiting characteristic personality traits. The *gamesman* was seen as the new, emerging leadership figure, oriented toward innovation, competition, and challenge. Other more traditional personality types were the *company man* (security-minded), the *craftsman* (production and quality-oriented), and the *jungle fighter* (power oriented). The analogies to Maslow's hierarchy are apparent: craftsman (production), company man (security and social acceptance), jungle fighter (power and esteem), and gamesman (self-actualization in meeting challenges).

The drive for self-actualization is the normative ideal of the managerial leader in the writings of researchers like Maslow, Zaleznik, and Maccoby. This is not to say, however, that actual leadership patterns correspond to this idea. Argyris (1962), in fact, has long emphasized that organizations routinely foster dependent immature relations. Likewise Maccoby's company man is far from the self-actualizing norm. Zaleznik, for his part, saw the inner-directed leader as the exception, not the rule.

In contrast to the ideal "self-actualizing leader," the more realistic norm is the "concerned manager" who provides employees with social recognition for a job well done. This image was publicized by the Hawthorne experiments (Roethlisberger, 1941) and was central to the human relations movement which arose in the 1930's. These experiments had demonstrated that when industrial engineering variables (e.g., light, pay incentives, work breaks) were altered in experimental groups, productivity rose. Surprisingly, however, productivity rose as well in the control groups. This "Hawthorne effect" showed administrative researchers that increased management concern for employers was a key motivator. During the 1930's and the postwar period the human relations movement preached the gospel of the new, concerned style of management.

The new style was taught to generations of public and private sector managers as the correct style of management. As discussed in Chapter 1, Douglas McGregor articulated it in *The Human Side of Enterprise* (1960) as "Theory Y." "Theory X" was the traditional, hierarchial style of management: top-down, one-way in communication, assuming subordinates must be coerced into being productive and believing that many preferred dependency. In contrast, Theory Y was presented as a new, more effective style; sensitive to human needs, showing concern for subordinates' views and assuming employees would be productive even without the close supervision of Theory X management. Most traits correlated with leadership are consistent with Theory Y or a self-actualizing approach but not with the authoritarian Theory X. Unfortunately, insufficient research exists to differentiate public leadership traits from those of private sector leaders.

Do Management Attitudes Lead to Organizational Effectiveness?

The trait of theory of leadership has considerable appeal. Though a given trait like "concern" doesn't necessarily lead to a given outcome like high productivity, it is hard to imagine leadership being successful without some combination of many of the named traits.

Some evidence exists that such traits *are* related to productivity. Nagle, (1954), for example, found that the trait of supervisory sensitivity (ability to discriminate among subordinates on the basis of their characteristics) was correlated at a high level ($r = 0.82$) with the productivity of their units as rated by superiors. Mills and Bohannon (1980) likewise found that police officers characterized by traits of dominance, intelligence, and autonomous achievement were more effective than their counterparts not so characterized.

Most evidence, however, shows only weak relationships of recommended leadership traits to organizational effectiveness. There are several reasons for this. First, attitudinal traits may not be translated by the manager into actual behavior. In a later section we will examine the behavioral approach to leadership, which addresses this problem. Second, what may be a good leadership attribute in one setting may be inappropriate in another. For example, Gitterman (1980) has found such "disapproved" traits as ethnocentrism, distrust of others, and high need for power to be characteristics of *successful* Soviet leaders. Researchers long ago discovered that there was little relation of personality traits to organizational effectiveness across differing situations (see Bird, 1940; Gibb, 1947; Stogdill, 1948).

A major reason for the finding of weak relationships has to do with the premises of trait theory. Trait theorists reasoned that good leadership attributes would lead to satisfied employees, and worker satisfaction would lead to effective work behaviors. While this seems plausible, research has found only a peripheral relationship between satisfaction and organizational productivity (see Brayfield and Crockett, 1955). For example, Vroom's (1964) study of nearly two dozen research efforts showed a very weak ($r = 0.14$) median correlation. Some have suggested that even this weak correlation is due to the effects of productivity on satisfaction, just the opposite of the trait theorists' assumptions (see Lawler and Porter, 1967).

As this evidence became generally known, researchers turned to the hypothesis that leadership behavior (not leadership attitudes) determined organizational effectiveness. This is not to say that the differences between the trait and behavioral approaches to leadership are sharp. Traits do suggest management behaviors. The trait of understanding, for example, suggests the behavior of two-way communication. The difference was one of degree. The trait approach emphasized the attitudes of the leaders; behaviors were secondary. The behavioral approach, in contrast, was generally concerned with the organizational climate of the group as reflected in broad patterns of management behavior. Students of the behavioral approach assumed that research would prove leader *behavior* to be more strongly related to organizational effectiveness than leader *attitudes and traits* had been.

BEHAVIORAL APPROACHES TO LEADERSHIP

Advocates of behavioral approaches to leadership study did not reject the findings of trait researchers. Attributes like sociability, fairness, or achievement-orientation were acknowledged to be important. But behavioralists argued that these attributes made little difference unless translated into leadership behavior. Behavior is, of course, a generic term which could be applied to almost any study of leadership. The behavioral approach to leadership is identified primarily with just three specific types of behavior. The first of these is *participatory management*, involving employees in democratic forms of agency governance. The second research focus concerns a *combination of task-oriented and people-oriented behaviors* thought by many to reflect an ideal leadership balance. The last focus studies behavior modification, path-goal, and other *instrumental behaviors* also advocated as keys to organizational effectiveness through leadership behavior. Each of these is examined in turn below.

Participatory Leadership Behavior

Participation, dealt with at greater length in Chapter 6, was the focus of the earliest major behavioral approach to the study of leadership. A seminal study of democratic leadership was that by Lewin, Lippitt, and White (1939). In research on children's clubs, these researchers created three different organizational climates. Under an authoritarian climate the leader made all decisions and allowed the group to see only one step at a time. Under a laissez-faire climate the leader acted as a passive resource for the club members. Under the democratic climate the leader pursued action on the basis of group discussion and decision.

Lewin found the authoritarian style led to high aggression and high dependency. Laissez-faire leadership led to low group performance and the emergence of a strong informal group leader. The democratic leadership style, in contrast, was associated with low aggression and high group performance. Later studies did not change this initial finding substantially. Kahn and Katz (1960), for example, found that in a variety of industries that high productivity section leaders were oriented toward employee interaction, whereas task-orientation prevailed in low-productivity sections.

Following Lewin, Coch and French (1948) documented a major cause of the apparent superiority of the democratic leadership style. These researchers found that subjects who participated in a decision were significantly more likely to accept and later carry it out. Similarly, recent research by Efran, Goldsmith, McFarland, and Sharf (1979) showed that securing verbal commitment beforehand led to higher performance than did three other methods tested: better information on work process, exhortation to try hard, or better monetary incentives. Participation invests the employee psychologically in the decision and reduces resistance to change.

The Institute for Social Research at the University of Michigan was a central force in studies of organizational participation and consequently "the Michigan studies" are classics of the literature on participatory leadership behavior. The Michigan studies showed the effects of participation were more complex than previously thought. Generalizing the democratic style as employee orientation and the authoritarian as production orientation, Katz, Maccoby, and Morse (1950) found managers could be high on *both* dimensions simultaneously. In another major experiment, Morse and Reimer (1956) found productivity increased under *both* participative and hierarchical leadership styles, although only the former increased employee satisfaction. Kahn (1956) also documented these results. A later review of forty-nine other studies by Anderson (1959) showed *no* clear relation of democratic leadership to organization performance. In summary, recent research (see Jermier and Berkes, 1979) continues to show a relationship of participation to employee satisfaction and even organizational commitment, but not necessarily to actual organizational performance.

A famous *Harvard Business Review* article by Slater and Bennis (1964) was titled, "Democracy Is Inevitable." This was thought to be so because participation provided better communication, consensus in decision-making, competency-based decisions, and utilization of organizational conflict. The Michigan studies and later social science research showed that participation led to satisfaction but not necessarily productivity (cf. Butterfield and Farris, 1974).

A second problem for advocates of organizational democracy was finding that participation was not a cause of productivity but only a mutual consequence of a more basic determinant—the propensity to innovate. Innovative organizations were found to be characterized by change, not only in participation but in many other productivity-related areas as well. For example, Marrow, Bowers, and Seashore (1967) studied the Harwood Manufacturing Company, often cited as a model democratic organization. These researchers found two-thirds of the reported productivity improvement to be due to industrial engineering improvement, better training, and personnel changes, *not participation per se*.

Another perspective alternative to organizational democracy argued that participation was effective, but only if part of a package of organizational changes. This argument was made by Rensis Likert (1961, 1967), who had studied four systems of leadership:

System 1. Exploitative authoritarian.

System 2. Benevolent authoritarian.

System 3. Consultative.

System 4. Participative.

Likert found System 4, the participative approach, to be superior—but only if it involved corresponding changes in supervision, decision-making, personnel systems, compensation systems, performance evaluation, employee training, and organizational communication. Otherwise, participative leadership would degenerate, Likert held, into benevolent authoritarianism.[1]

In addition to these modifications to the participative theory of leadership, many of the criticisms of the trait approach applied as well. Hofstede (1980), for example, found that in some cultures such as France, a non-participatory autocratic leadership style was often preferred, whereas in other countries such as Sweden, a participatory style received even more support than in the United States. Participation, like recommended personality traits, varies in effectiveness depending on the context. While it generally fosters employee satisfaction, too many other factors intervene to conclude that participatory leadership behavior will necessarily lead to greater organizational effectiveness. Given this conclusion, many students of the behavioral approach to leadership shifted from an emphasis on democratic leadership behaviors to a focus on social/task behaviors. This broader, less ideological focus was thought by many to incorporate the complex relationships found by the researchers on participative leadership.

Social/Task Leadership Behavior

The Michigan studies originated with a concern for democratic management but democratic participation soon came to be conceptualized in broad terms as "employee orientation," contrasted to "production orientation" (Katz and Kahn, 1951; Kahn and Katz, 1953). Other Michigan researchers expanded the concepts even further to compare "group maintenance functions" with "group achievement functions" (Cartwright and Zander, 1960; see also Zelditch, 1955). Implicit in this reconceptualization was the belief that some combination of social-oriented and task-oriented leadership behaviors might prove more effective than participatory behavior alone.

This alternative orientation was researched extensively in studies at Ohio State University, starting as early as 1945. In the period from 1945 to 1955, the Ohio State studies focused on two leadership behavior dimensions:

1. Consideration (C)   trust and respect for subordinates' ideas, facilitating two-way communication.

2. Structure, Initiation of (S)   initiation of plans, schedules, evaluations, and other task-structuring work activities.

The consideration-structure distinction of the Ohio State studies was similar to the earlier distinction between democratic and autocratic leadership. Consideration and structure, however, were much more broadly defined (see Stogdill, 1948; Flieshman, 1953; Halpin, 1954; Hemphill, 1954; Stogdill and Coons, 1957). Consideration, for example, included all forms of supportive interaction and concern regardless of actual participatory process or exercise of democratic powers. Structure included all task-organizing behaviors even if implemented in a non-autocratic manner.

Using these categories, Fleishman, Harris, and Burt (1955) came to conclusions similar to those at Michigan. High consideration did not lead to as high rated performance as high structuring behavior, though it was associated with higher satisfaction evidenced in lower absenteeism and fewer grievances. Some later researchers have also cast doubt that high consideration leads to better employee satisfaction, much less better organizational effectiveness (Gilmore, Beehr, and Richter, 1979). Factor analysis of hundreds of behavioral traits thus supported the contention that there were *two* underlying dimensions to leadership behavior —task structure as well as social concern.

Later research has frequently supported the Ohio State studies' reemphasis on the task dimension as co-equal if not superior in importance to the social dimension of leadership, including participatory behavior. Greene and Schriesheim (1980), for example, found that instrumental (task) leadership as well as supportive (social) leadership increased group arousal and cohesiveness in work. While supportive leadership had the edge in small and newly-formed groups, instrumental leadership seemed to be more effective in large group situations often encountered in bureaucracy.[2]

The Ohio State findings on the importance of a *combination* of task- and social-oriented behaviors were popularized immensely by two organization development specialists, Robert Blake and Jane Mouton (1964, 1966). Blake and Mouton used the consideration and structure dimensions, relabelled, in what they termed "the managerial grid" (Fig. 6). The four extreme corners and the center of this coordinate system identified five distinct leadership styles according to Blake and Mouton:

- 1,1 impoverished management style
- 1,9 country club style
- 9,1 authority orientation style
- 5,5 middle of the road style
- 9,9 team style

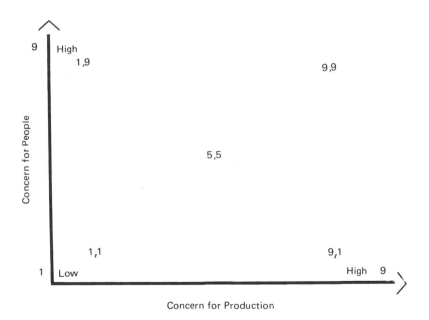

Figure 6. The managerial grid.

In citing the drawbacks of all but the 9,9 style, Blake and Mouton were simply re-iterating the earlier conclusions of Ohio State researchers and others who pre-scribed a combination of high consideration and high structure initiating behaviors for managerial leadership.[3]

There are many variants of these theories using social/task leadership behavior concepts.[4] One of the best-known is the life cycle theory of leadership associated with Hersey and Blanchard (1966, 1977, 1979). In a new organization, according to Hersey and Blanchard, the leader must emphasize structure and direction (Quadrant I) (Fig. 7). Later it is possible and desirable to emphasize both con-cern and structure (Quadrant II). At an even later stage of maturity the leader may be able to delegate structure concerns and concentrate on team building (Quadrant III). Occasionally an organization may progress to the most mature phase, where the leader may delegate both dimensions to subordinates and move on to other priorities (Quadrant IV).

As with the democratic leadership research, social/task theories of leadership have incurred substantial criticism. Fleishman and Peters (1962), for instance, found consideration/structure scores of managers were not related to their effec-tiveness as rated by superiors. Likewise, Korman (1966) found only a low relation between consideration/structure behaviors and organizational effectiveness. Sales (1968) also found no consistent relationship of structure to effectiveness, and only a low relation of consideration to effectiveness. Both Lowin and Craig (1968) and House, Filley, and Kerr (1971) found the consideration/structure categories highly contingent on setting. Employee competencies, for example, greatly in-

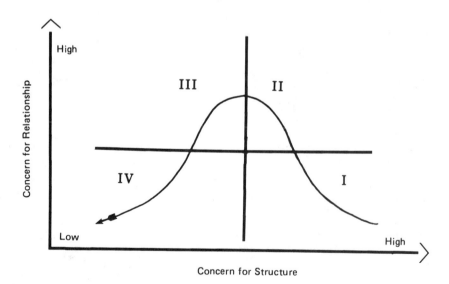

Figure 7. The life cycle.

fluenced closeness of supervision (structure) as did technology. Other research showed consideration/structure to be contingent on sex, with men being higher on structure and women on consideration (Kanter, 1977). Likewise consideration/ structure is contingent on group cohesiveness, with high structuring behavior being more effective for low cohesion groups (Schriesheim, 1980).

In summary, social/task theories of leadership behavior prescribe a clear norm for management. This is the action style high on *both* consideration and structure. It is "9,9" team management in Blake and Mouton's terms. Even the life cycle variant suggests that the high social, high task quadrant (Quadrant II in Hersey and Blanchard) is the most prevalent. Mounting evidence suggests, however, that this prescription is no more clearly related to organizational effectiveness than the participatory leadership concepts had been. Clearly, many other variables intervene. Leadership style and behavior are related to organizational effectiveness in a manner contingent on contextual variables. Contingency theories of leadership, discussed in a later section, build on this conclusion. First, however, we will conclude our discussion of behavioral approaches to leadership by examining a third major focus of that orientation.

Instrumental Leadership Behavior

In addition to study of democratic and social/task behaviors, a final major behavioral approach to the study of leadership is identified with *instrumental* leader behaviors. These include behaviors which clarify the relationship of means to ends for the individual employee (path-goal theories) or which reinforce desired employee patterns (behavioral modification theories). The former was introduced in Chapter 1 in the discussion of expectancy models, and the latter in the discussion of operant conditioning. What both path-goal and behavior modification theories have in common is a mutual emphasis on leader behavior which is instrumental to attaining the goals and rewards sought by the employee.

As set forth by House and Mitchell (1974), the path-goal theory of leadership is based on an expectancy theory of motivation [also called the VIE theory, focusing on valence/instrumentality/expectancy; see House, (1971)]. This theory states that motivational force (MF) is determined by the value of the goal to the participant (valence, V) and the expectation that a given effort will lead to the desired outcome (expectancy, E):

$$MF = V \text{ times } E$$

Expectancy/instrumentality theory is associated with the work of Vroom (1964), Porter and Lawler (1968), Graen (1969), and Nebeker and Mitchell (1974).

House and Mitchell sought to show how various leadership styles were instrumental to goal achievement. In each case a different management style is instrumental to the situation. Directive leadership (high structure) guides employees fac-

Path-Goal Contingencies

Style	Characteristics	When Instrumental
DIRECTIVE	clarifies roles, guides tasks, sets clear standards, schedules work	1. tasks are ambiguous *and* subordinates' personalities are authoritarian
PARTICIPATIVE	consults, takes suggestions seriously	1. subordinates are highly ego-involved in task 2. subordinates are highly nonauthoritarian personalities
SUPPORTIVE	friendly, concerned, makes work pleasant	1. task is stressful or dissatisfying
ACHIEVEMENT-ORIENTED	sets challenging goals, high performance standards, but shows confidence in subordinates	1. task is ambiguous and nonrepetitive

ing ambiguous tasks. Participative leadership (high consideration) mobilizes expression of ego-involved, nonauthoritarian subordinates. Supportive leadership (another type of high consideration) reduces stress in dissatisfying tasks. Achievement-oriented management encourages goal-attainment in tasks where opportunities for achievement are greatest. Complex situations may call for an appropriate combination of leadership styles, according to path-goal theory.

Path-goal theory is an expansion of earlier work on expectancy theory by M. G. Evans (1970, 1974). Evans argued that a high concern, high structure leadership style was associated with high group performance only if rewards were contingent on performance. Even earlier Bowers and Seashore (1966) had outlined four leadership styles similar to those in House's path-goal theory. House used expectancy theory to explain the relation of these leadership styles to various types of rewards (task accomplishment, ego involvement, stress reduction, goal attainment) in various situations.

Path-goal theory was a practical contribution to leadership research. Managers frequently overestimate the importance of formal rewards and underestimate the importance of task feedback clarifying path-goal relationships (Greller, 1980). Path-goal relationships may be clarified in individual work contracts with demonstrable success (Burgers, 1980). Although path-goal clarifying behavior does lead to greater job motivation, however, the strength of the relationship is low in most cases (Klimoski and Hayes, 1980). Thus, although path-goal concepts now often receive endorsement (Scanlon, 1979), the actual emplirical research supporting these recommendations is weak (Johns, 1978).

Some evidence exists that behavior modification is more effective than other, more diffuse forms of path-goal processes. Hersey and Blanchard (1980), for example, studied the effectiveness of various types of leadership behavior in the problematic situation of the disruptive worker. They found that high task-oriented leadership tended to exacerbate worker hostility, while high relationship-oriented leadership only rewarded disruptive behavior with attention. Most effective was a behavior modification style in which the leader ignored bad behaviors, set clear limits on bad behavior, and rewarded desired behavior.

Behavior modification has thus far received only limited testing, mostly in efforts to change such relatively concrete and specific behaviors as employee tardiness (Luthans and Kreitner, 1975). Behavior modification derives from broader notions about organizational change associated with Kurt Lewin (1947) and the study of group dynamics. Lewin saw change as a three-stage process involving 1) unfreezing (removal from the old environment, demeaning treatment, linking of reward to willingness to change); 2) change (identification of employee with new behaviors, internalization); and 3) refreezing (reinforcement of desired behavior). Lewin's studies of coaching of basketball teams and of training of U.S. Marines showed this sequence was effective in behavior modification. It is now commonly assumed that any effective leadership process must link rewards to desired behavior directly, but it is not clear that this is sufficient to achieve organizational effectiveness.

Summary

Research on leadership started with a concern for identification of leadership *traits*, so that this might be used as a basis for management selection and training. When the relationship of such traits to organizational effectiveness proved weak, researchers sought to emphasize specific leadership *behaviors*, starting with participative management. This democratic focus, and the later behavioral research on social/task and instrumental leadership behaviors, revealed the complexity of leadership and showed the futility of simple answers. By the 1960's and 1970's, students of leadership came to the view that leadership theories must take specific management situations into account. That is, earlier interest in broad generalizations (e.g., participative leadership always helps organizational effectiveness) was rejected in favor of theories tying particular behaviors to particular contingencies —hence the name "contingency theory."

CONTINGENCY APPROACHES TO LEADERSHIP

Contingency theories of leadership, also called situational theories, are unified by little other than a common rejection of the notion that good leadership is a direct function of having specified desirable leadership traits or set leadership behaviors. Contingency theorists examine a wide range of dimensions, seeking to develop relatively complex theories showing which type of leadership pattern is appropriate for a given cluster of situational factors.

The best-known contingency theory of leadership is that popularized in the writings of Fred E. Fiedler (1965, 1967, 1969, 1974, 1976; Fiedler and Chemers, 1974; Fiedler and Mahar, 1979). Fiedler examined the effect on organizational productivity of three situational variables: leader-member relations, degree of task structuring, and strength of leader authority. Productivity was measured objectively by the number of games won by sports teams, profits of businesses, or accuracy of bombing runs by Air Force teams. Fiedler found that task-centered styles (high structure) were associated with organizational effectiveness when these three variables were very favorable (good relations, structured tasks, strong authority) *or* when very unfavorable. For other, middle-favorability contingencies a relationship-centered style (high concern) was more effective.

The assumption was that an emphasis on structure rather than relationships was appropriate in the high-favorability contingency because there employees felt little need for participative meetings or other manifestations of a relationship-oriented approach. In the highly unfavorable contingency structure was more appropriate simply to assert direction and move toward goals. Such unfavorable settings lacked the basis for effective action through relationship-centered approaches alone.

Several objections have been raised to Fiedler's contingency theory. It is not predictive since leader-member relations cannot be predicted prior to group formation. It is not comprehensive since many other contingency variables can be posited. Csoka (1974), for example, found leader intelligence to be such an additional contingency [later investigated (Fiedler, Potter, Zais, and Knowlton, 1979)]. Greatest criticism centered on Fiedler's indirect method of measuring leadership style. Fiedler used a Least-Preferred Co-worker (LPC) scale (Fiedler, 1969) based on items like the following:

> *"Think of the person with whom you can work least well. He may be someone you work with now, or he may be comeone you knew in the past. Use an x to describe this person as he appears to you.*

helpful	_ _ _ _ _ _ _ _	*frustrating*
	1 2 3 4 5 6 7 8	
unenthusiastic	_ _ _ _ _ _ _ _	*enthusiastic*
	1 2 3 4 5 6 7 8	
efficient	_ _ _ _ _ _ _ _	*inefficient"*
	1 2 3 4 5 6 7 8	

Since LPC rating correlated with a relationship-centered management style, Fiedler used it as an operational way of measurement. A review by Graen, Alvares, and Orris (1970) found LPC theory still unproved. Research by Schneier (1975), Schriesheim and Kerr (1977) and Vecchio (1979) found relations involving LPC to be complex and weak.

In spite of its slim empirical validation Fiedler's contingency theory contained common-sense truths. Leaders who had "everything going for them"—strong authority, clear tasks, good staff relations—had little need to go beyond simple task orientation. Leaders with none of these favorable contexts dealt with a chaotic situation demanding strong, task-oriented leadership, though for opposite reasons. It seemed only in the in-between situations that relationship-centeredness would make a difference to organizational effectiveness.

Contingency Theory: Decision Relationships

Where Fiedler had examined task relationships (structure, authority, manager-employee relations), another theory developed by Vroom and Yetton (1973, Vroom, 1976) emphasized decision relationships as the key dimension on which the relation of leadership to effectiveness was contingent. Vroom examined six principle styles which fell into three groups: autocratic (A), consultative (C), and democratic or group (G). Though efficiency suggested a general preference for A over C or G, and for C over G, the more democratic styles might be considered preferable depending on seven decision rules:

1. INFORMATION. Whether the leader possessed the necessary information and experience to solve the problem alone.
2. TRUST. Whether subordinates could be trusted to make decisions based on organizational goals and priorities.
3. PROBLEM STRUCTURE. Whether the problem was unstructured, assuming the quality of the decision was important.
4. ACCEPTANCE. Whether subordinate acceptance was critical to implementation, assuming an autocratic approach would fail to assure acceptance.
5. CONFLICT. Whether employee conflict over the decision outcome was likely, assuming acceptance is critical.
6. FAIRNESS. Whether acceptance was critical *and* the quality of the decision was not important.
7. PRIORITY. Whether acceptance was critical *and* subordinates could be trusted.

These seven rules tended to favor a more democratic solution when a specific situation made them applicable.

The Vroom-Yetton model was presented as a normative prescription, not an empirical theory. Nonetheless, Vroom and Jago (1978) found that in 181 decision cases, two thirds were rated successful where managers' actual decisions conformed to the model outlined above. Only one-fifth of non-conforming cases were rated successful. Margerison and Glube (1979) likewise found strong support for the Vroom-Yetton model. In their research, leaders conforming to the model had workers with significantly higher productivity and satisfaction than did nonconforming managers.

Decision Rules and Leadership Styles

LEADERSHIP STYLE	DECISION RULES AFFECTING GIVEN STYLE
AI. Evaluate and decide on the basis of one's own information	1, 3, 4, 5, 6, 7
AII. Obtain information from subordinates but evaluate and decide oneself.	3, 4, 5, 6, 7
CI. Obtain evaluations as well as information from individual subordinates, but decide oneself	3, 5, 6, 7
CII. Obtain evaluations as well as information from subordinates via group discussion, but decide oneself.	6, 7
GI. (For individual problems). Share information with a subordinate, evaluate jointly, and reach a decision by mutual consensus.	
GII. (For group problems). Share information with group of subordinates, evaluate collectively, reach and follow democratic decision.	2

*Adapted from Vroom and Yetton (1973): 13, 145-146.

The decision contingencies supportive of a participative style (GII) were 1) the subordinates' acceptance being crucial and not otherwise assured; 2) assuming employees could be trusted to base decisions on criteria of organizational effectiveness; *or* 3) assuming the quality of the decision was not important.

Contingency Theory: Managerial Roles

The Vroom-Yetton model favored participatory leadership style only when the decision context required it, as when employee acceptance of the decision was crucial to its implementation and participation was crucial to acceptance. Expanding the focus on decision relationships to a more general examination of managerial roles has led other researchers to view participatory or high consideration leadership style as also contingent for its effectiveness on the *functional role* of the manager. Though this line of analysis antedates much of contingency theory discussed above, relatively little empirical testing of role-related theories has occurred. The hypothesis generated by the role theories are of interest, however, and so are reported here.

A critical determinant of managerial role is the organization's reward system, as typologized by French and Raven (1960):

1. coercive   based on fear
2. reward   based on recognition or remuneration
3. legitimate   based on formal position

4. expert   based on knowledge or skill
5. referent based on social appeal

In this scheme one would expect that coercive settings would be the least favorable to high consideration leadership styles, while referent settings would require managerial roles most favorable to such styles. Reward and legitimate settings would allow the most variation in leadership style, while expert settings might be expected to encourage laissez-faire styles (low consideration, low structure) due to their basis on individual competencies.

Another type of managerial role is based on the function of representation, as discussed by Miller (in Dubin, 1965), outlining four types of representation roles:

1. Representation of management (RM)
2. Representation of employees (RE)
3. Dual identity (DI)
4. Identification with fellow supervisors (FS)

In this analysis RE settings would be most supportive of high consideration leadership styles and RM settings the least. FS settings would allow the greatest variance, while a laissez-faire style (low consideration, low structure) would be associated with DI settings due to the tendency to withdraw in cross-pressured situations.

Finally, Price (1968: 48) distinguished a third type of managerial role typology:

Decision Roles

1. *Decision-making*: goal specification, progress measurement, selection of alternative courses or action
2. *Decision-enforcing*: sanctioning, monitoring, transmitting decisions, processing grievances

This, of course, corresponds to the familiar distinction between policy and program levels in agencies. Decision-making roles may be more supportive of high consideration styles of leadership because of the inherently greater social and interactive nature of these roles, whereas the inherently authoritative nature of the sanctioning and monitoring functions of decision-enforcing would be less supportive. Great variation would be possible and there is little research validation of this or other contingency theories based on managerial role.

Contingency Theory: Managerial Values/Subordinates' Values

As a final illustration of contingency theories of leadership, we may note a theory emphasizing yet another dimension: *managerial values* in relation to subordinates' values. Flowers and Hughes (1978) studied six basic value sets:

Value Relationships

1. *Existential*: value emphasis on human dignity and self-esteem; non-conforming, flexible, open.

2. *Sociocentric*: value emphasis on concern for people; harmonious, conflict-reducing, equalizing.
3. *Egocentric*: value emphasis on strength; seeking power, decisive, suspicious of others.
4. *Manipulative*: value emphasis on competition; risk-taking, productivity-emphasizing, gamesmanship.
5. *Conformist*: value emphasis on rule observance; loyal, business-like, consistent.
6. *Tribalistic*: value emphasis on teamwork; helpful, obedient, expecting performance.

Of these six value sets, the first three (existential, sociocentric, egocentric) are different dimensions of consideration (concern for people). The last three (manipulative, conformist, tribalistic) are dimensions of structure (concern for task). Using these value sets Flowers and Hughes theorized that the effectiveness of various leadership styles would be contingent on the prevailing value orientations of subordinates, as indicated on Table 3. As with role theory research, there is as yet no empirical validation of the value contingency theories of Flowers and Hughes.

Summary of Contingency Approaches

Contingency theorists have shown a long list of determinants of organizational effectiveness to be important in certain situations. These contingent factors include leader-member relations, degree of task structuring, and strength of leader authority (Fiedler); leader intelligence (Csoka); decision relationships and types (Vroom and Yetton); reward-related roles (French and Raven); representation-related roles (Miller); decision level (Price); and value relationships (Flowers and Hughes), to name a few. Contingency theory arose in reaction against single-factor theories of leadership, such as democratic theory. As a multifactor approach, however, contingency theory leads to such an extreme level of complexity of findings that the practicing public manager may wonder what its practical import may be. In the summary below we seek to address this question.

CONCLUSION

"The influence of supervisory behavior on productivity is small," Robert Dubin wrote nearly two decades ago (Dubin, Homans, Mann, and Miller, 1965). Little has happened since to change that judgment. Research has shown leadership style to be related to organizational effectiveness in highly complex and contingent ways which contrast with the expectations of early researchers that studies would soon vindicate the universal applicability of democratic management, "9,9" management, or other simple formulations.

Recent attempts to provide a theoretical framework for leadership research

TABLE 3. Flowers and Hughes Value Compatibility Matrix*

		Supervisory Value Role					
		Concern for People			Concern for Structure		
Subordinate Value Orientation		existential	sociocentric	egocentric	manipulative	conformist	tribalistic
Concern for People	existential	C	NC	PC	NC	NC	NC
	sociocentric	C	NC	PC	NC	NC	NC
	egocentric	NC	NC	NC	C	C	NC
Concern for Structure	manipulative	C	C	PC	NC	NC	NC
	conformist	NC	NC	PC	C	PC	NC
	tribalistic	NC	PC	PC	C	C	PC

C = Compatible   PC = Partly Compatible   NC = Not Compatible

*Vincent S. Flowers & Charles L. Hughes, "Choosing a Leadership Style," *Personnel*, January-February 1978, pp. 51-57.

61

Style	Pros	Cons
High S/Low C	efficient where appropriate; often consistent and fair; necessary in crises; some like parentalism	tends to lone-rangerism; over-reliance on too few; lowers morale, esp. for younger; for professionals can be inflexible; one-way communication lacks feedback, leads to errors
Low S/High C	wider information; participation ups commitment; conflict dealt with openly; develop people; more motivating for most	time consuming; can raise false expectations; can lose management control; can be an excuse for the abdication of leadership
High S/High C	many advantages of first two styles	high expectations of managers and employees; demand on time and energy; less consistency than High S/Low C; High S tends to undermine credibility of High C; requires delicate balance
Low S/Low C	self-management is ideal; allows priority for managers to develop new projects; minimizes overhead	requires very mature work-force; high risk, low control

are far more complex than earlier attempts. Earlier models utilized a two-dimensional grid based on two relatively specific dimensions such as consideration and structure. Recent models have utilized a three-dimensional grid based on very broadly defined axes which are themselves multidimensional. Luthans and Stewart (1977), for example, map leadership research onto the three dimensions of performance criteria variables, management variables, and situational variables. Likewise, Barrow (1977) uses leader characteristics, leader behavior factors, and environment factors as his three dimensions.

Because research results are so complex, ambiguous, and partial, there has been some tendency for practitioner-oriented leadership training efforts to continue to rely on the earlier, simpler, "common sense" theories. As Stockton (1980) recently noted, "group leadership training is currently at approximately the same place as training programs for individual counseling were ten years ago. There are competing training models in existence having very little evidence as to their efficacy."

There is some argument in favor of retaining the simpler theories. Blake and Mouton (1978), for example, have defended their work, writing, "Rejection of 'one best way' is equivalent to repudiating the proposition that effective behavior is based on scientific principles or laws. . . Shifting from an 'it all depends' to a 'one best way' concept of leadership is what supervisory training is—or should be about." That is, it may be argued that the purpose of theory is to help managers by identifying simple, actionable, effective interventions—not to reproduce all-too-complex reality in a confusion of theory. Certainly contingency theory is not a theory in any unified sense and most practitioners would indeed view it as simply saying leadership "all depends."

At the practitioner level, there is some consensus today on the relative benefits of high structure (S) or high consideration (C) leadership styles (see Owens, 1973):

The danger of this consensus is that practicing managers will be drawn into "common-sense" patterns which research would suggest are counterproductive. In spite of the youthfulness and complexity of leadership research, several generalizations are now possible. *First* popularly-recommended leadership styles marked by high participation and/or high consideration often lead to higher satisfaction but not significantly greater organizational effectiveness. *Second*, effectiveness is a function of many organizational variables of which leadership style is only one. *Third*, some of the most critical variables are those associated with clarifying the path-goal relationships which help the individual connect effort to performance to reward, though path-goal variables are not sufficient in themselves to assure high organizational effectiveness.

It is also possible to put forward a composite *profile* of the contingencies most favorable to participatory/high consideration leadership: In an agency in which such a leadership style is effective, the leader is also involved in other changes in decision-making, personnel, compensation, training, and the like. These changes give substance to participation or consideration and avoid its appearing merely symbolic or manipulative. Employees will hold values characterized by openness, flexibility, self-esteem, and support for democratic principles. The work situation will be neither new, unorganized, and anarchic on the one hand nor mature, stable, and self-maintaining on the other. Likewise, employee relations, task structure, and managerial authority in combination will present only moderate problems (neither consistent severe problems nor consistently no problems). The leader will not neglect task concerns or rewards for performance, and will emphasize participation and consideration only in those decision areas requiring employee acceptance of decisions.

In addition, it can be stated that there is an ideal profile of the effective leader regardless of the structure/consideration dimension. The effective leader will display many of the characteristics identified by the trait approach; inner direction, achievement orientation, expecting high standards, sociable, fair, understanding, aware of agency politics, self-confident, intelligent, expert in the field, fluent, and tall. Clearly these helpful traits do not assure high organizational performance. It can be said, though, that effective managers spend substantially more time on supervision, though not necessarily close supervision (Kahn and Katz, 1960). Such managers frequently ask for employee opinions and let employees receive feedback on their work (Mann and Dent, 1954). Above all, effective managers seek to adapt their leadership style and behavior to the situational context.

Such composite profiles drawn from leadership research reflect the limited state of the art. No research has validated an entire composite. These only reflect the assumption, untested, that the sum of specific leadership findings may be aggregated into a composite whole. Leadership research is at its strongest in puncturing simple generalizations based on "common sense:" that participatory management is uniformly desirable, that close supervision and engineered work standards will consistently yield higher organizational productivity, or that picking a leader with the right traits will assure good results. Since much of management selection and development rests on false assumptions like these, the contribution of leadership research is not insignificant. If managers can better diagnose the factors determining the appropriateness of various patterns of action, leadership theory research will have attained a useful objective.

ENDNOTES

[1] Other researchers have suggested more complex typologies of democratic management style. In contrast to Lippitt's three categories or Likert's four, Owens (1973) suggested five:

a. Autocratic   tough to parental
b. Bureaucratic   rigid rule-orientation
c. Diplomatic   salesperson for management
d. Participative   consultative to democratic
e. Free-Rein   sets goals but delegates policy decision process

As discussed below, however, Owens saw pros and cons to each approach according to the situation. The participative and 'free-rein' approaches were not viewed as intrinsically superior.

Tannenbaum and Schmidt (1973) proposed a seven-point scale of democratic management style:

a. Manager makes decision and announces it;
b. Manager "sells" decision;
c. Manager presents final idea and invites questions;
d. Manager presents tentative idea and invites questions;
e. Manager presents problem, solicits ideas, then makes the decision;
f. Manager sets limits, allows group to decide;
g. Manager allows group to decide within limits set by the manager's superior.

Like Owens, Tannenbaum and Schmidt believe no one style is ideal for all situations. Rather, they say, style must vary by the situation, the nature of the subordinates, and the personality of the manager.

[2] For a history of the Ohio State research see Shartle, 1979.

[3] Blake and Mouton (1967) combined the Ohio State dimensions with a *six-stage OD plan*:

a. GRID SEMINARS: Managers assess styles using the managerial grid, give and receive style critiques from team members.
b. TEAM DEVELOPMENT: Superior-subordinate meetings leading to team-wide agreements on goals and standards.
c. INTERGROUP DEVELOPMENT: Exchange and comparison of group images between headquarters and field, management and labor, other groups.
d. ORGANIZATIONAL BLUEPRINT: Organizational climate survey used as basis for organizational plan formulated by top management and discussed at each lower level.
e. IMPLEMENTATION: Members make commitments to courses of action supporting the organizational blueprint.
f. STABILIZATION: Reinforcing new behavioral patterns through training, team-building, and other forms or organizational development.

The grid seminar approach to organization has been widely used, primarily in the private sector.

Blake and Mouton's OD plan, with its emphasis on clear objectives, supportive climate, and superior-subordinate agreements and coaching, was reminiscent of management by objectives as implemented through organization development team-building techniques using the Ohio State leadership style categories.

[4] Among the many variants are those of R. F. Bales (1953, 1958) on socio-emotional versus task behaviors; F. C. Mann's three-factor theory (1965), focusing on human relations skills versus technical task skills versus administrative task skills; D. G. Bowers and S. E. Seashore's four-factor theory (1966) studying supportive versus interactive goal-emphasizing versus work-facilitating leader behaviors; or J. C. Wofford's five-factor theory (1967, 1971) studying order/group achievement versus personal enhancement versus personal interaction versus security/maintenance versus dynamic/individual achievement dimensions.

Perhaps the most popular other variant is W. Reddin's "3-D theory of management style," a three factor theory (Reddin, 1967, 1979). The term "3-D" refers to Reddin's adding an effectiveness dimension to the conventional consideration and structure dimensions. Reddin's categories thus correspond loosely to those of Blake and Mouton:

Blake and Mouton	*Reddin*
Impoverished	Deserter
Country Club	Developer
Authority orientation	Benevolent autocrat
Middle of the road	Bureaucrat
Team style	Executive

Reddin's categorical labels above apply when the style is applied appropriately and the effectiveness dimension is therefore high. Low effectiveness is also possible when styles are applied inappropriately:

Missionary	Reddin's label for a "Developer who so emphasizes relationships that production is sacrificed.
Autocrat	Label for a "Benevolent autocrat" who is so task-oriented that long-term working relationships are sacrificed.
Compromiser	Label for an "Executive" who is high on relationships and production, but is too easily influenced by short-term pressures.

A "deserter" is also described by Reddin as a low-effectiveness "bureaucrat." Though not original, Reddin's typology has achieved widespread popularity among organizational trainers and management appraisal consulting firms.

REFERENCES

Allport, F. H., *Social Psychology* (1924) (Boston: Houghton Mifflin).

Anderson, Richard C. (1959), Learning in Discussions, A Resume of the Authoritarian-Democratic Studies, *Harvard Education Review*, Vol. 29:pp. 201-215.

Argyris, Chris (1955), "Some Characteristics of Successful Executives, *Personnel Journal* (June):pp. 50-63.

――――(1960), *Understanding Organizational Behavior*, Homewood, Ill: Dorsey.

――――(1962), *Interpersonal Competence and Organizational Effectiveness*, Homewood, Ill.: Dorsey.

Bales, R. F. (1953), The Equilibrium Problem in Small Groups, pp. 111-161 in T. Parsons, R. F. Bales & E. A. Shils, eds., *Working Papers in the Theory of Action*, Glencoe, Ill: Free Press.

―――― Role and Role Conflict, in E. E. Maccoby, T. M. Newcomb, and E. L. Hartley (eds.) (1958), *Readings in Social Psychology, 3rd ed.* (New York: Henry Holt and Co.).

Bird, C., Leadership, in R. M. Elliott (ed.) (1940), *Social Psychology* (New York: Appleton-Century-Crofts) pp. 369-395.

Blake, Robert R. and Jane S. Mouton (1964), *The Managerial Grid*, (Houston: Gulf Publishing).

――――(1966), Managerial Facades, *Advanced Management Journal*, (July): pp. 29-36.

――――(1967), Grid Organization Development, *Personnel Administration* (January-February).

Blake, Robert R. and Jane S. Mouton (1978), What's New with the Grid? *Training and Development Journal*, (May):pp. 3-8.

Bowers, David G. and Stanley E. Seashore (1966), Predicting Organizational Effectiveness with a Four-Factory Theory of Leadership, *Administrative Scientific Quarterly*, Vol. 11, No. 2 (Sept.):pp. 238-263.

Brayfield, Arthur H. and Crockett, Walter H. (1955), Employee Attitudes and Employee Performances, *Psychological Bulletin*, 52(5) (Nov.):pp. 396-426.

Burgers, Sherry B., (1980) An Examination of the Use of Contracts in Groups, *The Journal for Specialists in Group Work*, Vol. 5, No. 2 (May), pp. 68-72.

Butterfield, D. A. and G. F. Farris (1974), The Likert Organizational Profile: Methodologycal Analysis and Test of System 4 Theory in Brazil, *Journal of Applied Psychology*, Vol. 59, No. 1 (February):pp. 15-23.

Campbell, John P. and Marvin D. Dunnett (1968), Effectiveness of T-Group Experiences in Managerial Training and Development, *Psychological Bulletin*, 70(2) (August):pp. 73-104.

Cartwright, D., and A. Zander. (1960) *Group Dynamics: Research and Theory*, 2nd ed. (Evanston, Ill.: Row, Peterson).

Coch, Lester and John R. P. French, Jr. (1948), Overcoming Resistance to Change, *Human Relations*, Vol. 1 (August):pp. 512-532.

Csoka, L. S. (1974), A Relationship Between Leader Intelligence and Leader Rated Effectiveness, *Journal of Applied Psychology*, Vol. 59, No. 1 (February):pp. 43-47.

Dubin, Robert; G. C. Homans; F. C. Mann; and D. C. Miller (1965), *Leadership and Productivity*, San Francisco: Chandler.

Efran, Jay S., Dennis Goldsmith, Peter J. McFarland, III, and Bonnet Short (1979), The Effect on Endurance of a Verbal Commitment vs. Exhortation, Task Information and Monetary Incentives, *Motivation and Emotion*, Vol. 3, No. 1 (March) pp. 93-101.

Evans, M. G. (1970), The Effects of Supervisory Behavior on the Path-Goal Relationship, *Organizational Behavior and Human Performance*, Vol. 5 (May): pp. 277-298.

————(1974), Effects of Supervisory Behaviors on Extension of a Path-Goal Theory of Motivation, *Journal of Applied Psychology*, Vol. 59 (April): pp. 172-178.

Fiedler, Fred E. (1965), Engineer the Job to Fit the Manager, *Harvard Business Review*, Vol. 43, No. 5 (Sept.-Oct.):pp. 155-122.

————(1967), *A Theory of Leadership Effectiveness* (N.Y.: McGraw Hill).

————(1969), Style or Circumstance: The Leadership Enigma, in *Psychology Today*. reprinted in W. E. Natemeyer, ed., *Classics of Organizational Behavior* (Oak Park, Ill.: Moore):pp. 210-216.

————(1974), The Contingency Model - New Directions for Leadership Utilization, *Journal of Contemporary Business*, Vol. 3, No. 4 (Autumn):pp. 65-79.

————and Martin Chemers (1974), *Leadership and Effective Management* (Glenview Ill.: Scott, Foreman.).

————(1976), The Leadership Game: Matching the Man to the Situation, *Organizational Dynamics*, Vol. 4, No. 3 (Winter):pp. 6-16.

Fiedler, Fred E. and Linda Mahar (1979), "A Field Experiment Violating Contingency Model Leadership Training," *Journal of Applied Psychology*, Vol. 6, No. 3 (June):pp. 247-254.

_____, Earl H. Butler, Mitchel M. Zais, and William A. Knowlton, Jr. (1979), "Organizational Stress and the Use and Misuse of Managerial Intelligence and Experience," *Journal of Applied Psychology*, Vol. 6F, No. 6 (Dec), pp. 635-647.

Fleishman, Edwin A. (1953), "The Description of Supervisory Behavior," *Journal of Applied Psychology*, Vol. 37, pp. 1-6.

_____, E. F. Harris, and H. E. Burtt (1955), *Leadership and Supervision in Industry* (Columbus: Ohio State University Bureau of Educational Research).

_____and Peters, D. R. (1962), "Interpersonal Values, Leadership Attitudes, and Management 'Success,' " *Personnel Psychology*, Vol. 15 (2):pp. 127-143.

Flowers, Vincent S. and Charles L. Hughes (1978), "Choosing a Leadership Style," *Personnel*, January-February:pp. 48-59.

French, John R. P. and Bertrum Raven (1960), "The Bases of Social Power," in D. Cartwright and A. F. Zander, eds., *Group Dynamics, 2nd Edition*, Evanston, Ill.: Row, Peterson, pp. 607-623.

Gibb, C. A. (1947), "The Principles and Traits of Leadership," *Journal of Abnormal Psychology*, Vol. 42, pp. 267-284.

Gilmore, David, L., Terry A. Beehr, David J. Richter (1979), "Effects of Leader Behaviors on Subordinate Performance and Satisfaction, A Lab Experiment with Student Employees," *Journal of Applied Psychology*, Vol. 64, No. 2 (April), pp. 166-172.

Gitterman, Margaret (1980), "Assessing the Personalities of Soviet Politboro Members," *Personality and Social Psychology Bulletin*, Vol. 6, No. 3 (Sept), pp. 332-352.

Graen, G. (1969), "Instrumentality Theory of Work Motivation: Some Experimental Results and Suggested Modifications," *Journal of Applied Psychology Monograph*, Vol. 53, pp. 1-25.

_____, K. Alvares, and J. Orris (1970), "Contingency Model of Leadership Effectiveness: Antecedent and Evidential Results," *Psychological Bulletin*, Vol. 74:pp. 285-296.

Greene, Charles N. and Chester A. Schrieshein (1980), "Leader-Group Interactions: A Longitudinal Field Investigation," *Journal of Applied Psychology*, Vol. 65, No. 1 (Feb.), pp. 50-59.

Greller, Martin M. (1980), "Evaluation of Feedback Sources as a Function of Role and Organizational Level," *Journal of Applied Psychology*, Vol. 65, No. 1 (Feb.), pp. 24-27.

Halpin, A. W. (1954), "The Leadership Behavior and Combat Performance of Airplane Commanders," *Journal of Abnormal and Social Psychology*, Vol. 49, pp. 19-22.

Hemphill, J. K. (1954), *A Proposed Theory of Leadership in Small Groups* (Columbus: The Ohio State University, Personnel Research Board Technical Report).

Hersey, Paul and K. A. Blanchard (1967), *Leader Behavior*, (Management Education and Development, Inc.).

_____, Alan C. Filley, and Steven Kerr (1971), Relation of Leader Consideration and Initiating Structure to R & D Subordinates' Satisfaction, *Administrative Science Quarterly*, Vol. 16 (March):pp. 19-30.

_____, and Terence R. Mitchell (1974), Path-Goal Theory of Leadership, *Journal of Contemporary Business*, Vol. 3, No. 4 (Autumn):pp. 81-97.

_____(1977), *Management of Organization Behavior*, (Englewood Cliffs, N.J.: Prentice Hall).

_____, and Kenneth H. Blanchard (1979), Life Cycle Theory of Leadership, *Training and Development Journal*, June:pp. 94-100.

_____, and Kenneth H. Blanchard (1980), The Management Change, *Training and Development Journal*, Vol. 34, No. 6 (June), pp. 80-98.

Hofstede, Geerte (1980), Motivation, Leadership and Organization: Do American Theories Apply Abroad? *Organizational Dynamics*, Summer, Vol. 9, No. 1, pp. 42-63.

Hornaday, J. A. and Baker, C. J. (1970), The Nature of the Entrepreneur, *Personnel Psychology*, (Spring):pp. 47-54.

House, R. J. (1971), A Path-Goal Theory of Leader Effectiveness, *Administrative Science Quarterly*, Vol. 16, pp. 321-338.

_____, and Terence R. Mitchell (1974), Path-Goal Theory of Leadership, Journal of Contemporary Business, Vol. 3, No. 4 (Autumn):pp. 81-97.

Jermier, J. M. and L. J. Berkes (1979), Leader Behavior in a Police Command Bureaucracy: A Closer Look at the Quasi-Military Model, Administrative Science Quarterly 24(1):pp. 1-23 (March).

Johns, Gary (1978), Task Moderators of the Relationship Between Leadership Style and Subordinate Responses, *Academy of Management Journal*, June: pp. 319-325.

Kabanoff, Boris and Gordon E. O'Brien (1979), Cooperative Structure and the Relationship of Leader and Member Ability to Group Performance, *Journal of Applied Psychology*, Vol. 64, No. 5 (Oct.):pp. 526-532.

Kahn, R. L., and D. Katz (1953), Leadership Practices in Relation to Productivity and Morale, in D. Cartwright and A Zander (eds.), *Group Dynamics* (Evanston, Ill.: Row, Peterson).

Kahn, Robert L. (1956), The Prediction of Productivity, *Journal of Social Issues*, Vol. 12:pp. 41-49.

Kanter, Rosabeth Moss (1977), *Men and Women of the Corporation* (N.Y.: Basic).

Katz, Daniel, N. Maccoby, and Nancy C. Morse (1950), *Productivity, Supervision, and Morale in an Office Situation*, (Ann Arbor, Mich.: Institute for Social Research).

Katz, Daniel and R. L. Kahn (1951), Human Organization and Worker Motivation, in L. R. Tripp (ed.), *Industrial Productivity* (Madison: Wisc.: Industrial
Relations Research Association, pp. 146-171.

Klimoski, Richard J. and Noreen J. Hayes (1980), Leadership Behavior and Subordinate Motivation, *Personnel Psychology*, Vol. 33, No. 3 (Autumn), pp.
543-556.

Knight, Patrick A. and Howard M. Weiss (1980), Effects of Selection Agent and
Leader Origin or Leader Influence on Group Member Perceptions, *Organizational Behavior and Human Performance*, Vol. 26, No. 1 (August), pp. 7-21.

Korman, Abraham K. (1966), 'Consideration,' 'Initiating Structure,' and Organizational Criteria - A Review, *Personnel Psychology*, Vol. 19, No. 4 (Winter):
pp. 349-361.

Lawler, Edward, III, and Porter, Lyman (1967), The Effect of Performance on
Job Satisfaction, *Industrial Relations*, 7(1) (Oct.):pp. 20-25.

Lewin, Kurt, Ronald Lippitt, and Ralph K. White (1939), Patterns of Aggressive
Behavior in Experimentally Created Social Climates, *Journal of Social
Psychology*, Vol. 10:pp. 271-299.

————, (1947) Frontiers in Group Dynamics, *Human Relations*, Vol. 1, No. 1
(June), pp. 5-41.

Likert, Rensis (1961), *New Patterns of Management* (N.Y.: McGraw Hill).

————(1967), *The Human Organization* (N.Y.: McGraw Hill).

Lowin, A. and J. R. Craig (1968), The Influence of Performance on Managerial
Style: An Experimental Object-Lesson in the Ambiguity of Correlational
Data, *Organizational Behavior and Human Performance*, Vol. 3:pp. 440-58.

Luthans, Fred and Robert Kreitner (1975), *Organizational Behavior Modification*,
Glenview, Ill.: Scott, Foresman.

————and Todd I. Stewart (1977), A General Contingency Theory of Management, *Academy of Management Review*, Vol. 2, No. 2 (April), pp. 181-195.

Maccoby, Michael (1976), *The Gamesman*, New York: Simon and Schuster.

Manley, J. Roger (1975), Have You Tried Project Management? *Public Personnel Management* (May-June), reprinted in J. M. Shafritz, ed., *The Public Personnel World* (Chicago: IPMA, 1977):pp. 326-335.

Mann, Floyd C. and James K. Dent (1954), *Appraisals of Supervisors and the Attitudes of Their Employees in an Electric Power Company*, Ann Arbor, Michigan: Institute for Social Research.

————(1965), Toward an Understanding of the Leadership Role in Formal
Organizations, in R. Dubin, G. C. Homans, F. C. Mann, and D. C. Miller,
Leadership and Productivity (San Francisco: Chandler Publishing Co.) pp.
68-103.

Margerison, Charles and Richard Glube (1979), Leadership Decision-Making:
An Empirical Test of the Vroom and Yetton Model, *Journal of Management Studies*, February:pp. 45-55.

Marrow, Alfred J., David G. Bowers, and Stanley E. Seashore (1967), *Management by Participation* (N.Y.: Harper and Row).

Maslow, Abraham (1954), *Motivation and Personality*, 2nd ed., (1970), New York: Harper and Row.

McGregor, Douglas (1960), *The Human Side of Enterprise*, New York: McGraw Hill.

Mills, Carol J. and Wayne E. Bohannon (1980), Personality, Characteristics of Effective State Police Officers, *Journal of Applied Psychology*, (Dec), Vol. 65, No. 6, pp. 680-684.

Morse, Nancy C. and E. Reimer (1956), The Experimental Change of a Major Organizational Variable, *Journal of Abnormal and Social Psychology*, Vol. 52 (Jan.):pp. 120-129.

Motowidlo, Stephan J. (1980), Effects of Traits and States Subjective Probability of Task Success and Performance, *Motivation and Emotion*, Vol. 4, No. 3 (September), pp. 247-262.

Nebeker, D. M., and T. R. Mitchell (1974), Leader Behavior: An Expectancy Theory Approach, *Organizational Behavior and Human Performance*, Vol. 11, pp. 355-367.

Owens, James (1973), The Uses of Leadership Theory, *Michigan Business Review*.

Porter, L. W. and E. E. Lawler (1968), *Managerial Attitudes and Performance*, (Homewood, Ill.: Irwin Dorsey).

Price, James L. (1968), *Organizational Effectiveness*, Homewood, Ill.: Irwin Dorsey.

Radin, Beryl A. (1980), Leadership Training for Women in State and Local Government, *Public Personnel Management*, Vol. 9, No. 2 (March-April) pp. 52-60.

Reddin, William J. (1967), The 3-D Management Style Theory, *Training and Development Journal*, (April):pp. 8-17.

Roethlisberger, F. J. (1941), *Management and Morale*, Cambridge, Massachusetts: Harvard University Press.

Sales, S. M. (1966), Supervisory Style and Productivity: Review and Theory, *Personnel Psychology*, Vol. 19:pp. 275-286.

Sank, L. (1974), Effective and Ineffective Managerial Traits Obtained in Naturalistic Descriptions from Executive Menders from a Super-Corporation, *Personnel Psychology*, 27(3) (Autumn):pp. 423-434.

Scanlon, Burt K. (1979), Managerial Leadership in Perspective: Getting Back to the Basics, *Personnel Journal*, (March):pp. 165-171.

Schneier, Craig E. (1978), The Contingency Model of Leadership: An Extension to Emergent Leadership and Leader's Sex, *Organization Behavior and Human Performance*, Vol. 21:pp. 220-239.

Schrieshein and Sikers (1977), Theories and Measures of Leadership: A Critical Appraisal of Current and Future Directions, in J. G. Hunt and L. Larson, eds., *Leadership: The Cutting Edge*, Carbondale: Southern Illinois University Press.

Schrieshein (1980), The Social Context of Leader-Subordinate Relations: An Investigation of the Effects of Group Cohesiveness, *Journal of Applied Psychology*, Vol. 65, No. 2 (April), pp. 183-194.

Shartle, Carroll L. (1979), The Early Years of the Ohio State University Leadership Studies, *Journal of Management*, Vol. 5, No. 2 (Fall), pp. 127-134.

Slater, Phillip E. and Warren G. Bennis (1964), Democracy is Inevitable, *Harvard Business Review* (March-April).

Starr, Barry M. and Terry Ross (1980), Commitment in an Experimenting Society: A Study of the Attribution of Leadership from Administrative Scen-
arios, *Journal of Applied Psychology*, Vol. 65, No. 3 (June), pp. 249-260.

Stockton, Rex (1980), The Education of Group Leaders: A Review of the Literature, *Journal for Specialists in Group Work*, Vol. 5, No. 2 (May), pp.
55-62.

Stogdill, R. M. (1948), Personal Factors Associated with Leadership: A Survey
of the Literature, *Journal of Psychology*, Vol. 25, pp. 35-71.

_____, and A. E. Coons (1957), *Leader Behavior: Its Description and Measure-
ment* (Columbus, Ohio: Bureau of Business Research, Ohio State University).

_____, (1974), *Handbook of Leadership*, New York: Free Press.

Vecchio, Robert P. (1979), A Dyadic Interpretation of the Contingency Model
of Leadership Effectiveness, *Academy of Management Journal*, Vol. 22(3):
pp. 590-600.

Vroom, Victor (1964), *Work and Motivation*, N Y : Wiley.

_____and P. W. Yetten (1973), *Leadership and Decision-Making* (Pittsburgh:
University of Pittsburgh).

_____(1976), Can Leaders Learn to Lead? *Organizational Dynamics*, Vol. 4,
No. 3, (Winter):pp. 17-28.

_____and Arthur G. Jago (1978), On the Validity of the Vroom-Yetten
Model, *Journal of Applied Psychology*, (April):pp. 151-162.

Wofford, J. C. (1967), Behavior Styles and Performance Effectiveness, *Personnel
Psychology*, Vol. 20, pp. 461-496.

_____(1970), Managerial Behavior, Situational Factors, and Productivity and
Morale, *Administrative Science Quarterly*, Vol. 16, pp. 10-17.

Zaleznik, Abraham (1977), Managers and Leaders: Are They Different? *Harvard
Business Review* (May-June): reprinted in J. L. Gibson, J. M. Ivancevich, and
J. H. Donnelly, eds., *Readings in Organizations, 2nd Ed.*, Dallas: Business
Publications, 1979, pp. 158-175.

Zelditch, M. (1955), Role Differentiation in the Nuclear Family: A Comparative
Study, in T. Partsons, R. E. Bales, et. al., eds., *Family Socialization and
Interaction Process*, Glencoe, Ill: Free Press.

ROLE BEHAVIOR

Managerial leadership, discussed in Chapter 3, depends critically on the ability of the manager to recognize, understand, utilize, and possibly change the patterns of behavior characteristic of the agency's employees. Behaviors are routinized over a period of time, allowing them to become anticipated by the manager and other organizational members. Such established behavior patterns are reinforced positively or negatively by sanctions applied by the manager or the informal work group. Sets of sanctioned, expected behaviors are called *roles*. Role management is an essential aspect of the administrative function in the public sector as well as the private.

There are many types of roles. Two broad dimensions divide roles into functional and cultural roles. *Functional roles* include patterns based on administrative task or function. For example, there are roles associated with the traditional administrative functions of planning, organizing, staffing, directing, coordinating, reporting, and budgeting. Benne and Sheats (1948) set forth ten such roles:

    I. TASK ROLES
        1. *Seeking information* and data
        2. *Giving information* and data
        3. *Initiating* ideas, proposals, concepts, or plans
        4. *Clarifying* ideas, proposals, concepts, or plans
        5. *Coordinating* group ideas, proposals, concepts, or plans
        6. *Orienting* the group toward goal-achievement
        7. *Establishing* outside contacts for the group (a *gatekeeper* role)

    II. GROUP-MAINTAINING AND GROUP-BUILDING ROLES
        1. *Supporting participation* of all group members

2. *Encouraging compromise* and *harmonizing viewpoints*

3. *Reducing tension* (e.g., through humor)

Likewise, Mintzberg has put forward a different set of ten: interpersonal roles (figurehead, leader, liaison), informational roles (monitor, disseminator, spokesman), and decisional roles (entrepreneur, disturbance handler, resource allocator, negotiator). As with the Ohio State studies of leadership, there is some evidence these functional roles may be reduced to those which are relationship-centered (e.g., liaison, disseminator, spokesperson, figurehead) and those which are task/decision-oriented (e.g., monitor, disturbance handler, resource allocator, negotiator) (see Shapira and Dunbar, 1980).

The second dimension involves *cultural roles*, such as those based on nationality, race, or sex. For example, Hofstede (1980: 59) has found that decision-making roles vary by nationality. Studies of cultural roles within a given nation, in contrast, have found fewer administrative differences. Lefkowitz and Fraser (1980), for instance, found no differences between blacks and whites on need for achievement and need for power, controlling for education. Similarly, a variety of studies have found no difference by sex. Muldrow and Bayton (1979) found no differences by sex on any of six decision task variables studied. Weaver (1980) found no sex differences in job satisfaction. Schneier and Bartol (1980) found no sex differences on group performance or on a variety of sociometric and interaction analysis measures. Sadd (1979) found femininity was not related to fear of success, self-deprecation, or insecurity as is sometimes alleged.[1]

Any given employee will hold a variety of roles, each with its own set of sanctioned expectations. In addition to cultural roles such as being a woman, a black, or a member of the social upper class, one may hold various functional roles such as being the quality controller, being the union steward, or simply the person who organizes the agency's parties. From the point of view of the administrator, managing the many roles of many employees, four questions arise. First, why do people conform to roles and when is conformity most likely or useful? Second, how does role conflict occur and what are its consequences? Third, how do role conformity and role conflict affect the emergence within the agency of an informal organization parallel to the formal structure? And last, when informal roles and organizations are incompatible with formal and necessary functions, how can role change occur? The remainder of this chapter is organized around these four questions.

ROLE CONFORMITY

Although conformity is often disparaged, organizations could not hold together without it. The inducement of rewards and the force of authority are powerful motivators but no organization can function effectively unless its members share widespread acceptance of and conformity to organizational roles. Role conformity is intrinsic to bureaucratic organization because without it the separation of roles from personalities would be impossible. Organizational continuity in the face of personnel turnover depends on efficient socialization of new organizational members to dominant values, procedures, and social orientations of the agency.

From a management perspective it is perhaps fortunate that powerful forces to conform exist in the work group. This was demonstrated in the classic experiments of Solomon Asch (1952). Asch placed his subjects in a group of ostensible peers who were actually Asch's assistants. Such groups were given the task of guessing the length of a line. When the assistants all agreed on the wrong length the subject usually went along. (Asch, 1951) and others (Weiner, 1958) showed that such conformity is most likely when the subject is ambiguous. Management-related areas characterized by high ambiguity include such matters as perceived promotion criteria and behaviors thought instrumental to promotion, policies of political leadership of the agency and behaviors thought consistent with these, or work team norms and associated behaviors. We may thus expect that role conformity is particularly salient to the study of public management.

While the tendency to conform is a powerful force and while it is operative in many management-related areas, it is more pronounced for some individuals and for some situations than for others. Conformity is greatest when agency members . . .

- belong to a cohesive group (Lott and Lott, 1965)
- believe others in the group are successful and competent
- expect to remain in the group
- are highly motivated upon entrance into the group (Schein, 1968)
- are themselves authoritarian in personality (Nadler, 1959)
- lack self-confidence (Velley and Lamb, 1957)
- are dealing with issues outside their own specialty (Raia and Osipow, 1970)
- are less intelligent (Bass et al., 1953)

The prototypical profile of a high-conformity situation would thus be one in which an authoritarian person of low self-confidence joins an organization which he or she has intensely desired to join and with which he or she expects to remain. The organization is composed of a close-knit group of individuals who are competent and successful. The new member may be of lower intelligence or be dealing with issues outside those of their main talent. In such a situation conformity is highly predictable. Such extremes are not necessary for conformity, however. Because of the dynamics of conformity and exclusion, almost all individuals conform most of the time to most organizational expectations.

The Dynamics of Conformity and Exclusion

Conformity to group norms starts even before joining the organization. Anticipatory socialization is the process by which the individual takes on the characteristics of the group to which he or she aspires. Graduate students may begin to attend professional meetings, management aspiring employees may start wearing suits to work, or new intellectual and social interests may be fostered in imitation of the culture of the group into which the organization member seeks to rise.

Organization selection processes may complement anticipatory socialization. The organization may become biased toward recruitment of individuals of the "right type," seeking individuals who will "fit in." Through training, apprenticeship, or mentoring (cf. Johnson, 1980) the organization seeks to socialize selected employees into desired roles. As Caplow (1964) has noted, this socialization process may involve four distinct steps:

1. acquiring a new self-image which reflects organizational norms
2. acquiring new relationships and abandoning those dissonant with the organization
3. adopting new values which reflect organizational goals
4. adopting new modes of behavior which conform to organizational norms.

By taking on the behaviors of the organization the individual is simply living up to expectations. This is the "Pygmalion effect," whereby subordinates commonly take on positive or negative behaviors according to the expectations of superiors (see Rosenthal and Jacobson, 1968; Livingston, 1969).

Whenever an individual joins an organization he or she enters into a sort of psychological contract (see Levinson, Price, Munden and Sulley, 1962.) In this contract the individual's conformity to organizational expectations is exchanged for the benefits of belonging. Those who accept the contract involved in job offers are more likely to do so if the interviewer emphasizes the personal career interest of belonging (Alderfer and Cord, 1970). When organizational realities like pay, conditions, and recognition are close to what was contracted for, individuals are more likely to stay on in the organization (Dunnett, Arvey, and Banas, 1973).

Just as the psychological contract involves expectations by the individual it also involves organizational expectations of the individual. "A price," de la Porte has explained, "is set for admission and recognition in the form of certain values and rules of behavior to be respected by group members at all times" (de la Porte, 1974). For example, in *Men and Women of the Corporation* (1977), Kanter found "A tremendous value was placed on team membership and getting along with peers; 'peer acceptance' was considered a factor in promotions. 'Individual performers' were generally not promoted" (Kanter, 1977).

Organizations may regard many behaviors as relevant and appropriate for conforming behavior but only some will be regarded as pivotal. In these areas strong sanctions emerge against nonconformity (Schein, 1970). Such pivotal behavioral norms were found to cluster in ten areas by de la Porte (1974):

1. organizational pride
2. performance

3. cost-effectiveness
4. teamwork
5. planning
6. supervision
7. training and development
8. innovation
9. customer relations
10. honesty and security

All organizational members who deviate from pivotal group norms will be subject to sanction. Sanction typically begins with receipt of increased communication directed toward encouraging conformity (Schacter, 1951; Schacter, 1959; Emerson, 1954; Berkowitz and Howard, 1959). Continuation of nonconformity after this initial stage will bring escalating sanctions eventually leading to rejection from the group in most instances (Festinger, 1950; Sampson and Brandon, 1964). It is no exaggeration to say that the non-conformist may easily take on the characteristics of an organizational leper in extreme cases. But why do social organizations routinely allow and encourage such sanctioning activity? What positive functions are served by conformity which may prevent a more tolerant management from accepting normative deviation from organizational expectations?

The Positive Functions of Conforming

From an organizational viewpoint conformity is a method of dealing with actual or potential conflict. Conformity involves the cooptation of existing and potential critics or rivals, strengthening the organization. By placing such individuals under conformity-inducing group pressures, a weakness may be transformed into a strength. Cooptation may occur not only with regard to employees but also with regard to external interest representatives, who may be given advisor or other status. The Tennessee Vally Authority, for example, acquired substantial power through cooptation of representatives of such interests as the Farm Bureau, the Department of Agriculture, land grant colleges, and extension services (see Selznik, 1949, 1957). Organizations which tend to emphasize cooptation in management tend to have a higher degree of effectiveness (Price, 1968).

It should be noted that, like gravity, cooptation is a two-way force. At times, as with the hiring of a token minority member, cooptation is unilateral and organizational norms may be relatively unchanged. At other times, including the TVA example above, however, cooptation may lead to mutual accomodation of affected interests and real change in organizational norms. Short of mutual accomodation, cooptation may reduce consensus (Price, 1968).

Conformity may be based on personal factors rather than organizational. Conformity tends to increase popularity, for example (Argyle, 1957). It also reduces cognitive dissonance in group membership and may make work more satisfying. Back (1951) found that conformity based on personal attraction led to a work climate in which task requirements were viewed as intrusions. Likewise, he found conformity based on membership prestige led to low risk-taking in task performance.

Conformity is most positive in function when based on the task itself. Socialization to professional norms is typically of this type. Back (1951) found that task-based conformity was associated with an intensive and efficient work process. An example is provided in a case study by Trist and Banforth (1957). These researchers found that when new, supposedly superior technology disbanded highly cohesive teams of coal miners, productivity fell markedly. Conformity may involve an espirit-de-corps which promotes organizational effectiveness in a manner more significant than does technology. The promotion of task-based conformity—as by the promotion of staff professionalization—is therefore a potentially productive and important management objective.

The Negative Functions of Conformity

Management must be equally sensitive to possible negative impacts of organizational conformity, however. There are numerous good reasons for the popular negative reaction to the concept of conformity. Prime among these is the tendency toward suboptimization. That is, the forces of conformity are most effective at the small group level. The norms of the subgroup, however, are often *not* the norms of the organization in microcosm. The organization may efficiently socialize individuals to subgroup norms while failing to do so for organizational norms.

Robert K. Merton observed this tendency in his classic 1940 essay on bureaucratic structure. He wrote, "espirit-de-corps and informal social organization which typically develops in such structures often leads the personnel to defend their entrenched interests rather than to assist their clientele and elected higher officials" (Merton, 1978). Subgroup norms may involve such negative behaviors as withholding information or goal displacement (elevating means to become ends in themselves, as when bureaucracies become locked into self-defeating procedural technicalities). More broadly, conformity may simply reinforce professional biases —what Veblen called "trained incapacities." This is particularly true in agencies organized along professional-functional lines.

Irving Janis's *Victims of Groupthink* (1972) details errors arising from overreliance on a closed subgroup, even one at the top of an organization. Janis examined four major policies: the Bay of Pigs invasion decision, Pearl Harbor, the invasion of North Korea, and the escalation of the Vietnamese War. In each case he documented a pattern of "groupthink" or harmful conformity:

- negative feedback was avoided
- warning signals were ignored
- critics were stereotyped and dismissed
- unanimity became a pivotal group norm
- "mindguard" roles developed to protect the leader from inputs deemed harmful

- self-censorship emerged
- discrepant information was rationalized
- no attempt was made to empathize with views outside the subgroup

Janis concluded that consensus seeking became so dominant in cohesive policy groups studied that a realistic appraisal of the alternatives became no longer possible. Groups which are too homogenous and conforming may lack the diversity of resources needed for effective problem solving.

Conformity and cohesion achieved through reaction against a common enemy, as in Janis's foreign policy cases, often is negative in organizational impact. Resort to emphasis on an external foe is an ancient and effective tactic to secure unity and conformity. In management as well as politics, a negative external environment is associated with greater cohesiveness. As Hickson (1961) has shown, however, conformity based on external threat is also associated with restriction of output and lower productivity. Likewise, Seashore (1954) has found that while very high group cohesion sometimes creates strong production orientation, in general as cohesiveness increases, employee-perceived production pressure decreases. Though this tendency is not a major organizational force it does suggest that conformity may just as well serve the social norms of the work unit as it can the production norms of the agency.

In extreme cases conformity may actually serve neither organization nor subgroup or individual goals. Harvey (1974) labelled this the "Abilene Paradox," alluding to a family incident in which his family took a long, hot, arduous trip to Abilene, Kansas. On returning it was discovered that no one really wanted to go. Each was conforming to the perceived value preferences of the other. Citing Watergate scandals of the Nixon presidency as an illustration, Harvey argued that such "trips to Abilene" are not uncommon in bureaucracies. They are merely one example of many types of role conflict—conflict between individual needs and behaviors elicited by organizational roles, whether formal agency roles or informal subgroup roles.

ROLE CONFLICT

Role conflict arises because individual needs conflict with role demands, because of divergent expectations of a given role by different agency members, or because the same individual may hold two or more conflicting roles simultaneously. These are called person-role conflict, intrarole conflict, and interrole conflict respectively. Person-role conflict, for example, occurs when what an individual values contradicts what is expected of his or her role. A valued image as a "nice guy" may conflict with a personnel analyst's role as an evaluator of performance of marginal employees (Keeley, 1977). Religious obligations may conflict with job requirements for service at specified times. Person-role conflict is a universal organizational problem requiring individualization of supervisory practices, reward structures, and other management policies.

Intrarole conflict occurs when organizational members have different, conflicting expectations of a given person's role. A common example is that of boundary roles—roles interfacing the agency with the environment, including other agencies. Those occupying boundary roles are subject to intense expectations to represent organizational norms (the expectation of organization members) and to accommodate to the norms of other agencies in the environment (external expectations). Boundary role incumbents are subject to particular stress. Role management for such individuals may require job rotation, training and resocialization opportunities, or rest and recreation (see Adams, 1976; Wall, 1974). Intrarole conflict is also evident in first-line supervisory roles (e.g., foremen). Such role incumbents must represent employees to higher management and represent higher management to employees. This "in the middle" position is also stressful and requires a compensating management policy (see Mann and Dent, 1954; Walker, Guest, and Turner, 1956).

Interrole conflict occurs when an individual holds two or more roles which are in tension with each other. Typical is the manager who has risen through professional ranks. Examples are the doctor who becomes a hospital administrator or the professor who becomes a university dean. Such individuals often hold strong self- and peer-imposed professional expectations which may conflict with their new jobs. Academic deans, for example, may be torn between pressures for cost cutting (an administrative norm) and pressures for professional excellence (a professional norm).

All types of role conflict are examples of cognitive dissonance (Festinger, 1957). Cognitive dissonance is the stress induced when a person values two things which conflict with each other. Needs may conflict with job expectations, or the expectations of one person or group may conflict with another's. The level of cognitive dissonance in each case depends on two factors:

1. *Intensity of values*: the stronger the positive or negative rewards, whether material or symbolic, the more intense the dissonance. Values are intensified when the associated expectations are articulated more frequently, more forcefully, or by individuals of greater importance to the individual's reference system.
2. *Intensity of constraints*: the stronger the constraints preventing the individual from simultaneous satisfaction of competing values, the greater the dissonance. Role overload is a common example as is role ambiguity. In the former there is too much task burden while in the latter there is too little task direction. (Interestingly, role overload may also cause dissonance since underload may create boredom or lowered esteem.)

Cognitive dissonance has been shown to be a powerful force having substantial effect on management. Pettigrew (1972), for instance, has estimated that millions of workdays are lost annually due to the stress of role conflict. House and Rizzo

(1972) have correspondingly found that reduction of role ambiguity reduced turn-over and increased job satisfaction. Ambiguity and conflict in role performance are particularly negative to 1) lower-level employees, perhaps because they lack control over job definition and hence experience contradictory role expectations as intractable and frustrating (Caplan and Jones, 1975); 2) introverts (Kahn, Wolfe, Quinn, and Sneck, 1964); 3) individuals having high need-achievement (Johnson and Stinson, 1975; Schuler, 1975); and 4) individuals with a high need for clarity (Lyons, 1971).

When role conflict occurs individuals seek to reduce dissonance in one of several ways:

1. *Withdrawal*: individuals may seek to isolate themselves from both conflicting values, as by avoiding persons apt to articulate one or the other of two competing role expectations. A classic example was the tendency of Catholic members of Communist unions in the 1940's to become apolitical rather than have to choose between their union or their church.
2. *Transformation*: individuals may seek to alter one value to elim-inate dissonance with the other, as by changing personal values to conform to organizational norms. Mixed work groups may sacrifice representativeness to pick a higher-status individual as leader in order to project an image consistent with perceived organizational expectations (e.g., selection of white males in mixed groups; see Webber, 1974; Aries, 1976).
3. *Rationalization*: individuals may change their perceptions to eliminate dissonance, as when enforcement officials ignore civil liberties infractions thought necessary to effectiveness in crime reduction (cf. Festinger, 1958).
4. *Aggression*: individuals may express stress through hostility, as when managers frustrated in goal achievement vent their frus-tration on subordinates (see Dollard, Doob, Miller, and Sears, 1939, for the classic formulation of frustration-aggression theory).

The supervisor who seeks to manage role conflict within the organization tries not so much to eliminate role conflict (which is often intrinsic to organization design) as to channel its impact away from deviant behavior and toward organizational ends.

DEVIANCE

Reactions to dissonance, as through withdrawal or aggression, are the basis for deviance within the organization. Deviance may take extreme forms such as alco-holism, drug addiction, or chronic absenteeism. Milder examples include the coffee-break group which comes to an informal understanding about keeping the work pace down in order to have a more relaxed atmosphere. Deviance exists whenever employees choose to devalue or evade organizational norms in order to confer legitimacy on other informal norms of their own.

Deviance is most likely among those whose mobility is dependent on an outside reference group (e.g., certain specialists) or among those with no hope for mobility. Kanter, for example, has noted the tendencies of secretaries to ignore company norms of impersonality and task orientation. "The secretarial function," Kanter noted (1977) "represented a repository of the personal inside the bureaucratic. . . some secretaries were largely defined out of the mobility game, they could afford to carry on the human side of the office." Likewise, Gouldner (1957) has noted the greater deviance of "cosmopolitans" (those with strong external professional affiliations) compared to "locals" (see also Consalvi, 1960).

Many other factors may increase the likelihood of deviance, including the amount of dissonance experienced by the role incumbent. Individual deviation is increased by physical separation of the employee from the work group (Allen, 1965; Kiesler, 1960). Similarly, group deviation is increased by the physical isolation of the work group from the rest of the organization (Roethlisberger and Dickson, 1939).

Extreme forms of deviance (e.g., alcoholism) are increasingly recognized as major management problems requiring formal programs (e.g., counseling). More subtle forms of deviance such as rationalization and formation of subgroup norms inconsistent with agency policy are often overlooked but may be even more damaging to the organization. In some cases deviance may be regarded as a tolerable idiosyncracy of an otherwise "good group citizen" (Hollander, 1958, 1964). Others may be tolerated as negative role examples (Dentler and Erickson, 1959). These are exceptions to the generally strong reaction of organizations against deviance.

MANAGING ORGANIZATIONAL ROLES

Early in this century management theory embraced a "scientific" approach which emphasized industrial engineering (e.g., time and motion studies). It was only with the 1930's that management theory began to emphasize what was called the manager's "responsibility to lead." That is, new stress was laid on the view that the manager's job, perhaps the primary job, was to manage organizational role expectations and conflicts—not simply apply industrial production techniques.

The new viewpoint was associated with such individuals as Elton Mayo and Chester Barnard. Mayo had worked with the Hawthorne experiments (see Roethlisberger and Dickson, 1939). These had suggested the importance of informal group norms in restricting production. This in turn had implied the need for management concern for employee needs. Barnard, a telephone company executive, was among the first organization theorists to describe management in non-Weberian terms: an intrinsically cooperative effort resting on a moral purpose inculcated by the manager (see Perrow, 1979: 65-73; Selznik, 1957).

More recently Rensis Likert (1961) has emphasized similar themes in the concept of "supportive management." Supportive management called for the constructive use of conflict, the explicit examination of goals, and a new emphasis on the basic work group:

1. *Constructive use of conflict.* Organizations may develop to higher levels only by tapping the creative forces represented in conflict management. Conflict management, not blind encouragement of conformity, was most suited to organizations seeking rapid change in the modern environment.

2. *Explicit examination of goals.* Argyris (1957) and others argued that the role demands of most organizations are incompatible with the needs of healthy individuals. Both to integrate personal goals with organizational goals and to reduce role ambiguity (a major generator of stress), goal clarification efforts are central to the manager's organization development role.

3. *Emphasis on the basic work group.* This emphasis is now central to management because of the recognition of the importance of the basic work group in socialization of the individual to conformity with or deviance from organization norms. For example, the work group may be enhanced through increasing its social density, a strategy which has been found to reduce role stress and, through greater job feedback, reduce role ambiguity (Szilagyi and Holland, 1980; on measuring role ambiguity see Breaugh, 1980).

An organizing framework for these three emphases is career development. In fact, sometimes role management is used interchangeably with career development. Career development, is a vehicle for managing role conflicts. Withdrawal may be channeled into climbing (mobility), aggression into constructive criticism and competition, transformation into anticipatory socialization, and rationalization into personal and management development. A comprehensive career development strategy is far more than training or counseling. It is a basis for organizational control and change which operationalizes organizational assumptions about motivation and leadership discussed in Chapters 1 and 2.

It is often assumed that career development is achieved through conformity alone (Mills, 1953; Whyte, 1955). Evidence by Porter and Lawler (1968a, 1968b), however, suggests that upward mobility is most likely to come through differentiating oneself through superior performance, not by being the same as one's co-workers. On the other hand, as Kornhauser has shown in his studies of auto workers (1965), organizations can crush employee motivation by blocking mobility. The alternative to management control through a career development strategy is often the development of powerful, informal social groups within the organization—groups developed by employees to satisfy individual needs not recognized in agency policy.

INFORMAL ORGANIZATION

More than any other single objective, role management is concerned with the agency's response to informal organization. Informal organization is the set of un-authorized behaviors which are routinized parts of the organizational culture of the agency. Informal organization may promote deviant goals, organization goals, or both. It was the promotion of deviant goals, however, which first placed the topic of informal organization high on the agenda of students of administration.

In the Hawthorne plant of the Western Electric Company, Roethlisberger and Dickson, working with Elton Mayo, found that the informal organization of work-ers could countervail management's carefully-designed incentive systems (Roeth-lisberger and Dickson, 1939). In their "Bank Wiring Room" experiment fourteen workers in a separated work environment were placed on a group piecework plan under which the more the group produced, the more its members received in in-come. Contrary to engineering theory, Roethlisberger and Dickson found that the hypothesized group pressure to increase the paycheck through higher productivity did *not* materialize. Rather, informal group pressures were mobilized to restrict output. High producers were labelled "rate-busters" while low producers were termed "chiselers." Pressure was put on inspectors to be "one of the guys." The more intelligent and dexterous workers often had the lowest output. Informal group norms centering on such goals as pleasant job conditions and "spreading the work" (job security) proved more powerful than management's incentive pay-cen-tered control system.

Informal Organization as a Threat

Early views of informal organization were generally pessimistic. In their classic an-thology, *Papers on the Science of Administration* (1937), Luther Gulick and Lyn-dall Urwick adopted the essentially negative view of informal organization found in the Hawthorne studies (Gulick and Urwich, 1937). Informal organization was seen as the inevitable consequence of bad management. Scientific management, in contrast, would avoid the emergence of harmful employee roles not officially sanc-tioned. It sought to do this through highly detailed task procedures and time schedules which left virtually no discretion to the rank-and-file employee. Disciples of scientific management sought to break each task into exact sequences of mo-tions which had to be done at prescribed speeds (time-and-motion studies). Locked into rigidly prescribed patterns, in theory there was no opportunity for the rise of informal, unsanctioned group behavior. In reality, however, discontent over the tight supervision which scientific management entailed led to employee resentment, informal resistance, and even unionism.

Gulick and Urwick argued that sound management proceeded from scientific management's assumptions of detailed specification of tasks and schedules accord-ing to identifiable principles of administrative science such as clarity of hierarchical lines of authority and adoption of optimal spans of control. When bad management tolerated unclear lines of authority, they argued, workers misunderstood or forgot central organization purposes. Soon workers devoted their energies to their own individual ends and informal workgroup goals. Likewise, when bad management allowed too large a span of control (as in French bureaucracy), accountability broke down and was replaced by informal organization.

Fear of informal organization was intensified by another principle of administrative science: homogeneity. This principle called for organization of homogenous work groups (e.g., like professionals grouped in staff departments). Since such groups were thought to suffer occupational biases and to be oblivious to the needs of other units, it was particularly important that these groups not be left to develop their own directions. Gulick and Urwick argued forcefully that only clear, hierarchical control administered through a manageable span of control could prevent the dangerous emergence of informal groups which would usurp the powers of management.

Later sociological research popularized the view that informal organization was pervasive and generally negative in association. For example, William Foote Whyte's *Street Corner Society* (1943) was a notable study demonstrating a high degree of informal organization even in street corner gangs. Whyte's later work, *Money and Motivation* (1955b), showed similar informal organization in work groups. Ways in which workers defeated time-and-motion studies through informal work groups were highlighted in this study. Output restriction was also detailed in numerous other studies which attributed it to such poor management practices as inadequate job security, inadequate reward systems, or unpopular speed-ups (Collins, Dalton, 1948; Roy, 1952; Viteles, 1953; Hickson, 1961).

In the public sector much the same conclusions were reached in Blau's classic study of a New York City employment office (Blau, 1955). Blau found that employment counselors often followed informal group norms rather than agency policies. They would fail to share job listings, neglect job counseling, fail to match the best person to the best job, and show favoritism or discrimination against certain clients. These and other forms of deviance came about through informal group attempts to make work more satisfying and to thwart a quantitative management performance control system.

Informal Organization as an Opportunity

Chester Barnard, a founder of modern organization theory, introduced an opposite perspective in the midst of this research supporting a negative management view of informal organization. Barnard, a telephone company executive, argued that informal organization served three highly important and positive functions.

1. *Communication.* Informal communication channels afforded by informal organization allowed more rapid and flexible inter-

actions and responses that would be possible under strict hierarchical organization.

2. *Cohesiveness.* Informal organization was a powerful socializing
system regulating members' willingness to serve and contribute
to team spirit and mobilization, thereby stabilizing management
authority.

3. *Support.* Informal organization provided mutual support for
informal group members, enhancing their feelings of self-respect
and independence of action.

Barnard thus saw informal organization as a complement to formal organization.
In a two-way influence process formal organizations created and shaped informal
organizations, but they also reflected the organizational culture engendered by
them. This concept leads directly to concern for role management as a central
function of the administrator.

Much postwar research has reinforced Barnard's positive view of informal organization. In studies of WWII soldiers, for example, Shils (1950) found that informal primary groups contributed to self-confidence and reduced fear. Consequently, soldiers in such groups were less likely to surrender. Similarly, research
on Korean War prisoners by Schein (1956) showed the Chinese method of con-
sciously preventing informal group formation (through constant prisoner rotation)
led to lower morale, greater sickness, and fewer escapes.

This military research confirmed Mayo's findings that management practices
which promoted informal organization (e.g., allowing group rest periods for socialization) led to increased worker satisfaction and productivity (Mayo, 1946). The
desirability and inevitability of informal groups was vividly popularized through
Roy's (1960) widely-circulated case study of "banana time." Conversely, Trist
and Bamforth's (1951) famous study of English coal mining showed how a new
technology which disrupted informal organization could lead to plummeting
productivity.

Informal Organizations: Summary

It is now recognized that informal organization is critical even in high-control settings like prisons (Social Science Research Council, 1960). In government agencies
where authority is less pervasive, even more reliance must be placed on norm-en-
forcing social pressures of the informal group. On the other hand, limits must be
drawn on Barnard's enthusiasm for informal groups. Perrow (1979), for example,
has charged that Barnard saw no negative effects in informal organizations because
he thought such groups would serve only personal goals which would be overridden
by the collective goals of the organization. In reality, informal groups may reinforce collective ends different from those of the agency.

Informal work groups represent a powerful force which is not necessarily deviant (as Gulick implied) nor necessarily beneficial (as Barnard suggested). Rather,

informal organization is an almost-inevitable facet of organizational life with which the manager must contend. Changing (or reinforcing) informal norms for organizational ends is increasingly recognized as a central management function. It is at the heart of organization development attempts to understand and manage organizational culture and it is central to the role management function of the administrator.

MANAGING ROLE CHANGE

The need for role management is not new. Mary Parker Follett's advocacy of opening up communication and using conflict constructively embodied similar concerns nearly a half century ago (Follette, 1940). Nor is this a need which should be foreign to students of public administration. Theodore Caplow, for example, has shown how role management is relevant even in university settings. Because of discrepancies between university-conferred authority rankings and profession-conferred statuses, Caplow noted, role conflict is common (Caplow and McGee, 1958). Management strategy in universities is often to be passive, allowing power to lie where it might. Caplow charged this laissez-faire attitude is a failure of role management which contributed to a kind of "lawlessness" and heightening of conflict.

While some might argue that normative "lawlessness" is in fact the freedom needed for university survival, Caplow's example does strongly suggest the need for an explicit approach to role management. Indeed, the great upsurge in organizational development in the last two decades reflects this. This growth has been somewhat restrained by the pragmatic and practical ethos of American management (Guth and Jaguiri, 1965; England, 1967; Lick and Oliver, 1974). Nonetheless, organization development techniques like team-building (see Dyer, 1977) have become commonplace in public administration. Since organization development in public administration is surveyed elsewhere (e.g. Golembiewski, 1977; Golembiewski and Eddy, 1978), we may simply note that virtually all of its forms seek formal or informal role change as part of a conscious managerial change effort.

Role management techniques have also become commonplace in individual-centered and intrapersonal interventions. These range from stress reduction (Frew, 1977) to sensitivity training (Back, 1972) to life/career planning (Storey, 1978) to role negotiation as part of management by objectives (MBO) or other goal-centered control systems (Carroll and Tosi, 1973). In each of these the focus is on employment of role-changing techniques drawn from social psychology, counseling, and learning theory. In each, management takes an active role in the change process. Informal organization and organizational culture is not taken as a "given," nor is it assumed that role development is a "personal matter" outside the scope of concerns of the manager.

In many ways all of organizational behavior research impacts role management.

As a way of focusing discussion, only two typical approaches will be discussed: 1) de la Porte's strategy based on survey feedback (de la Porte, 1974); and 2) Janis's strategy based on decision-making theory (Janis, 1972). Both approaches involve three phases, as do most role management interventions. These three phases are assessment, goal-setting, and commitment. The assessment phase is devoted to problem awareness. The goal-setting phase is focused on problem definition and choice. The commitment phase involves choice implementation.

In the *survey feedback model* management administers a survey instrument. De la Porte's instrument calls for measurement of organizational culture in ten dimensions, such as planning, supervision, honesty. The confidential results are assembled and a graphic "normative profile" is drawn up. This profile helps agency members become aware of mutually perceived problems (and strengths). Group sessions are held throughout the organization, starting at the top, to promote problem awareness and to help members identify existing group norms.

In later group meetings cooperative action is undertaken to establish group goals. "Excellence points" may be identified as standards toward which the agency aspires. Goals may be prioritized and new relationships and procedures recommended. In the commitment phase (the later group meetings), commitment to priorities and recommendations is authoritatively endorsed by top management first, then by consensus or votes in lower-level meetings throughout the agency. Provisions are made for recognition of performance on commitments. An explicit evaluation procedure is established along with a schedule of reviews and opportunities for further decision-making in relation to the change process.

Janis's *decision-making model* provides an alternative approach to role change. In the assessment phase he argues for establishment of "devil's advocate" roles, legitimating the critical evaluator role, and encouraging conflict. This overthrow of customary group norms against conflict and dissensus must be accompanied by efforts to establish a climate in which leaders accept criticism. Use of outside consultants as facilitators may further expand the range of critical roles injected into the decision-making process. The rotation of "devil's advocate" roles also encourages individual sensitivity enhancement.

In Janis's goal-setting phase planning groups are established. Management refrains from stating priorities at this time and the planning group instead begins with a survey of similar plans and goals by rival organizations. After the group sets initial goals, reactions are sought from all the stakeholders in the decision, both within and without the agency. In the commitment phase, additional planning groups may be created throughout the organization or the original planning group may split into subgroups. Subgroups reach conclusions which are tentative. At a subsequent meeting each group member is called upon to express possible doubts. Only after this process are decision-making groups merged and a final decision sought through consensus or vote.

Both de la Porte's and Janis's strategies could be applied to cognitive matters apart from role change. Typically, however, each is a structured approach to role change in which problem identification and goal-setting are used as vehicles for commitments to new modes of behavior. To the extent the problem area upon which the agency focuses is process- rather than policy-oriented, both strategies will involve role change as an evaluative criterion for management.

Both approaches have advantages and disadvantages. The survey-feedback approach has the advantage of addressing group norms comprehensively, directly, and in a manner providing empirical feedback to group members. In spite of possible abuses (Ilgen, Fisher, and Taylor 1979); feedback is essential to role learning (Meyer, Kay, and French, 1965). Feedback can establish a systematic goal-setting and commitment-making process throughout the whole organization (see Nadler, 1977; Golembiewski and Hilles, 1979). Dangers include possible premature consensus on values and goals and possible bias toward manipulation by top management.

The advantage of the decision-making approach of Janis is its action-oriented, narrower focus on decision-making as the basis for change. It provides more explicitly for legitimation of divergent norms and perspectives, greater utilization of conflict, and is potentially more participatory, thereby enhancing commitment. A prime danger of this approach is the possibility that "devil's advocates" may be stereotyped and ignored after a *pro forma* hearing. A second weakness is its inability to address "nondecisions—potential issues which never reach the explicit decision stage. This would be illustrated by an agency which, due to demographic changes, shifts from a lower- to a middle-class clientele. While this may revolutionize the nature of the agency, it may occur without ever being addressed in explicit decision-making processes.

In summary, role conflict, informal organization, and issues of conformity and deviance powerfully affect organizational life. Management must respond through conscious strategies of role management. These strategies are multifaceted and may involve objectives pertaining to motivation, leadership, communication, and virtually any of the other organization behavior topics treated in this volume. Traditional roles and organization culture are difficult to change. Frequently change interventions require the catalyzing influence of an outside professional (Bion, 1959; Argyris, 1969). A participatory approach improves role understanding and commitment to role change (Miller, 1980). All approaches involve assessment, goal-setting, and commitment phases and, as such, bear much in common with organization development techniques. Default on role management responsibilities is associated with the emergence of informal organization and organizational culture commonly deviant from agency norms. Without an appropriate managerial response to the challenge of role management, whether by the traditional "natural leader" or the contemporary "OD specialist," the agency will have a poor basis for organizational communication and decision-making, the topics of Chapters 4 and 5.

ENDNOTES

[1]Of course, not all studies have found sex independent of behavioral effects relevant to management. Zammuto, London, and Rowland (1979) found that males reporting to males resolved conflict more through withdrawal than did males or females reporting to females. Likewise, males reporting to males used less confrontation than females reporting to females. Donnell and Hill (1980), although finding no sex differences on most variables studied, did find women to be more achievement motivated but less open and candid with colleagues compared to men. Humphreys and Shrode (1978) found more similarities than differences by sex, but did find that women had more difficulty with budgetary and less difficulty with conceptual decisions than did men. The strength of these relationships is such that they cannot be construed as contradicting the conclusion of Donnell and Hill (1980): that "Women, in general, do not differ from men, in general, in the ways they administer the management process."

REFERENCES

Adams, J. Stacy (1976),   The Structure and Dynamics of Behavior in Organizational Boundary Roles,   in M. W. Dunnette, ed., *Handbook of Industrial and Organizational Psychology* (Chicago: Rand McNally).

Aldefer, C. P. and C. M. Cord (1970),   Personal and Situational Factors in the Recruitment Interview,   *Journal of Applied Psychology*, Vol. 54:pp. 377-385.

Allen, V. L. (1965),   Situational Factors in Conformity,   in L. Berkowitz, ed., *Advances in Experimental Social Psychology*, Vol. 2 (N.Y.: Adademic Press): pp. 145, 146.

Argyle, M. (1957), *The Scientific Study of Social Behavior* (London: Methuen).

Argyris, Chris, (1957), The Individual and the Organization: Some Problems of Mutual Adjustment, *Administrative Science Quarterly*, Vol. 2, No. 1 (June): pp. 1-24.

_____(1969),   The Incompleteness of Social Psychological Theory,   *American Psychologist*, Vol. 24:pp. 893-908.

Aries, E. (1976),   Interaction Patterns and Theories of Male, Female, and Mixed Groups,   *Small Group Behavior*, Vol. 7, No. 1:pp. 7-18.

Asch, Solomon E. (1952), *Social Psychology* (Englewood Cliffs, N.J.: Prentice-Hall).

_____(1957),   Effects of Group Pressure Upon the Modification and Distortion of Judgments,   in H. Guetzkow, ed., *Groups, Leadership and Men* (Pittsburgh: Carnegie Press).

Back, K. W. (1951),   Influence Through Social Communication,   *Journal of Abnormal and Social Psychology*, Vol. 46:pp. 190-207.

_____(1972), *Beyond Words; The Story of Sensitivity Training and Encounter Groups* (N.Y.: Russell Sage Foundation).

Barnard, Chester I. (1938),   Informal Organizations and Their Relation to Formal

Organizations, in *Functions of the Executive* (Harvard), reprinted in W. E. Natemeyer, ed., *Classics of Organization Behavior* (Oak Park, Ill.: Moore, 1978):pp. 239-243.

Bass, Bernard M., C. R. M. Gehee, W. C. Harkins, D. C. Young, A. S. Gebel (1953), Personality Variables Related to Leaderless Group Discussion, *Journal of Abnormal and Social Psychology* (January):pp. 120-28.

Benne, K. and P. Sheats (1948), Functional Roles of Group Members, *Journal of Social Issues*, Vol. 4, No. 2 (Spring):pp. 41-49.

Berkowitz, L. and R. C. Howard (1959), Reactions to Opinion Deviates as Affected by Affiliation Need (n) and Group Member Interdependence, *Sociometry*, Vol. 22:pp. 81-91.

Bion, W. E. (1959), *Experiences in Groups* (N.Y.: Basic).

Blau, Peter (1955), *The Dynamics of Bureaucracy* (Chicago: University of Chicago Press).

Breaugh, James A. (1980), A Comparative Study of Three Measures of Role Ambiguity, Journal of Applied Psychology, Vol. 65, No. 5 (Oct.):pp. 584-589.

Caplan, R. and V. Jones (1975), Effects of Work Load, Role Ambiguity, and Type A Personality on Anxiety, Depression, and Heart Rate, *Journal of Applied Psychology*, Vol. 60, No. 6 (Dec.):pp. 713-719.

Caplow, Theodore and R. J. McGee (1958), *The Academic Marketplace* (N.Y.: Basic).

_____(1964), *Principles of Organization* (N.Y.: Harcourt, Brace, and World).

Carroll, S. and W. Tosi, Jr. (1973), *Management by Objectives* (N.Y.: Macmillan).

Collins, O., M. Dalton, and D. Roy (1946), Restriction of Output and Social Cleavage in Industry, *Applied Anthropology*, Vol. 5, No. 3:pp. 1-14.

Dalton, M. (1948), The Industrial 'Rate-Buster': A Characterization, *Applied Anthropology*, Vol. 7:pp. 5-18.

Dentler, R. A., and K. T. Erickson (1959), The Functions of Deviance in Groups, *Social Problems*, Vol. 7:pp. 98-107.

Dollard, John, L. W. Doob, N. E. Miller, O. H. Mowrer, and R. R. Sears (1939), *Frustration and Aggression* (New Haven: Yale).

Donnell, Susan M. and Jay Hill (1980), Men and Women as Managers: A Significant Case with No Significant Difference, *Organizational Dynamics*, (Spring) Vol. 8, No. 4:pp. 60-77.

Dunnette, M. D., R. D. Arvey, and P. A. Banas (1973), Why Do They Leave?, *Personnel* (May-June):pp. 25-39.

Dyer, William G. (1977), *Team Building* (Reading, Mass.: Addison-Wesley).

Emerson, R. M. (1954), Deviation and Rejection: An Experimental Replication, *American Sociological Review*, Vol. 19:pp. 688-693.

England, George W. (1967), Personality Value Systems of American Managers, *Academy of Management Journal* (March):pp. 53-68.

Festinger, Leon (1950), Informal Social Communication, *Psychological Review*, Vol. 57:pp. 271-282.

_____(1957), *Theory of Cognitive Dissonance* (N.Y.: Harper and Row).

Festinger, Leon (1958),   The Motivation Effect of Cognitive Dissonance,   in G. Lindzey, ed., *Assessment of Human Motives* (N.Y.: Rinehard and Co.):pp. 65-86.

_____, S. Schacter, and K. Bark (1950), *Social Pressures in Informal Groups* (N.Y.: Harper and Row).

Follett, Mary Parker (1940), Dynamic Administration (N.Y.: Harper and Row).

Frew, D. (1977), *The Management of Stress* (Chicago: Nelson-Hall).

Golembiewski, Robert T. (1977), *Public Administration as a Developing Discipline: Part 2, Organization Development* (N.Y.: Marcel Dekker).

Golembiewski, Robert T. and W. B. Eddy, eds. (1978), *Organizational Development in Public Administration* (N.Y.: Marcel Dekker).

Golembiewski, Robert T. and R. J. Hilles (1979), *Toward the Responsive Organization: The Theory and Practice of Survey/Feedback* (Salt Lake City: Brighton Publishing Co.).

Gouldner, Alvin W. (1957),   Cosmopolitans and Locals: Toward an Analysis of Latent Social Roles,   *Administrative Science Quarterly*, Vol. 2, No. 3 (Dec.): pp. 281-292.

Gulick, Luther and Lyndall Urwick, eds. (1937), *Papers in the Science of Administration* (N.Y.: Institute of Public Administration).

Guth, William D. and Renato Jagiuri (1965),   Personal Values and Corporate Strategies,   *Harvard Business Review* (Sept.-Oct.):pp. 125, 126.

Harvey, Jerry B. (1974),   The Abilene Paradox: The Management of Agreement, *Organizational Dynamics* (Summer):pp. 128-146.

Harvey, O. J. and C. Consalvi (1960),   Status and Conformity to Pressures in Informal Groups,   *Journal of Abnormal and Social Psychology*, Vol. 60:pp. 182-187.

Hickson, D. (1961),   Motives of Workpeople Who Restrict Their Output,   *Occupational Psychology*, Vol. 35, No. 1 (Jan.-Feb.):pp. 111, 112.

Hofstede, Geerte (1980),   Motivating Leadership and Organization: Do American Theories Apply Abroad?,   *Organizational Dynamics*, (Summer), Vol. 9, No. 1:pp. 42-63.

Hollander, E. P. (1958),   Conformity, Status, and Idiosyncracy Credit,   *Psychological Review*, Vol. 65:pp. 117-127.

_____(1964), *Leaders, Groups and Influence* (N.Y.: Oxford).

House, R. and J. Rizzo,   Role Conflict and Ambiguity as Critical Variables in a Model of Organizational Behavior,   *Organizational Behavior and Human Performance*, Vol. 7, No. 3 (June):pp. 467-505.

Humphreys, L. W. and W. A. Shrode (1978),   Decision-Making Profiles of Female and Male Managers,   *MSU Business Topics* (Grad. School of Business Administration: Michigan State University) 26(4):pp. 45-51 (Autumn).

Daniel R. Ilgen, Cynthia D. Fisher, and M. Susan Taylor (1979),   Consequences of Individual Feedback on Behavior in Organizations,   *Journal of Applied Psychology*, Vol. 64, No. 4 (August), pp. 349-371.

Janis, Irving L. (1972), *Victims of Groupthink* (N.Y.: Houghton Mifflin).

Johnson, Mary C. (1980), Mentors–The Key to Development and Growth, Training and Development Journal, Vol. 34, No. 7 (July) pp. 55-57.

Johnson, T. and J. Stinson (1975), Role Ambiguity, Role Conflict, and Satisfaction: Moderating Effects of Individual Differences, *Journal of Applied Psychology*, Vol. 60, No. 3 (June):pp. 329-33.

Kahn, R., E. Wolfe, R. Quinn, and J. Sneck (1964), *Organizational Stress: Studies in Role Conflict and Performance* (N.Y.: Wiley).

Kanter, Rosabeth Moss (1977), *Men and Women of the Corporation* (N.Y.: Basic).

Keeley, N. (1977), Subjective Performance Evaluation and Person-Role Conflict Under Conditions of Uncertainty, *Academy of Management Journal* (June): pp. 301-314.

Kelley, H. H. and T. W. Lamb (1957), Uncertainty of Judgment and Resistance to Social Influence, *Journal of Abnormal and Social Psychology*, Vol. 55: pp. 137-139.

Kieler, C. (1969), Group Pressure and Conformity, in J. Mills, ed., *Experimental Social Psychology* (N.Y.: MacMillan): ch. 11.

Kornhauser, A. (1965), *Mental Health of the Industrial Worker* (N.Y.: Wiley).

Lefkowitz and Allan W. Fraser (1980), Assessment of Achievement and Power Motivation of Blacks and Whites, *Journal of Applied Psychology*, (Dec.), Vol. 65, No. 6:pp. 685-696.

Levinson, H., C. R. Price, H. J. Munden, and C. M. Sulley (1962), *Men, Management and Mental Health* (Cambridge: Harvard).

Lick, Edward J. and Bruce L. Oliver (1974), *Academy of Management Journal* (Sept.):pp. 549-554.

Likert, Rensis (1961), *New Patterns of Management* (N.Y.: McGraw-Hill).

Livingston, J. S. (1969), Pygmalion in Management, *Harvard Business Review*, Vol. 47, No. 4:pp. 81-89.

Lott, A. J. and B. E. Lott (1965), Group Cohesiveness as Interpersonal Attraction: A Review of Relationships with Antecedent and Consequent Variables, *Psychological Bulletin* (Oct.):pp. 259-309.

Lyons, T. (1971), Role Clarity, Need for Clarity, Satisfaction, Tension, and Withdrawal, *Organizational Behavior and Human Performance*, Vol. 6, No. 1 (Jan.):pp. 99-110.

Mann, F. C. and J. K. Dent (1954), The Supervisor: Member of Two Organizational Families, *Harvard Business Review*, Vol. 6 (Nov.-Dec.):pp. 103-112.

Mayo, Elton (1946), *The Human Problems of an Industrial Civilization* (Cambridge: Harvard Graduate School of Business Administration).

Miller, Ernest C. (1980), Hire in Haste–Repent at Leisure: The Team Selection Roles at Graphic Controls, *Organizational Dynamics* (Spring) Vol. 8, No. 4: pp. 2-26.

Mills, C. Wright (1953), *White Collar: The American Middle Classes* (N.Y.: Oxford).

Mintzberg, H. (1973), The Nature of Managerial Work (N.Y.: Harper and Row).

Muldrow, Tressie W. and James A. Bayton (1979), Men and Women Executives and Processes Related to Decision Accuracy, *Journal of Applied Psychology*, Vol. 64, No. 2 (April):pp. 99-106.

Nadler, David A. (1977), *Feedback and Organization Development* (Reading, Mass.: Addison-Wesley).

Nadler, E. B. (1959), Yielding, Authoritarianism, and Authoritarian Ideology Regarding Groups, *Journal of Abnormal and Social Psychology*, (May):pp. 408-410.

Perrow, Charles (1979), Complex Organizations: A Critical Essay, 2nd Ed. (Glenview, Ill.: Scott Foreman).

Pettigrew, A. (1972), Managing Under Stress, *Management Today* (April):pp. 99-102.

Porte, P. C. Andre de la (1974), Group Norms: Key to Building a Winning Team, *Personnel* (Sept.-Oct.):pp. 121-127.

Porter, L. W. and E. E. Lawler (1968a), What Job Attitudes Tell About Motivation, *Harvard Business Review*, Vol. 46, No. 1:pp. 118-126.

_____(1968b), *Managerial Attitudes and Performance* (Homewood, Ill.: Irwin Dorsey).

Price, James L. (1968), *Organizational Effectiveness; An Inventory of Propositions* (Homewood, Ill.: Irwin Dorsey).

Raia, J. R. and S. H. Osipow (1970), Creative Thinking Ability and Susceptibility to Persuasion, *Journal of Social Psychology*, Vol. 28:pp. 181-186.

Roethlisberger, F. J. and W. Dickson (1939), *Management and the Worker* (Cambridge: Harvard).

Rosenberg, L. A. (1961), Group Size, Prior Experience, and Conformity, *Journal of Abnormal and Social Psychology*, Vol. 63:pp. 436, 437.

Rosenthal, P. and K. Jacobson (1968), *Pygmalion in the Classroom* (N.Y.: Holt, Rinehart, and Winston).

Roy, Donald F. (1960), Banana Time: Job Satisfaction and Informal Interaction, *Human Organization*, Vol. 18, No. 4.

Roy, E. (1952), Quota Restriction and Goldbricking in a Machine Shop, *American Journal of Sociology*, Vol. 57:pp. 427-444.

Sadd, Susan, *Sex Roles and Achievement Conflicts* (1979), *Personality and Social Psychology Bulletin*, Vol. 5, No. 3 (July):pp. 352-355.

Sampson, E. E. and A. C. Brandon (1964), The Effects of Role and Opinion Deviation on Small Group Behavior *Sociometry*, Vol. 27:pp. 261-281.

Schacter, Stanley (1951), Communication, Deviation, and Rejection, *Journal of Abnormal Social Psychology*, Vol. 46:pp. 190-207.

_____(1959), The Chinese Indoctrination Program for Prisoners of War *Psychiatry*, Vol. 19:pp. 149-172.

_____(1968), Organizational Socialization and the Profession of Management, *Industrial Management Review*, Vol. 9:pp. 1-16.

Schacter, Stanley (1971), The Individual, the Organization, and the Career: A Conceptual Scheme, *Journal of Applied Behavioral Science*, Vol. 7:pp. 401-426.

Schein, E. H. (1956), The Chinese Indoctrination Program for Prisoners of War, *Psychiatry* Vol. 19:149-172.

_____(1970), *Organizational Psychology*, (Englewood Cliffs, N.J.: Prentice-Hall).

Schneier, Craig Eric & Kathryn M. Bartol (1980), Sex Effects in Emergent Leadership, *Journal of Applied Psychology*, Vol. 65, No. 3 (June):pp. 341-345.

Schuler, R. (1975), Role Perceptions, Satisfaction, and Performance: A Partial Reconciliation, *Journal of Applied Psychology*, Vol. 60, No. 6 (Dec.):pp. 683-687.

Seashore, Stanley E. (1954), *Group Cohesiveness in Industrial Work* (Ann Arbor, Mich.: Institute for Social Research, University of Michigan).

Selznik, Philip (1949), *TVA and the Grass Roots* (Berkeley: University of California).

_____(1957), *Leadership in Administration* (N.Y.: Harper and Row).

Shapira, Zur and Roger L. M. Dunbar (1980), Testing Mintzberg's Managerial Role Classification Using an In-Basket Simulation, *Journal of Applied Psychology*, Vol. 65, No. 1 (Feb):pp. 87-95.

Shils, E. A. (1950), Primary Groups in the American Army, in R. K. Merton and P. F. Lazarsfeld, eds., *Continuities in Social Research* (N.Y.: Free Press).

Social Science Research Council (1960), *Theoretical Studies in the Social Organization of the Prison* (N.Y.: SSRC).

Storey, W. (1978), Which Way: Manager-Directed or Person-Centered Career Pathing, *Training and Development Journal* (Jan.):pp. 10-14.

Szilagyi and Winford E. Holland (1980), Changes in Social Density Relationships with Functional Interaction and Perceptions of Job Characteristics, Role Stress, and Work Satisfaction, *Journal of Applied Psychology*, Vol. 65, No. 1 (Feb.):pp. 28-33.

Trist, E. L. and K. W. Bamforth (1951), Some Social and Psychological Consequences of the Longwall Method of Goal-Getting, *Human Relations*, Vol. 4, No. 1 (Feb.):pp. 3-38.

Viteles, M. A. (1953), *Motivation and Morale in Industry* (N.Y.: Norton).

Walker, C., R. Guest, and A. Turner (1956), *The Foreman on the Assembly Line* (Cambridge: Harvard).

Wall, J. A. (1974), Some Variables Affecting a Constituent's Evaluation of a Behavior toward a Boundary Role Occupant, *Organizational Behavior and Human Performance*, Vol. 11:pp. 390-408.

Webber, R. A. (1974), Majority and Minority Perceptions: Cross-Cultural Teams, *Human Relations*, Vol. 27, No. 9:pp. 873-889.

Weaver, Charles N. (1980), Job Satisfaction in the U.S. in the 1970's, *Journal of Applied Psychology*, Vol. 65, No. 3 (June):pp. 364-367.

Weiner, M. (1958), Certainty of Judgment as a Variable in Conformity Behavior, *Journal of Social Psychology*, Vol. 48:pp. 257-263.

Whyte, William Foote (1943), *Street Corner Society* (Chicago: University of Chicago).

Whyte, William Foote (1955), *The Organization Man* (N.Y.: Simon and Schuster).

_____(1955b), *Money and Motivation* (N.Y.: Harper).

Zarmarta, Raymond F., Manuel London, and K. M. Rowland (1979), Effects of Sex on Commitment and Conflict Resolution, *Journal of Applied Psychology*, Vol. 64, No. 2 (April):pp. 227-231.

COMMUNICATION

In any organization, communication is critical to effective management. Mintzberg, in a now classic study on the nature of managerial work, describes the manager as the "nerve center" of his organization's information. The unique access of the manager to all subordinates and special outside contacts confers the power to acquire information.

> In effect, the manager is his organization's generalist with the best store of non-routine information . . . as monitor the manager continually seeks and receives information from a variety of sources in order to develop a thorough understanding of the organization and its environment . . . as disseminator the manager sends external information into his organization and internal information from one subordinate to another . . . as spokesman the manager must transmit information to various external groups . . . [and] serve outsiders as an expert in the field in which his organization operates. (Mintzberg, 1973.)

Mintzberg names "sharing information" as a key area of concentration for managers seeking to improve their effectiveness.

Applying Mintzberg's categories to the activities of public sector executives Lau et al. (1980) found the communication role to be central to effective management. In an analysis of work diaries Lau (et al.) found that a sample of Navy executives spent 22 percent of their time in informational roles: monitoring internal and external information, interpreting, integrating, brainstorming information internally, and transmitting plans, policies, actions, and results to outsiders. (Lau, 1980.)

Though a critical activity of public sector managers, communication as a phenomenon is not well understood. Often it is defined in terms of its most limited meaning, the directive a manager issues to a subordinate. We propose a more comprehensive description of the process of communication in this chapter. Then we explore both verbal and nonverbal types of communication, the structure of communication, and the important skill of listening. We conclude with the consideration of a proposed approach to assessing communication effectiveness: the communication audit.

COMMUNICATION AS A PROCESS

The field of organizational communication, lodged in the interstices of the disciplines of organizational behavior and speech communication, lacks a prevailing paradigm which would lend unity to its content. Goldhaber reports that in a recent review of twenty-six organizational communication textbooks, thirty-nine major topics were explored. But no topic was covered in every book and the majority of topics were covered in less than one-half of the textbooks. (Goldhaber, 1979.) However, Goldhaber mentions a few concepts which gain general support in this literature review.

1. Organizational communication occurs within a complex open system which is influenced by and influences its environment;
2. Organizational communication involves messages and their flow, purpose, direction, and media; and
3. Organizational communication involves people and their abilities, feelings, relationships, and skills. (Goldhaber, 1979.)

We adopt the working definition for organizational communication proposed by Tortoriello. Organizational communication, he says, is the study of the flow and impact of messages within a network of interactional relationships. (Tortoriello, 1978). This definition is enriched by Goldhaber's description, which portrays this communication as a process where messages are created and exchanged within an organizational environment which produces uncertainty. (Goldhaber, 1979.)

The virtue of these definitions is that they incorporate David Berlo's now classic statement on the "process" character of communication:

> "If we accept the concept of process, we view events and relationships as dynamic, ongoing, ever-changing, continuous. When we label something as a process, we also mean it does not have a beginning, an end, a fixed sequence of events. It is not static, at rest. It is moving. The ingredients within the process interact; each affects all of the others . . ." (Berlo, 1960.)

Figure 8 is a representation of these definitions which provides the conceptual tools for discussing communication in public sector organizations.

Communication is about creating and exchanging messages. A message means the symbol or symbols we perceive and to which we attach meaning in communication. Messages may be verbal (speeches, lectures, conversations) or nonverbal

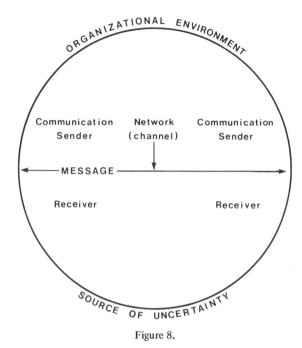

Figure 8.

(body language, physical characteristics, vocal cues, personal space) (Goldhaber, 1979).

Whether verbal or nonverbal, the messages that are created and exchanged in an agency travel over channels called communication networks. Communication networks flow from roles and structures that vary from agency to agency. Networks may be formal or informal, and they may channel information vertically or horizontally.

Messages are communicated through an interaction process. There is constant mutual feedback between sender and receiver so that both parties are communicators, or givers and receivers, at the same time. (Tortoriello, 1978.) The environment within which communication occurs is a significant part of the communication picture, because of its role in shaping both process and contents of communication. Environmental factors in public sector organizations, including clients, funding bodies, and legislative and executive officials, often shape communication networks, while changes in political and social and economic environment ensure a ubiquitous uncertainty for public sector managers. Some communication scholars define the principal function of communication as the reduction of uncertainty. (Farace, Monge, Russell, 1977.) Since historically government agencies are established to cope with problems unresolved in the private sector, the level of uncertainty—the gap between information and information held—is heightened for the public manager.

Following Berlo's lead contemporary communication theorists are quick to point out the dangers in describing the communication activity in terms of its discrete components:. senders, receivers, messages, channels, networks. When we examine the components of communication we freeze a process that in the real world is dynamic and constantly changing. Our analytical purpose is served only if we keep in mind the whole as we study its parts.

Communication as we usually think of it in an organization is intentional, conscious, directed and purposive. For example, the director of the Division for Social Services wants to make her decisions known, inform her employees about a new case management program, tell them how it will be implemented, and obtain sufficient information from the case workers to evaluate the new system at each stage of the implementation process. But sometimes managers communicate unconsciously. For example, the same director repeatedly checks her watch while in a conversation initiated by a social worker who is disgruntled about the paperwork generated by the new system. We established earlier that a message is a symbol to which we attach meaning. In the first instance, the social service director is using the symbols of verbal communication. In the second example non-verbal symbols were used to communicate meaning.

Watzlawick, Beavin, and Jackson (1967) capture the significant differences between verbal and nonverbal communication by aligning each type of communication with two distinct systems: the digital and the analogic. Digital communication is like an on/off switch; analogic communication is like a rheostat. Content messages tend to be transmitted in digital form through verbal communication, which consists of individual sounds, words, and sentences. Nonverbal communication such as voice tone, friendliness, and attentiveness transmits analogic messages. Variation occurs by discrete steps in digital communication, by degree in analogic communication. The analogic, nonverbal communication is more likely to communicate a relationship message, the digital, verbal communication a content message. All communications have content and relationship dimensions.

VERBAL COMMUNICATION

In Organizations, verbal communication takes place through three distinct types of encounters. Each encounter utilizes its own techniques or vehicles for communication. In *Encounter 1*, fact, opinions, and ideas are conveyed by management to employees. Techniques typically employed are policy procedure manuals, employee directives, letters, memos, operational guidelines, and internal agency newsletters. *Encounter 2* captures various forms of joint consultation in the organization, between management and unions or within work units (teams, project members, etc.). Vehicles typically utilized to facilitate this process are structured meetings and problem solving sessions. (Here nonverbal messages may also transmit meaning.) *Encounter 3* refers to the dialogue between an individual employee, or applicant, and a manager. This process unfolds through normal day-to-day discussion, occurs as part of periodic performance review or, for the potential employee or promotee, may take place in a formal interview. *Encounter 3* communication has a very strong nonverbal dimension.

Considering verbal communication in terms of these three sets of organizational encounters helps isolate, and freeze for exampnation purposes those places where communication might break down. Typically barriers to effective organizational communication arise in the effort to translate a specific message through a given medium. Communication breakdown may result from characteristics of the medium or the message. Figure 9 highlights these vulnerable points in the process. With breakdown points identified, the manager can focus on effective remedies.

In the context of *Encounter 1* communication, breakdown may be occasioned by the words chosen or by the medium employed. In some governmental cultures the medium itself impedes effective communication, as in Thailand where the anonymous letter is a "time-honored tradition within the Thai government," (Krannich, 1979). In the U.S. the medium of the written word is generally acknowledged as a useful tool in organizational communication. But in terms of the choice of words, every student of government is familiar with the popular criticism leveled against bureaucratic writing. Examples of bureaucratic gobblegook abound in the popular press, with a current favorite being the phrase "radiation enhancement weapon" used by the Department of Defense to describe the neutron bomb. One recent proposal to enhance the clarity of communications offers a tool ". . .which rearranges and consolidates content in order of priorities and restricts the uses of verbs to one, written in the active voice and adjacent to the subject." (Silverman, 1980). This "optimum legibility formula" (OLF) stipulates a seven point formula for effective and efficient written communication:

1. Write the complete message as quickly as possible, without premeditated compliance with OLF restrictions.
2. Determine the purpose for the message by listing three or four potential sentence subjects.
3. Decide what to write by answering the six basic journalistic questions: who, what, when, where. why, and how.
4. Rearrange sentences in order of priority, consolidating all sentences with identical or synonymous verbs.
5. Place verbs immediately following their subjects.

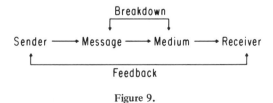

Figure 9.

6. Eliminate all linking verbs.
7. Use one verb per sentence.

Sometimes *Encounter 1* communication breaks down because managers think that every detail needs to be communicated. Employees typically don't want to know everything there is to know about their agency. The most important and desired information falls into the following categories:

- *Job security*—facts on the agency's stability, plans for the future growth, intention to expand or reduce the work force, commitment to fair treatment of employees.
- *Opportunity for advancement*—facts on how employees can get ahead, increase their income, improve their working conditions.
- *Status and recognition*—facts on why the employee's job is important; how his "team" rates with the public; how the employee himself has contributed to its success.
- *Personnel benefits*—facts on the material advantages of working for government agencies; how its job benefits compare to other plans in government and private industry.
- *What's expected in return*—facts on job performance criteria; procedures, policies and rules; standards of conduct; expected level of effort, contribution, and cooperation. (Public Personnel Administration, 1973.)

Beyond communicating these items, managers need to be sensitive to information overload.

Encounter 2 communication, where joint consultation takes place in a meeting setting, provides management with an opportunity to evaluate employee responses unmatched by any other medium. Employees may be reluctant to put in writing a criticism that will surface naturally in a group setting. Gestures and facial expressions, between and among the participants, provide helpful clues as to attitudes in a group. Employees may be more likely to raise questions at a meeting than through other channels for upward communication. And the general verbal as well as non-verbal reaction of the group will help the meeting's convener determine the majority perspective on any individual topic. (Public Personnel Administration, 1973.)

Communication in such a meeting often falters because of inattention to the structure of the meeting itself. Improperly planned and structured meetings impede communication by failing to encourage the communication for which the meeting exists, by stressing the wrong message, or by producing a cynicism in employees about the effectiveness of participation. Baker provides some guidelines to ensure meetings are effective mediums for communication. (Baker, 1979.) Before calling a meeting a manager should:

1. determine alternatives to holding meeting
2. clearly establish purpose

 3. limit attendance
 4. distribute agenda in advance
 5. circulate background material
 6. choose an appropriate meeting time
 7. place a limit on the meeting and on each item.
During the meeting the manager must be sure to:
 1. start and end on time
 2. place important items at top of agenda
 3. assign time keeping and minutes responsibility
 4. end the meeting with a unifying or positive issue
 5. summarize what has been accomplished
 6. coordinate time of next meeting.
And after the meeting the manager should take time to:
 1. provide timely and complete minutes
 2. follow through on decisions
 3. conduct a periodic evaluation of the meeting.

In *Encounter 3* type communication the messages are transmitted back and forth between an individual manager and a current or potential employee. Effective communication in this one-to-one exchange is highly dependent on the personalities involved. (Strategies encouraging supervisor-subordinate communication will be addressed under the topic performance appraisal in Chapter 10). What needs stress here is that an individual's satisfaction at work has been traced empirically to the quality of communication interaction experience. Communication can both reduce uncertainty (Thayer, 1968) and satisfy needs for affiliation (Timm and Wilkins, 1977). Timm (1978) has argued that supervisor to subordinate communication behavior should be viewed as part of the organizational reward system.

Whereas in *Encounter 1* and *Encounter 2* communication the message is carried largely by words, *Encounter 3* falls into the realm of interpersonal communication where non-verbal messages carry the burden of meaning. The employment interview presents one case where the importance of non-verbal transactions in *Encounter 3* communication has been well-documented. Several studies have found the importance of the articulative and nonverbal behavior (eye contact, gesturing, smiling, appropriate tone) in receiving a favorable evaluation in a job interview. (Imoda and Hakel, 1977; McGovern, 1977; Washburn and Hakel, 1973; Wexley, Fugito, and Malone, 1975.) We turn now to an in depth discussion of the nonverbal dimension of communication.

NONVERBAL COMMUNICATION

Nonverbal communication occurs when a message is transmitted by a means other than the spoken or written word. Nonverbal communication constitutes a significant proportion of any message transmitted during a communication event. Harris (1970) suggest that sixty-five percent of social meaning in face-to-face communication is carried by the nonverbal message. According to Mehrabian (1971), 93 percent of general meaning can be attributed to nonverbal messages and only 7 percent to verbal. The role of nonverbal communication in interpreting organizational interactions is increasingly recognized as critical. Lewis sums up the current assessment of its importance in these words: "Most of us speak at least one oral language, but everyone speaks a nonverbal language. Communication analysts tend to agree that perhaps most of the expression of emotional and motivational states occurs on nonverbal levels and is communicated by facial and paralinguistic use." (Lewis, in Tortoriello, 1978.) Tortoriello concludes, "probably more feeling and intentions are communicated nonverbally than through all the verbal methods combines." (Tortoriello, 1978.) The definition of nonverbal communication adopted here is that of Tortoriello; ". . . the exchange of messages primarily through nonlinguistic means including; kinesics (body language), facial expressions and eye contact, tactile communication, space and territory, environment, paralanguage (vocal but nonlinguistic cues), and the use of silence and time." (Tortoriello, 1978.)

Using the analogic label to describe nonverbal communication systems as opposed to the digital definition for verbal communication helps to identify and thus to eliminate a major source of communication breakdown. Breakdown occurs when problems arise in translating analogic messages into digital messages. When communicators try to fit the continuous into the discrete, information may be lost or seriously misrepresented. A first step to avoid communication breakdown due to the existence of nonverbal as well as verbal messages is to identify more precisely the modes of nonverbal communication.

Kinesics or Body Language a well documented mode of nonverbal communication, has been categorized by Ekman and Friesen (1969) into five types of expressions. *Emblems* are nonverbal behaviors that stand for words: the sign OK, and the peace sign, for example. Often emblems are used to reinforce a verbal message. *Illustrators* are forms of nonverbal behavior that literally illustrates a message: the parking attendant points to a space while commanding "park here." *Affect displays* are facial movements which send a message, either intentional as in sticking a tongue out to communicate insult, or unintentional, when a shy employee blushes in response to a compliment from the manager. *Regulators* such as turning one's eyes away from the speaker to signal loss of interest or nodding one's head to keep communication going regulate all communication. Finally, *adapters* are nonverbal behaviors learned in childhood which meet some need, but which the speaker may not notice. Touching one's head to relieve an itch which in private you might scratch is one example.

Facial Expressions and Eye Contact are a second category of nonverbal communication. The most visible indicator of emotions and feelings is probably the face (Goldhaber, 1979). But it is eye contact that has been the subject of the most extensive investigation in organizations. Goldhaber summarizes our knowledge about eye contact under the following points:

1. Eye contact seems to occur when people are seeking feedback, when an individual wants to signal open communications, and when an individual is asking for inclusion.
2. Women appear to engage in more eye contact than do men.
3. Eye contact increases as communicators increase the distance between themselves.
4. Eye contact may produce anxiety in others.
5. Eye contact does not occur when people want to hide their feelings, when people are physically close, in some competitive situations, when listeners are bored, and when an individual does not want social contact. (Goldhaber, 1979.)

Tactile Communication a third nonverbal mode, may be the most primitive form of message sending. Nancy Henley suggests that the message sent is often a message of dominance. In our culture, persons of higher status are permitted to touch others, but it would be a notable break of etiquette for a person of lower status to touch their superiors. (Henley, 1977.)

Space and Territory has been studied extensively by ethologists who report that dominant animals in a group have a territory which is distinguished from that of other animals by its greater size. Space and territory emerge in the organizational world as nonverbal communicators of status and power. Mehrabian (1971) notes:

> "Higher-status persons of a social group have access to more locations and have more power to increase or restrict immediacy vis-a-vis others than lower status members. . .For instance, among persons of different status within the same institution, such as a school, a business, or a hospital, high-status individuals are assigned larger and more private quarters." (p. 34.)

In other words, the higher you are up in the organization the better you are able to protect your territory and the more territory you have to protect.

Environment referring to both the building and rooms in which we work and the arrangements of movable objects like furniture around us can influence our communication patterns. A desk may serve as a marker to establish personal space. When an office is arranged so that chairs are grouped together, this signals intimacy and informality. When chairs are lined up in front of desk, this is a sign that the desk's occupant has authority and power.

Paralanguage the tone and variation accompanying verbal messages is a sixth nonverbal mode which may either compliment or contradict a verbal communication. Tortoriello, et al. suggest that paralanguage may explain attraction and repulsion between communicators, even when comprehension of a message is unaffected.

> *"In one organization a woman was next in line for a promotion. However, her boss told her that a certain personal characteristic kept her from getting the job. Only after asking a colleague for advice did she learn that one of her most annoying personal characteristics was her high-pitched strident voice. Since the new position would require public relations work and representing the company to the public, it was felt that the image she would present would be a negative one. The stereotypically high-strung and extremely tense individual is often associated with having a high-pitched voice." (Tortoriello, 1978.)*

Finally, the use of *silence and time* shades the meaning of messages between and among people. Silence can indicate support or opposition, create uneasiness, provide a link between messages or sever a relationship. (Tortoriello, 1978.) Time can be an indicator of status, as when a subordinate waits for hours to see a supervisor, or it can be an acknowledgement of mutual respect, when manager and subordinate organize their schedules so as to conserve each other's time.

Everyone in an organization can become a more effective communicator through increased awareness of nonverbal messages and their impact. Nonverbal messages may serve to repeat, substitute, contradict, complement, or regulate communication. (Koehler, 1981.)

VERTICAL AND HORIZONTAL COMMUNICATION

Thus far we have discussed the substance of communication as it is transmitted verbally and nonverbally. We turn now to the channels along which messages flow. What are the patterns of communications in organizations? What effects do the different patterns have on the organizational process? What factors create particular communication patterns?

Within organizations, communication is the foundation of control and coordination. The formal organization dictates the channels for information flow: vertical in direction for formal transactions rooted in the principles of authority and hierarchy and horizontal in direction for transactions emanating from job function. (Goldhaber, 1979.)

Vertical communication may be "down-the-line" or "up-the-line." (Conboy, 1979.) According to Katz and Kahn, down-the-line channels are used to communicate five types of messages.

1. Job instructions—direction on how to do a specific task.

2. Job rationale—information about how one task relates to other tasks in the organization.
3. Procedures and practices—messages indicating the rules of the game in the organization.
4. Feedback—messages telling individuals about their performance on the job.
5. Indoctrination of goals—messages about overall organizational goals and the relationship of the individual goals to organizational goals (Katz and Kahn, 1966.)

Logic would suggest that down-the-line communication messages should become more elaborate as they move through levels of the hierarchy, because at each level more specific details might be added to ensure comprehension by subordinates, and because employees want necessary information from their supervisors. But Conboy reports that in fact remarkable attrition occurs as messages move down the hierarchy. One study of 100 industrial managers yielded average information acquisition figures as follows for down-the-line communication.

- Board of Directors—100 percent of communication content
- Vice Presidents—67 percent
- General supervisors—56 percent
- Plant managers—40 percent
- Foremen—30 percent
- Workers—20 percent

Another issue in downward communication concerns how information acquisition is perceived by different people in the organization. One study conducted by Likert indicated that supervisors may overestimate the amount of information known by subordinates. Employees often complain that they don't receive enough information about their job performance. (Katz and Kahn, 1966.) Often the information that is added as the message proceeds down the organizational hierarchy may change the meaning originally intended. But the communication downward may also falter because, as noted earlier, managers may overload employees with messages like bulletins, memos, and announcements, many of which may be of marginal interest to them. Sometimes filtering, or shortening, changing, and lengthening messages as they move down, and power grabbing, or not sharing messages, also frustrate downward communication.

Up-the-line communication occurs when messages flow from subordinate to superior. Typically these messages ask questions, provide feedback or offer new ideas. According to Planty and Machaver (1952) upward communication should be fostered for four reasons:

1. It indicates the receptivity of the environment for downward communication

2. It facilitates acceptance of decisions by encouraging subordinate participation in the decision-making process.
3. It provides feedback on subordinate understanding of downward communication.
4. It encourages submission of valuable ideas.

Several management theorists have argued that openness of communication between subordinates and superiors is critical to maintaining a successful organizational climate (Havey, 1966; Likert, 1967; Burke and Wilcox, 1969, Jablin, 1979). Yet researchers have discovered that subordinates are afraid to tell superiors how they feel (Vogel, 1967), they distort information they give their bosses (Read, 1962; Downs, 1967; Athanassia, 1973; O'Reilly and Roberts, 1974a), and they feel that passing negative information to a boss may bring punishment (Blau and Scott, 1962; Argyris, 1966).

Two of the obstacles inhibiting downward communication particularly impede upward communication: filtering and power grabbing. The filtering upward occurs as employees tend to report information that makes them look good and keep silent information that casts them in a poor light. Also, the alienated worker can simply refuse to share information with supervisors because of his desire to maintain some control, however meager.

Upward filtering has received considerable research attention. It is usually measured directly, by asking respondents to indicate their degree of openness with their superiors, or else indirectly, by measuring the agreement between superiors and subordinates on subordinates work problems and responsibilities (Monge, Edwards, Kirste, 1979). Factors found to affect upward filtering include the subordinate's satisfaction (Burke and Wilcox, 1969), the subordinate's trust in the superior (Roberts and O'Reilly, 1974), and the subordinate's own mobility aspirations (Maier, Hoffman, and Tead, 1963; Read, 1962).

Research shows that openness in communication in general will prevail when 1) both superiors and subordinates perceive each other as willing and receptive listeners; and 2) both refrain from responses which might be perceived as neutral-negative or nonaccepting (Jablin, 1979). In a practical vein, Goldfarb concludes from his research on upward communication that "the most effective method for encouraging upward communication is sympathetic listening during the many day-to-day information contacts within the department and outside the workplace." (Goldhaber, 1979.)

So far we have focused on vertical communication, which emphasizes the formal control structure of an organization, its hierarchy, and chain of command. Horizontal communication, in contrast, emanates from functional relationships outlined in the structure of jobs. It refers to the messages exchanged between and among the people and units at the same level in the organizational hierarchy. While the amount of vertical communication may be higher in the typical organization, where estimates of vertical communication run as high as 67 percent (Porter and

Roberts, 1973), horizontal communication remains important. Estimates of the amount of horizontal communication hover in the 30-40 percent range (Porter and Roberts, 1976). However much communications research suggests the vertical system would be nearly unworkable without considerable flow of information laterally (Burns, 1954; Dublin, 1962; Dubin and Spray, 1964; Guetzkow, 1965; Simpson, 1959).

Typically horizontal communication is initiated in order to coordinate tasks, solve problems, share information, and/or resolve conflict. (Goldhaber, 1979.) Though it is a critical part of effective communication in an organization, horizontal communication may falter because of rivalry and specialization of work units without communication avenues linking them, or lack of incentives or rewards for effective communication. As remedies for poor horizontal communication Conboy proposes the following:

1. Boldly and clearly announce the expectation that horizontal communication will occur.
2. Put into place mechanisms like routing systems to ensure that horizontal communication takes place.
3. Design reward systems to reinforce good horizontal communication and discourage hoarding information. (Conboy, 1976.)

The hierarchical structure of organizations and the functional description of jobs or tasks prescribe certain vertical and horizontal communication patterns in organizations. Also, informal communication networks operate within the work units throughout the organization. Conboy defines networks as ". . . social communication circuits involved in particular activities." (Conboy, 1976.) Networks specify who talks to whom, how far communicating units are from one another in the network, and ground rules to be followed in communication.

The location of an individual in a communications network may have significant implications for the organization. Research has found that certain people occupy "key communicator" roles for some topics of concern to the organization; they serve as links between larger groups of people (Taylor, Farace, and Monge, 1976; Albrecht, 1978). These "key" people are the ones who most members of the organization can reach through relatively few channels. They might link groups but are not themselves members (a manager with three reporting units) or they might be group members who have linkages to one or more other groups (Taylor, 1977). Research suggests significant differences in how key communicators and nonkey communicators relate to the organization. Key communicators identify more with their jobs, are more satisfied with downward directed messages, perceive themselves to be closer to management and believe their jobs to be more central in the overall environment. (Albrecht, 1979.) To the extent that such communication linkages affect assumptions people have about their organization, managers need to keep in mind the communication location of subordinates.

Poole identifies three aspects of communication networks that determine the shape of communication networks operative in an organization: centrality (the degree to which an individual is at the crossroads of an information flow), connectedness (the degree to which members are inter-linked), and dominance (the degree to which information flow is one-way or two-way). (Poole, 1978.) Four network designs that have been studied extensively are the wheel, the chain, the circle and the all channel or star. Figure 10 depicts each for five person groups.

Research clearly indicates that the shape of the network influences the process of communication as well as the behavior of individuals in the network. Thus these findings hold implications for both job satisfaction and productivity within the organization. The wheel network, where the hub holds the unique role in collecting, evaluating and dispensing information, seems to work best where tasks are simple. Obviously the person at the hub is a critical factor, but this highly centralized communication network achieves high speed and accuracy on simple tasks. On the satisfaction dimension, the person at the hub reports high satisfaction while persons in the spoke positions report low satisfaction. The wheel pattern also produces low flexibility to change. The chain network yields the same general results as the wheel, but with a higher level of job satisfaction than the wheel provides. The circle design, where relationships are symmetrical, produces high consistency and uniformity in group operation. Job satisfaction is high, a sense of participation is experienced. On the down side the circle takes time to operate and accuracy may be low. The all channel, sometimes called the star design, provides high versatility and flexibility. The high involvement provided by everyone to everyone channels, yields personal high satisfaction, but task satisfaction may be lower because of the time-consuming character of this network. Table 4 summarizes these findings.

These findings on networks are based mainly on studies where groups perform simple tasks. Some studies, however, indicate that with more complex problems, the circle network may result in faster and more accurate performance than the wheel. (Shaw, 1954; Mears, 1974.) Other studies show that all groups within the star and chain networks eventually reach the same levels of performance regardless of structure, whether the focus is on simple or on complex tasks. (Carzo, 1963.) Conboy draws three broad conclusions from a review of research on networks:

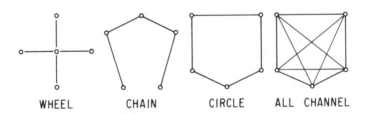

WHEEL   CHAIN   CIRCLE   ALL CHANNEL

Figure 10. Communication network designs.

TABLE 4. Networks*

	Wheel	Chain	Circle	Star
Speed of Performance	Fast	Fast	Slow	Slow
Accuracy	Good	Good	Poor	Poor (in early stages)
Job Satisfaction	Very poor	Poor	Very good (personal)	Very good (personal)
Flexibility to job change	Slow	Slow	Fast	Fast

*Adapted from Alex Bavelas and Dermat Barrell, "An Experimental Approach to Organization Communication," *Personnel*, March 1951, pp. 370-371 and Conboy, pp. 31, 32.

1. . . .the design of a network has a major influence on the outcomes processed by that network.
2. . . .there is no universal design. Form and function should be matched according to circumstances.
3. . . .any human communication network should be seen as subject to change, modifiable according to the needs of each subsequent task. (Conboy, 1976.)

Thus far our discussion of networks has focused on individual group members as communicators. As Poole (1978) points out, these network analyses can be generalized to organizational units to provide a macro-level view of communication flow. Viewing the units as the communicators, Poole has analyzed how information, once transmitted, is integrated and evaluated by work units. This research helps managers by pointing out the way organizations typically respond to information problems.

Poole describes how organizations cope with the need to integrate and evaluate information. He focuses on two aspects of needed information: its availability, which refers to how easily obtainable and suited to its needs the work unit perceives the information to be, and its uniformity, the variability of information requirements over time. Figure 11 represents the methods prominent at five points along these uniformity, availability dimensions.

When information is high in availability and high in uniformity the single employee who works with the information takes on the job of evaluating and integrating it. Information is typically transmitted by forms. But when the individual finds this direct use of information unsatisfactory he goes to the source to clarify it, seeks feedback through informal group meetings. If uniformity of information decreases while availability remains high the proper response is to suppress the rate of information input or increase the variety of sources of information.

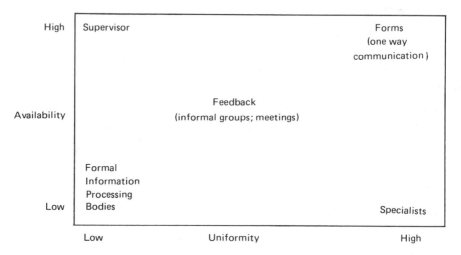

Figure 11. How organizational units cope with information problems. *Adapted from M. S. Poole. An Information Task Approach to Organizational Communication," *The Academy of Management Review*, vol. 3, 1978, pp. 493-504.

The supervisor is in the best position to take these steps and so the person in that role serves to evaluate and integrate information under these conditions. However if the uniformity of information remains high and the availability decreases specialists or experts can best cope with the integration and evaluation challenge by determining the informations suitability. Finally when information is very low in availability and uniformity formal information processing bodies will develop to cope with it. Often regular committees are appointed to evaluate new information. (Poole, 1978.)

Poole's contribution is useful in pointing out the close relationship between the character of information and the response of organizations to it. As Figure 11 suggests, the character of the information controls the proper vehicle for response. While most network studies in communication describe communication patterns and explore their effects on organizational processes (Guetzkow, 1965; Terreberry, 1968; Ference, 1970), Poole attempts to provide information on factors that create communication patterns and processes in the first place. (Poole, 1978.)

The public sector manager works in a difficult communication environment. Often critical information is unavailable, especially in problem areas that yield little information about solutions, such as rehabilitation of prison populations. Under these circumstances managers can't afford a network of organizational communication which diminishes useful information. Understanding both the impact of different structures of communication and the capacity of information to shape organizational response keeps the public manager on top of a major organizational challenge.

LISTENING

Communication is a process through which messages are sent and received along the channels described above. But the transaction involves at least two communicators and the success of the experience is highly dependent on the listening skills of each. Studies show that we spend nearly one-half of our communication time listening. For public or private sector managers, listening is a critical part of the role: as a source both of new ideas and of understanding employees.

Though the importance of listening is critical to effective management, most of us get low marks in this communication skill. Under normal listening conditions most people, within 24 hours, lose 75 percent of the information gained in a 10-minute presentation. The culprit is poor listening habits. (Nichols, 1962.) Carl Weaver attributes this inattentiveness to the personal risk involved in taking another's ideas seriously (Weaver, 1972). Huseman identifies typical barriers to listening: (Huseman, 1976)

- attending to stimuli that serve to satisfy our own needs
- not attending to stimuli that do not conform to our own models of the world
- . . . filtering based on our own frame of reference. . .

Managers need to be sensitive to the purpose of listening in order to sharpen their listening skills. Charles Kelly differentiates between two types of listening guided by distinct purposes. Deliberative listening is listening for information. It includes the ability hear, analyze and recall information and draw conclusions from it. (Kelly, 1962.) Empathetic listening is listening for understanding. The empathetic listener participates in the spirit of his or her environment as a receiver of communication. (Kelly, 1962.) Often empathetic listening is called active listening.

Leonard differentiates these types of listening by motivation of the listener:

> *"The active or empathetic listener strives first to understand the speaker, while the deliberative listener wants first to analyze what the speaker said. In deliberative listening. the listener strives to understand the message for the purpose of using the information contained in the message. Primarily, the listener attempts to evaluate the message. But with active listening, the listener first wants to understand the person, to see and to feel what he or she feels. Deliberative listening is primarily a feeling process. . ." (Leonard, 1981.)*

Research suggests that good listening habits can be developed. Regarding deliberative listening or listening for information, 10 guides to good listening proposed by Ralph Nichols have now become part of the conventional wisdom.

1. Find an area of interest in what is being said. Ask yourself: what is the speaker saying that I can use?
2. Judge the content and not the delivery style of the speaker.
3. Withhold evaluation of the speaker's point until you completely comprehend it.
4. Be attentive to central ideas of the speaker, not collection of the facts.
5. Be flexible and adaptable in methods of recording key points of the speaker.
6. Give the speaker your conscious attention; don't fake attention.
7. Resist distractions from the environment.
8. Gain experience through practice in hearing difficulty, expository material. Exercise your mind.
9. Identify emotion-laden words that tend to impair your ability to perceive and understand and through reflection and discussion try to diffuse the emotional impact of such words on you. Such words might be redneck, pervert, communist, right-winger, lesbian.
10. Apply the spare time in listening to thinking about what is being said. Most people think about 4 times the rate at which speaking occurs. Use that spare time. (Nichols, in Huseman, 1970.)

While useful, these guidelines for listening principally address deliberative listening, which is focused on information gathering. But as Leonard notes, the good listener listens for *all* the meanings, those behind the words, not just the obvious meanings. Prerequisites for active listening include:

1. "The listener must want to listen." The desire to listen is highly correlated with the ability to know what to do generally in an interpersonal situation, to be in touch with yourself and what's going on inside of others.
2. "...the listener must be willing to suspend judgment." This point goes beyond merely withholding judgment until the cognitive material is totally comprehended. It invites the listener to genuinely see the issue from the other's point of view.
3. "...the listener must allow and encourage the statement of feelings by the other." Feelings need to be expressed and accepted before dealing with them.
4. "...the listener must be aware of his or her own feelings, and be prepared to integrate them into the interaction where appropriate." (Leonard, 1981.)

But beyond these prerequisites for active listening, the messages actually communicated to the speaker by your behavior, shapes the communication encounter.

A person skilled in active listening is sensitive to the nonverbal cues he or she is emitting. Usually labeled "attending behavior" these nonverbal (typically physical) communications tell the speaker, "I'm here, I am interested in you. I want to listen." (Leonard, 1981:16). Leonard includes in attending messages the following:

- facing the other person squarely
- adopting an open posture
- leaning toward the other
- maintaining good eye contact
- being relatively relaxed
- reflecting attention through facial expressions
- attending with vocal cues (Leonard, 1981)

Of course many factors external to the communicators influence the quality of interpersonal communication in an organization. Sometimes these factors may be beyond the manager's control. Typical external factors in organizational settings are poor physical conditions such as noise, poor acoustics, a gloomy atmosphere, and uncomfortable or inappropriate furniture and the relative status of the communicators. For the public manager, status is sometimes determined by subtle political relationships relevant in a communication encounter. Awareness of these constraints will focus the listener's attention on taking them into proper account in a communication.

In summary, we note that listening is a skill that can be cultivated. We have pointed to some of the strategies for increasing both deliberative and active listening effectiveness. It is well worth a manager's time and energy to adopt these strategies. A good listener makes better decisions, stimulates better speaking, and is more likely to enjoy the communication experience. (Huseman, 1970.)

THE COMMUNICATIONS AUDIT

Effective communication is a prime factor in achieving organizational effectiveness (Greenbaum, 1974; Barnard, 1938; Bavelas, 1951; Dorsey, 1957; Katz and Kahn, 1966). A growing body of applied research attempts to synthesize our accumulated understanding of the dynamics of communication and develop it from data collection instruments that can ascertain how well the communication system is working in an organization. Howard Greenbaum's work on the organizational communication audit advances an outline for managers to follow in assessing communications. At the organizational level the communications audit provide for three stages:

- factfinding; data on the organization's history, objectives, structure, leadership style, organizational character and communication system is maintained and developed.

TABLE 5. Communication audit network analysis instrument

During a typical workday, I usually communicate about work-related matters
with the following people through the following channels:

	Identi-fication	Formal Organizational Structure	Informal (Grapevine) Organizational Structure
Executive			
Stenographer-Secretary	0001	– A B C D E	– A B C D E
Senior Stenographer	0002	– A B C D E	– A B C D E
Executive Secretary	0003	– A B C D E	– A B C D E
Assistant executive director	0004	– A B C D E	– A B C D E
Assistant manager	0005	– A B C D E	– A B C D E
Telephone operator	0006	– A B C D E	– A B C D E
Executive director	0007	– A B C D E	– A B C D E
Administration and Finance			
Assistant director for administration	0008	– A B C D E	– A B C D E
Typist	0009	– A B C D E	– A B C D E
Accounting clerk	0010	– A B C D E	– A B C D E
Accounting clerk typist	0011	– A B C D E	– A B C D E
Assistant accountant	0012	– A B C D E	– A B C D E
Senior accountant	0013	– A B C D E	– A B C D E
Typist	0014	– A B C D E	– A B C D E
Stenographer	0015	– A B C D E	– A B C D E

Key: A = not at all important
      B = somewhat important
      C = fairly important
      D = very important
      E = extremely important

*From Gerald Goldhaber. *Organizational Communication*. Dubuque, Iowa, Wm. C. Brown
Pub., 1979, 2nd Ed., pp. 355-357.

- analysis: the extent to which existing practices are achieving objectives of the major communication networks and goals of the organization.
- evaluation and reporting; conclusions based on analysis are drawn about the efficiency and effectiveness of the overall communication system. (Greenbaum, 1974.)

The International Communication Association has developed a standardized system of five instruments for conducting communications audits in organizations. The five measurement tools are the questionnaire survey, interview, network analysis, communication experiences, and communication diary. They can be used independently or in combination to yield information on the communication health of an organization. Tables 5 and 6 provide illustrations of these two tools. The Network Analysis (Table 5) is particularly helpful in providing information on the operational communication network. Respondents report the typical amount of communication with each individual in their unit and with critical personnel outside the unit. Computer analysis identifies all communication links so managers can more readily identify critical actors in communication systems. The communications questionnaire provides for gaining information about the appropriateness of the amount of down-the-line information provided to employees. Respondents indicate both their perception of the amount of information currently received and the amount they would really like to have. Table 6 identifies all of the topics included in this questionnaire.

In effective agencies communication systems and individual communication behaviors are sensitive to changes in mission, goal and environment. The communication audit offers some guidelines for monitoring both communication be-

TABLE 6. Questionnaire Survey Topics

Topic	Number of Items
1. Amount of information received and needed from others on selected topics	26
2. Amount of information sent and needed to be sent to others on selected topics	14
3. Amount of follow-up or action taken and needed on information sent to others	10
4. Amount of information received and needed from selected sources	18
5. Timelines of information received from key sources	6
6. Amount of information received and needed from selected channels	16
7. Quality of communication relationships	19
8. Satisfaction with major organizational outcomes	13
9. Demographic information	12
Total	134

havior and climate within the agency. Since communications behavior and climate may enhance or limit an organization's awareness of changed conditions managers can't afford to ignore this element of organizational life.

Public managers, in particular, need to be aware of the multiple means for analyzing communication within the organization. This need is heightened because the functional tasks of the public organization often lack goal clarity and because the political environment of many agencies demands frequent reordering of priorities.

REFERENCES

Albrecht, T. (1978), Communication and Perceptions of Organizational Climate: An Empirical Analysis. Unpublished Ph.D. Dissertation, Department of Communication, Michigan State University. Cited in Albrecht, 1979.

Albrecht, T. (1979), The Role of Communication in Perception of Organizational Climate. *Communication Yearbook 3*, edited by Dan Nimmo, New Brunswick, New Jersey; Transaction Books: pp. 343-357.

Argyris, C. (1966), Interpersonal Barriers to Decision Making. *Harvard Business Review* (March-April) 44:pp. 84-97.

Athanassiades, J. C. (1973), The Distortion of Upward Communication in Hierarchical Organization. *Academy of Management* 16:pp. 207-227.

Baker, H. Kent (1979), How to Make Meetings Meaningful. *Management Review.* 67:pp. 45-47.

Barnard, Chester I. (1938), *Functions of the Executive.* (Cambridge, Mass.: Harvard University Press).

Bavelas, Alex, Barrett, D. (1951), An Experimental Approach to Organizational Communication. *Personnel* 27:pp. 366-371.

Bell, Daniel (1979), Communications Technology - For Better or For Worse. *Harvard Business Review* 57:pp. 20-45.

Berlo, David K. (1960), *The Process of Communication.* (New York: Holt, Rinehart and Winston).

Boudewyn, Adri G. (1977), The Open Meeting - A Confidential Forum for Employees. *Personnel Journal* 56:pp. 192-194.

Blau, P. M. and W. Scott (1962), *Formal Organization.* San Francisco: Chandler.

Burke, R. J. and D. S. Wilcox (1969), Effects of Different Patterns and Degrees of Openness in Superior-Subordinate Communication on Subordinate Job Satisfaction. *Academy of Management Journal*, 12:pp. 319-326.

Burns, T. (1954), The Direction of Activity and Communication in a Departmental Executive Group. *Human Relations* 7:pp. 73-97.

Carzo, R. (1963), Some Effects of Organizational Structure on Group Effectiveness. *Administrative Science Quarterly* 8:pp. 393-424.

Cathcart, R. S., Samovar, L. A. (1974), *Small Group Communication: A Reader.* Second edition. (Dubuque, Iowa: Wm. C. Brown Company Publishers).

Conboy, William A. (1976), *Working Together: Communication In A Healthy Organization.* (Columbus, Ohio: Charles E. Merrill).

Dorsey, John T., Jr. (1957), A Communications Model for Administrators. *Administrative Science Quarterly* 2:pp. 307-324.

Downs, A. (1967), *Inside Bureaucracy.* Boston: Little Brown.

Dubin, R. (1962), Business Behavior Behaviorally Viewed, in G. B. Strother (Ed.) *Social Science Approaches to Business Behavior.* Homewood, Ill.: Dorsey Press.

Dubin, R. and S. Spray. (1964), Executive Behavior and Interaction. *Industrial Relations* 4:pp. 99-108.

Eckman, P., and W. Friesen (1969), "The Repertoire of Nonverbal Behavior: Categories, Origins, Usage, and Coding." *Semiotica* 1:pp. 49-98.

Farace, R. V., Monge, P. R., Russell, H. M. (1977), *Communicating and Organizing.* Reading, Mass: Addison-Wesley.

Ference, T. (1970), Organizational Communication Systems and the Decision Process. *Management Science* 17:pp. 83-96.

Galbraith, J. (1973), *Designing Complex Organizations.* MA: Addison-Wesley.

Goldhaber, Gerald M. (1979), *Organizational Communication.* Dubuque, Iowa: Wm. C. Brown, Co.

Greenbaum, Howard H. (1974), The Audit of Organizational Communication. *Academy of Management Journal* 17:pp. 739-754.

Guetzkow, H. (1965), Communication in Organizations. James March (ed.), *Handbook of Organizations.* Chicago: Rand-McNally.

Hage, J., Aiken, M., Marrett, C. (1971), Organization Structure and Communication. *American Sociological Review* 36:pp. 860-871.

Hall, R. (1962), Intra-Organization Structural Variation. *American Sociological Review* 7:pp. 395-308.

Haney, W. V. (1967), *Communications and Organization Behavior - Text and Cases* (2nd ed.) Homewood, Ill.: Irvin.

Harris, D. B. (1970), Human Intelligence - Its Nature and Assessment. *American Journal of Psychology.* 83(3):pp. 455-457.

Henley, Nancy M. (1977), *Body Politics: Power, Sex and Nonverbal Communication.* Englewood Cliffs, New Jersey: Prentice Hall.

Hollandsworth, J. D., Jr., Kazelskis, R., Stevens, J., Dressel, M. E. (1979), Relative Contributions of Verbal, Articulative, and Nonverbal Communication to Employment Decisions in Job Interview Setting. *Personnel Psychology.* 32:pp. 359-367.

Huseman, Richard C., James M. Tahiff, and John Hatfield (1976), *Interpersonal Communication in Organizations.* (Boston: Holbrook, 1976).

Huseman, R. C., Logue, C. M., Freshley, D. L. (1970), *Interpersonal and Organizational Communication.* Boston: Holbrook Press Inc.

Imada, H. S. and Hakel (1977), Influence of Nonverbal Communication and Rater Proximity on Impressions and Decisions in Simulated Employment Interviews. *Journal of Applied Psychology*. 62(3):pp. 295-300.

Jabin, Frederic M. (1978), Message Response and "Openness" in Superior-Subordinate Communication. *Communications Yearbook 2* edited by Brent D. Rubin. New Brunswick, New Jersey: Transaction Books.

Katz, Daniel, Kahn, Robert (1966), *The Social Psychology of Organizations*. (New York: Wiley).

Katz, R., Tushman, M. (1979), Communication Patterns, Project Performance, and Task Characteristics: An Empirical Evaluation and Integration In An R & D Setting. *Organizational Behavior and Human Performance*. 23:pp. 139-162.

Kelley, Charles M. (1970), Actual Listening Behavior of Industrial Supervisors As Related to Listening Ability, General Mental Ability, Selected Personality Factors and Supervisory Effectiveness. Unpublished Ph.D. Dissertation. Purdue University. 1962. Excerpt first published in Cathcart, Robert S. and Samovar, Larry A. *Small Group Communication: A Reader*. (Dubuque, Iowa: William C. Brown Company Publishers). cited by Leonard (1981).

King, Corwin P. (1978), Keep Your Communication Climate Healthy. *Personnel Journal*. 57:pp. 204-206.

Kirkpatrick, Donald L. (1978), Communications: Everybody Talks About It, But . . . *Personnel Administrator*. 23:pp. 46-50.

Koehler, J. W., Anatol, K. W. E., Applbaum, R. L. (1981), *Organizational Communication: Behavioral Perspectives*. (New York: Holt, Rinehart and Winston).

Krannick, Ronald L. and Caryl Rae Krannick. (1979), Anonymous Communications and Bureaucratic Politics in Thailand. *Administration and Society*. 2(2): pp. 227-248.

Lau, Allan W., Newman, A. R. (1980), The Value of Managerial Work in the Public Sector. *Public Administration Review*. 11:pp. 513-520.

Lawrence, P., Lorsh, J. (1967), *Organizations and Environment*. (Cambridge, MA: Harvard University Press).

Leonard, Rebecca. (1981), Active Listening: Skilled Interpersonal Communication. Unpublished Manuscript. Department of Speech Communication. North Carolina State University.

Lewis, Phillip V. (1975), *Organizational Communications*. (Columbus, Ohio; Grid). Cited in Thomas R. Tortoriello. See entry for Tortoriello (1978).

Likert, R. (1967), *The Human Organization*. New York: McGraw-Hill.

Likert, R. (1959), Motivational Approach to Management Development. *Harvard Business Review* 37:pp. 75-82.

Maier, N. R. F., L. R. Hoffman, W. H. Read (1963), Superior-Subordinate Communication. *Personnel Psychology* 16:pp. 1-11.

McGovern, T. V., Tinsky H. E. A. (1978), Interviewer Evaluations of Interviewee Nonverbal Behavior. *Journal of Vocational Behavior* 13(2):pp. 163-171.

Mears, P. (1974), Structuring Communication in a Working Group. *The Journal of Communication* 24:pp. 71-79.

Mehrabian, Albert. (1971), *Silent Messages*. (Belmont, California: Wadsworth Publishing Company, Inc.).

Mintzberg, Henry. (1973), *The Nature of Managerial Work*. (New York: Harper and Row Publishers).

Monge, Peter R., Jane A. Edwards, Kenneth K. Kirste (1978), The Determinants of Communication Structure in Large Organization: A Review of Research *Communication Yearbook 2*. ed. by Brent D. Rubin. New Brunswick, New Jersey: Transaction Books.

Nadler, D. A. (1979), The Effects of Feedback on Task Group Behavior: A Review of the Experimental Research. *Organizational Behavior and Human Performance* 23:pp. 309-338.

Nichols, R. G. (1962), Listening Is Good Business. *Management of Personnel Quarterly* 2:p. 4.

O'Reilly, C. and K. Roberts (1974), Information Filtering in Organizations. *Organizational Behavior and Human Performance* 11:pp. 253-265.

Patten, Thomas H., Jr. (1978), Open Communication Systems and Effective Salary Administration. *Human Resource Management* 17:pp. 5-14.

Planty, Earl and William Machaver (1952), "Upward Communications: A Project in Executive Development". *Personnel* 28-4:pp. 304-318.

Poole, M. S. (1978), An Information Task Approach to Organizational Communication. *The Academy of Management Review* 3:pp. 493-504.

Horizontal Communication in Organizations. *Administrative Science Quarterly* 4:pp. 188-196.

Porter, L. W. and K. H. Roberts (1976), Communication in Organizations. in M. Dunnette, (ed.) *Handbook in Industrial and Organizational Psychology*. Chicago: Rand McNally: pp. 1553-1589.

Public Personnel Administration: Policies, Practices, and Procedures. (1973), Communicating With Employees. Englewood Cliffs, New Jersey: Prentice-Hall.

Read, W. H. (1962), Upward Communication in Industrial Hierarchies. *Human Relations* 15:pp. 3-15.

Roberts, K. H. and O'Reilly, C. A. (1974), Failures in Upward Communication in Organizations. *Academy of Management Journal* 17:pp. 205-215.

Romoff, Mark. (1978), Employee Communications in the Federal Government. *The Canadian Business Review* 4:pp. 36-39.

Samaras, John T. (1980), Two-Way Communication Practices for Managers. *Personnel Journal* 59:pp. 645-648.

Shannon, Wayne E. (1978), One Person Communication. *Training and Development Journal* 32:pp. 20-24.

Shaw, M. E. (1954), Some Effects of Unequal Distribution of Information Upon Group Performance in Various Communication Networks. *The Journal of Abnormal and Social Psychology* 50:pp. 547-553.

Shuler, R. S. (1979), A Role Perception Transactional Process Model for Organizational Communication—Outcome Relationships. *Organizational Behavior and Human Performance* 23:pp. 268-291.

Silverman, B. R. S. (1980), The Optimum Legibility Formula: A Written Communications System. *Personnel Journal*. (July) 59, 7:pp. 581-583.

Simpson, R. L. (1959), Vertical and Horizontal Communication in Organizations *Administrative Science Quarterly* 4:pp. 188-196.

Summers, Donald B. (1977), Understanding the Process By Which New Employees Enter Work Groups. *Personnel Journal* 56:pp. 394-397.

Taylor, J. (1977), Communication and Organizational Change: A Case Study. Unpublished Ph.D. dissertation, Department of Communications, Michigan State University. Cited in Albrecht, 1979.

Taylor, J., R. Farace and P. Monge (1976), Communication and the Development of Change Among Educational Practitioners. Paper presented to the World Education Conference, Honolulu, Hawaii. Paper cited in Albrecht, 1978.

Terreberry, S. (1968), The Evolution of Organizational Environments. *Administrative Science Quarterly* 12:pp. 590-613.

Thayer, L. (1968), *Communication and Communication Systems*. (Homewood, IL: Richard D. Irwin).

Timm, P. R., Wilkens, P. L. (1977), *A Model of Perceived Communication Inequity and Job Dissatisfaction*. Paper presented at the National Meetings of the Academy of Management, Kissimmee, FL.

Timm, Paul R. (1968), Worker Responses to Supervisory Communication Inequity An Exploratory Study. *Journal of Business Communication* 16:pp. 11-24.

Tortoriello, Thomas R., Blatt, Stephen J., Devine, Sue (1978), *Communication In the Organization: An Applied Approach*. (New York: McGraw Hill).

Truell, George F. (1978), Communication Styles: The Key to Understanding. *Personnel Administrator* 23:pp. 46-48.

Van de Ven, A., Delbecq, A., Koenig, R. (1976), Determinants of Coordination Modes Within Organizations. *American Sociological Review* 41:pp. 322-338.

Vogel, A. (1967), Why Don't Employees Speak Up? *Personnel Administration* 30: pp. 18-24.

Washburn, P. V. and Hakel, M. C. (1973), Visual Cues and Verbal Content As Influences on Impressions Formed After Simulated Employment Interviews. *Journal of Applied Psychology* 58(1):pp. 137-141.

Watzlawick, P., Beavin, J. H., Jackson, D. D. (1967), *Pragmatics of Human Communication - A Study of Interactional Patterns, Pathologies, and Paradoxes*. (New York: W. W. Norton and Company, Inc.)

Weaver, Carl H. (1972), *Human Listening: Processes and Behavior*. (New York: Bobbs-Merrill Co., Inc.).

Wexley, K. N., Fugita, S. S., Malone, M. P. (1975), Applicants Nonverbal Behavior and Student-Evaluators' Judgements in a Structured Interview Setting. *Psychological Reports* 36(2):pp. 391-394.

DECISION-MAKING

The management of the decision-making process is often equated with the study of management. It is thought to be the generalized process to which other considerations of leadership, motivation, role management, and communications are subservient. Herbert Simon, perhaps the most influential of the postwar organization theorists, interpreted complex organizations in terms of a decision-making framework. The decision-making approach is also at the core of contemporary political science methodology, with its special concerns for analysis of public organizations.

The decision-making approach is particularly pertinent to public management. Partly this is because decision-making raises the political aspects of public administration. In the private sector many decisions on priorities flow almost undiscussed from universal acceptance of the logic of the profit motive. In the public sector, in contrast, almost any issue area may become politicized and thrust into the center of decision-making. At the same time, public sector organizations are typically forced to perform at a higher level of accountability to many publics and this, too, not only brings greater importance to decision-making processes but makes them the objects of public access efforts. Greater accountability, whether actual or merely potential, leads to more formality and less flexibility in the public sector.

Because of these pressures and constraints the management of the decision-making process is critical in public management. Much of public administration literature is directed to this one arena. Essentially two schools of thought have emerged in the early literature.

One emphasizes planning approaches to decision-making, calling for assumptions of organizational rationality. The other focuses on incremental decision-making and is based on assumptions about the benefits of market-like forces in the setting of priorities, substituting the market place of influences for the economic market place. These two schools were pitted against each other in an important debate between liberals and conservatives after World War II.

The first two sections of this chapter present by turn the early liberal case for planning and the post-WW II conservative critique of planning in government. It was in the context of this debate that Herbert Simon advanced his decision-centered approach to public administration in his classic work, *Administrative Behavior* (1945). A third section of the present chapter treats this viewpoint which, for a time, seemed to emerge as a preferable alternative to rational or incremental models of planning and decision-making.

Later, in the 1960's and 1970's, participatory approaches to decision-making were advanced as better models. These are discussed in a fourth section. Although participatory management (discussed in greater detail in Chapter 7) declined in the late 1970's and early 1980's its influence has continued to be felt through empirical studies of individual and group decision-making. These studies, outlined in a fifth section of this chapter, generally support the utilization of participatory group decision-making. The focus, however, is on appropriate management of such processes. As with contingency theories of leadership, a variety of complex factors seem to constrain the potential of group decision-making processes. Alternatives to group decision-making, the delphi and nominal group techniques, are therefore presented next. The chapter closes with a general discussion of the management of decisionmaking by the practicing public administrator.

PLANNING AND RATIONAL MODELS OF DECISION-MAKING

When students think of decision-making, they often assume a rational model. First, goals are set. Second, goals are broken down into a timetable of interim objectives. Obstacles to achievement of objectives are inventoried. For each obstacle, alternative solutions are surveyed and the optimal one selected. Solutions are spelled out into task matrices which relate resources (personnel, materials) to these tasks. Tasks are assembled into a rational, sequential plan through Program Evaluation and Review Techniques (PERT) or other planning processes. Later, costs and benefits are tracked through program budgeting as a data base for evaluation and possible revision of the plan selected.

The vision of rational planning was at its peak in the United States in the 1930's and 1940's. A symbol of this vision was the National Resources Planning Board, directed by Charles Merriam, a leading political scientist of the 1930's. Political scientists of that era had begun to condemn the "ramshackle character of our national legislative machine," as Edwin Corwin put it in his 1931 presidential address to the American Political Science Association (APSA) (Corwin, 1932). Corwin called on political scientists to put aside questions of power and influence and instead concentrate on issues of government management and planning.

This orientation was epitomized the following year when Henry Dennison, an industrialist, was invited to present his views to the APSA on "The Need for the Development of Political Science Engineering," (Dennison, 1932). Related groups such as the Brookings Institution pointed toward the planning models of the French and German advisory economic councils (Lorwin, 1931). By 1934, a vast American literature on social planning was available (see Brooks and Brooks, 1933, 1934), ranging from Chamber of Commerce reports to Harry Laidler's *Socialist Planning and a Socialist Program* (1932). George E. G. Catlin wrote, "The blessed word Mesopotamia of the last decade was 'rationalization'; of this decade, it is planning" (Catlin, 1932).

In a decade, social planning emerged from a concept bordering on sedition to one accepted by nearly all segments of American society. There was a relative consensus in the planning literature on the general vision of using state power to achieve regulation, security, and fairness. Typical was Rexford Tugwell's *Industrial Discipline and the Governmental Arts* (1933). Tugwell, a close advisor of President Roosevelt, argued that the alternative to class conflict in the Depression was a co-operative effort of social planning and regulation of the economy. Social planning themes were predominant in such New Deal innovations as the Blue Eagle (NRA) code authorities and the Tennessee Valley Authority (TVA). Indeed, the vision of national social planning through a country-wide network of TVA-type authorities was promoted by liberal congressmen well into the late 1940's.

Although the vision of national planning fell from grace after World War II, one should not think it disappeared. At the micro-organizational level it prospered with the rise of program planning and budgeting systems (PPBS) in industry in the 1950's and government in the 1960's. At the intergovernmental level, the vision of rational planning was enshrined in the 1971 institution of "A-95 clearinghouses" by the U.S. Office of Management and Budget. Both PPBS and the A-95 clearing-houses illustrated governmental attempts to force disparate agencies and jurisdictions to rationalize and coordinate their efforts. Both also were intended to provide top administrators with rational planning tools for centralized decision-making.

The argument for a rationally planned approach to decision-making in the public sector was strong. One of the most sophisticated arguments on its behalf was Karl Mannheim's *Freedom, Power, and Democratic Planning* (1950). Planning was necessary, he argued, because of the collapse of free markets under American capitalism. The rise of large, relatively uncontrolled groups—corporations, unions, interest groups—had eroded the self-regulating marketplace. The collapse of this traditional coordination device, along with the decline of religion as a social control and the failure of the independent regulatory commissions, meant that America needed new forms of social coordination.

Since Mannheim rejected totalitarian-type planning, he argued that new, democratic forms of planning had to be found. He believed these would involve governmental control over the growing monopoly power of the corporations, centralization in most areas of decision-making, strong legislative oversight, social education for democratic citizenship, and governmental initiatives to foster citizen access and group competition.

Although many European democracies moved in directions indicated by Mannheim, America did not. A decade later Gunnar Myrdal (1960) made the same arguments for planning. Although many liberals looked to Sweden, Britain, or West Germany for models of governmental decision-making, direct planning was not a dominant preference even for liberals. Instead, liberals looked to indirect planning through Keynesian economics. Briefly, Keynesianism held that the economy could be controlled by fiscal (e.g., taxes, deficits) and monetary (e.g., interest rates, money supply) policies without recourse to direct means like wage and price controls or nationalization of industry. In fact, postwar liberals believed Keynesian fiscal and economic policies would achieve most of the objectives previously claimed for national social planning. Keynesianism, moreover, was believed to provide a model for doing this on a decentralized basis without resort to odious economic commands, quotas, and controls.

A symbol of this shift in liberal thought was the replacement of Merriam's National Resources Planning Board by the Keynesian-oriented Council of Economic Advisors after World War II. The CEA's indirect controls meant public administration's future did not depend on its capacity to evolve sophisticated rational planning techniques for decision-making. Keynesianism was seen as a means of compensating for the decline of market competition and the consequent erosion of faith in control through Adam Smith's "invisible hand" (the competitive economic market).

Interest in planning approaches to decision-making was somewhat restored in the late 1960's and 1970's when Keynesian economics proved incapable of dealing with simultaneous recessionary and inflationary tendencies in the American economy. Civil rights, environmental, consumer, and other social movements of this period also helped resurrect belief in the need for direct controls and authoritative and systematic governmental planning.

Certainly such approaches to decision-making characterize the contemporary American planning profession. As a recent national study of American planners concluded, planners "reflect their liberal idealism in the commitment to the idea that society can control its future evolution in both a rational and equitable fashion through the medium of public authority in the form of positive government" (Vasu, 1979). In contrast to the liberal planning ethos of professional planners, however, the conservative critique of planning approaches to decision-making has been more influential in many aspects of American public administration.

THE CONSERVATIVE CRITIQUE OF PLANNING

Historically, the debate over rational models of decision-making (most planning approaches) emerged from the broader clash of socialism and capitalism. Responding to socialist advocates of governmental planning, depression-era conservatives argued that rational, comprehensive planning models made assumptions that exceeded human capacities for integration and coordination. In practice, the critics charged, such decision-making approaches were misguided and undesirable.

Conservative economists like Friedrich Hayek argued against socialist planning in books like *Collectivist Economic Planning* (1935) and *The Road to Serfdom* (1944). They argued that whenever possible governmental planning should yield to market mechanisms in the making of social decisions. By this they meant that the competition of private producers would, if left to itself, provide the most efficient housing, transportation, recreation and other needs of the nation. In addition to the argument that bureaucrats were invariably noninnovative and government agencies prone to stagnation, it was also held that planning was the antithesis of freedom because, unlike the subtle influence of market forces, planning could only be implemented through coercive directives. Above all, planning was deemed to be inherently inferior because of the absence of a governmental criterion akin to the profit criterion in market decisions based on prices. Unable to set values by a market, governmental planning was seen as inevitably degenerating into elite coercion of the masses "for their own good." Planning was "the road to serfdom."

The conservative, market-oriented perspective on decision-making was popularized in the United States by scholars at the University of Chicago. These included such individuals as Michael Polanyi, Milton Friedman, Edward Banfield, and Charles Lindblom. Writing in *The Logic of Liberty* (1951), Michael Polanyi's arguments illustrated this influential school.

Polanyi held that the complex tasks of modern government could be managed only by a market-like system of mutual adjustments which were incremental in nature. That is, Polanyi rejected decision-making by central planners in favor of a give-and-take bargaining process in which a "marketplace" of ideas and influence groups eventually led to a compromise more appropriate than experts would have made. This incrementalist or bargaining perspective was held to be in contradiction to the planning perspective. Citing Soviet war communism of the 1919-1921 period, Polanyi argued that central planning led to administrative chaos. The choice was between totalitarian central planning or incrementalist decision-making under capitalism. Middle solutions like "market-socialism" were held to be contradictions in terms, unworkable in practice.

These themes were picked up by Milton Friedman, a Chicago economist who later became famous as an advisor to the Nixon and Reagan administrations. In his *Capitalism and Freedom* (1962), Friedman also took the view that there are only two ways to coordinate governmental decision-making: through central planning or through markets. Planning, however, was intrinsically coercive. Worse, it was unresponsive to democratic preferences. Whereas the market could make billions of decisions reflecting consumer preferences, government responded only through a single yes-no decision every fourth year at presidential election times. The result, Friedman held, was that most governmental programs were unnecessary and undesirable. This analysis led Friedman to a policy of "denationalizing" schools, abolition of professional licensing, termination of social security and public housing, private development of parks and recreation, and other policies substituting private market forces for governmental services.

There are numerous reasons why central planning rarely lives up to expectations. Many were summarized by Charles Lindblom in an enormously influential article in the *Public Administration Review*, titled "The Science of Muddling Through" (Lindblom, 1959). In public administration, decisions often affect many objectives: efficiency, service, equity, accountability, and so on. When values conflict the administrator has no overriding decision criterion akin to the profit motive in the private sector. Even where values are clear, the public decision-maker may lack information on the alternative solutions to the problem. Such information can be costly to obtain, if it can be obtained at all. Information costs may be in terms of time, effort, and expense. Incurring such costs may generate an information overload that the agency is incapable of dealing with. Or the information-gathering effort, while comprehensive, may take too much time for the election-oriented political leader.

Even if values are clear and alternatives comprehensively documented, the public decision-maker may still often fail. Means-ends knowledge is often missing. For example, the means to reduce poverty are not well understood. Many policy alternatives are innovative and social science is too primitive to be able to predict the effects. Diffuse benefits like "social welfare" or environmental quality may be difficult to measure, compounding the problem. Even more fundamentally, decision-makers may not even be able to understand what the problem is, let alone comprehensively understand the alternatives. Crime, for instance, is recognized as a problem area, but decision-makers disagree about whether crime is primarily an economic problem (poverty), a psychological problem (criminal personality), a sociological problem (broken families), or whatever. Typically, the nature of the problem will be dependent on situational factors. Also typically, social science will lack an adequate situational theory of the problem. That is, while social scientists may understand some general dynamics of a problem, they may not be able to apply this knowledge to differing concrete situations. While theories will abound, the state of the art will not allow the decision-maker to proceed confidently with policy choice and implementation.

Decision-making by planning in a computational sense can occur only when there is agreement on both goals and means (Nalbardian and Klinger, 1980). Moreover, rational planning works best when the decision has to do with distributive rather than redistributive matters (Skok, 1980). Distributive policies deal with allocation of resources, whereas redistributive policies—like some land use regulation—deal with reallocating resources from one group to another. Redistributive questions involve far more political intensity and bargaining—something more amenable to incrementalism.

Because of these limits, empirical studies have frequently shown that national investment in research for rational planning in government is often wasted. Weiss, in *Social Science Research and Decision-Making* (1980). found that not only is research frequently not utilized but governmental decision-makers were so bound by incrementalism and bargaining that they typically disavowed making broad decisions of the type toward which research was directed. Staats (1980) noted this perception of low decision-making discretion and hence low need for planning studies when, as head of the Government Accounting Office, he looked into the neglect to utilize research at the federal level.

The conservative criticism of planning is not limited to the public sector, of course. For instance, in a recent survey of two dozen American and European corporations Peters (1979) found that the traditional notion of planning-deciding-implementing was not descriptive of what actually occured in decision-making. Instead Peters found that senior managers received single-option policy papers from subordinates, not ones with comprehensively-developed alternatives. Most of the time of senior managers was spent on "fighting fires" (day to day problems). Little if any time was left for such managers to become involved in policy decision-making while the options were still genuinely open. This was made worse by the tendency of subordinates to shield senior managers from negative feedback. Once the policy option was outlined for the manager, the manager often vacillated for months or years before deciding. The decision did not flow immediately from the analysis of problems or from the preceding planning effort.

HERBERT SIMON AND DECISION-MAKING THEORY

If the conservative critique was effective in highlighting the limits of the rational planning model of decision-making, public administration was not won over to the proposed solution of substituting private market goods for governmental services in such areas as recreation and education. Instead, many social scientists sought to erect an alternative decision-making theory which was premised neither on central planning of the radical type nor on abdication to the marketplace as some conservatives advocated. Among the earliest and most influential of these social scientists was Herbert Simon.

From the incrementalist literature on public decision-making it sometimes appeared that governmental decisions were made by thousands of small choices by bureaucrats, with no real control from the top. The image was presented of the political marketplace. Often implied was the notion that it was like the freely competitive economic marketplace, which was not controlled by any consumer or producer. In contrast, research has shown that governmental agencies *are* controlled by decision-makers. Agency outcomes are not the mere resultant of the market-like effect of thousands of small bureaucratic choices of "the system." For example, it has been shown that the higher one's hierarchical rank the more likely one is to participate in decisions (Zeitz, 1980) and change in top public leadership does have a strong and pervasive effect on the substance of decision outcomes (Bunce, 1980).

Simon was aware of these realities. He knew also, however, that as later research would prove, few managers actually decided things by rational searches for alternative solutions for anticipated problems (cf. Moore and Anderson, 1954). The nature of decision-making had to be conceived as a model lying somewhere in between marketing and incrementalism on the one hand and rational comprehensive planning on the other. Simon set forth his compromise model in two famous works, *Administrative Behavior* (1945) and *Models of Man* (1957), and one co-authored with James G. March, *Organizations* (1959).

Simon's model centered on the concepts of bounded rationality and satisficing. *Bounded rationality* meant that decision-makers do plan, but only by searching a few available alternatives, only by seeking to assess a few of the consequences of each, and only using highly simplified assumptions about cause and effect. *Satisficing* meant that decision-makers did not really seek the optimal solution, only the first solution that satisfied the minimal criteria they deemed necessary. These concepts were soon widely accepted because they preserved the planning function of the decision-maker but were much more realistic in depicting actual practice.

Simon recognized that many decisions did have the appearance of being the uncontrolled results of incremental choices by "the system" or "the marketplace." These he called *programmed decisions*. Unlike nonprogrammed decisions in which the leadership decision-making role was apparent, programmed decisions were characterized by standard operating routines which left little discretion for those involved. Even routinized decisions were not lacking in control. Actually a key function of management is the design of those routines and even more important, promulgation and maintenance of the norms and values which make them work. Simon argued for the importance of the managerial role of socialization of employees to organizational patterns, particularly norms of efficiency and economizing. Like many other functions at top levels of management, this role was not reducible to planning calculations or laws of management science—but neither was it determined by an impersonal, uncontrolled marketplace of incremental choices.

Decision-making under bounded rationality is not rationality in the ordinary sense. There is not an expectation that decision-makers are rational in the sense of comprehensive planning. Decisions are seen not as the result of calculations but rather of premises. Premises may be previous decisions (which the bureaucrat takes as givens and does not reexamine), preferences and values of superiors, or action rules incorporated into standard operating procedures. Premises simplify decision-making. This is essential in a real world in which many decisions must be made under time pressure, but it does mean bureaucratic decision-making is only quasirational.

What difference does Simon's decision-making theory make for the practicing agency head in the field? First, it suggests that not too much investment of time and resources be sunk into the tools of the planners, analysts, and scientific managers. It suggests efforts to design tight, comprehensive, quantitative performance control systems or other centrally planned solutions to complex organizational problems may be misguided. Second, it suggests that the manager is wise to invest time and energy into organizational efforts which clarify management's goals, socialize employees to them, and specify them into standard routines. This should not be done in a rigidly planned manner, but it is not a waste for the manager to spend a great deal of time in setting the proper climate in the agency. Third, it suggests that the agency head should devote time and resources to improving organizational communications. Subordinates must be made aware of values set at higher levels.

Top management must receive feedback on whether standards are realistic. All levels need to share in a common bank of information about past decisions, organizational objectives, and operating procedures. These communication needs require an abandonment of strictly hierarchical lines of communication but they do not involve an uncontrolled free market. Simon spent a great deal of time seeking to show how his theory translated into practice through the design and formalization of complex communication patterns which reinforce values which are set at the top and specified for the employee in operating routines.

In summary, Simon's work represented a critique of the traditional organization theories of men like Weber and Taylor. Simon emphasized the limits of rationality and criticized scientific management principles of hierarchical communication, unitary authority lines, and optimization in decision-making. He also emphasized the importance of managerial control, not through planning instruments, but through influence over organizational values, communications patterns, and operating procedures. Simon's concept of decision-making quickly became accepted by most social scientists as the best description of organizational behavior to that time.

Moreover, Simon's later emphasis on detailed examination of the decision-making process in case studies also led the way in a new emphasis on case studies in schools of business and public administration. The case approach stood in clear contrast to either scientific management or human relations orientations of Simon's day, both of which centered on seeking certain universal rules or laws of management. Simon's decision-making approach rejected these two viewpoints, saying that they couldn't answer fundamental management questions due to their abstract level of analysis. By examining communications patterns in various decision contexts and drawing conclusions specific to individual case situations, Simon's work was a forerunner of behavioralism and later situational theories of management.

Critics and Revisionists

In the ensuing three decades, Simon's decision-making theory of organizational behavior was itself subjected to as intense criticism as that to which he had put earlier theories. Human relations advocates often saw Simon's model as one in which all values are determined at the top and employees are indoctrinated like automatons into blind allegiance. This seemed to remove all room for self-actualization of the individual (Argyris, 1973a; response by Simon, 1973). In actuality, however, Simon's model was not inconsistent with self-actualization, as Argyris (1973b) has noted. This is because Simon's concept of rationality was a bounded one which left much room for employee choice and creativity. Though this point was central to Simon's critique of comprehensive rationality, Simon's focus on economizing/efficiency as the dominant organizational value continued to draw the criticism of organizational humanists seeking the fulfillment of other values in agency life (see Guerreiro-Ramos, 1980).

A more fundamental criticism of Simon's model was posed by Charles Perrow (1972). Perrow noted research showing that organizational goals were often largely symbolic. Far from manipulating employees like robots, goals were often of little influence—far less than Simon's theories suggested (see Meyer and Rowan, 1977; Perrow, 1978). Other research cited by Perrow indicates that even bounded rationality may be an inadequate description of reality. Instead it may often happen that rather than a decision-maker searching a few alternative solutions to a problem, agency staff with preconceived interest in certain types of solutions will influence the organization to search about for problems which are good experimental arenas for those solutions, ignoring perhaps more important problems which aren't (see Cohen, March, and Olsen, 1972; March and Olsen, 1976). Perrow noted many of these discrepancies between Simon's theories and empirical research. He concluded that while Simon's model was indeed superior to its predecessors, there was a need for a more complex contingency theory of organizational behavior.

That is, Perrow argued that previous theories had been insufficiently complex. Although Simon's emphasis on influence patterns and socialization to dominant values was more complex than the contingency theory of Fiedler (discussed previously in Chapter 2), even Simon did not capture the true complexity of actual patterns of decision-making. Perrow had much the same criticism of other social scientists who had presented variants to Simon's model. Notable among these was Amitai Etzioni's mixed-scanning model, which acknowledged the impossibility of comprehensive planning but sought to defend the feasibility of rational planning of specific program alternatives after a far less rational scanning and selection process had narrowed the alternatives drastically (Etzioni, 1967).

The problem was that Etzioni's model, like Simon's, still assumed the primacy of management's goals. But as McCaskey (1979) has found, decisions are commonly recognized after the fact and goals are defined after action is taken. "Clearly," McCaskey concluded, "we need alternatives to goal-directed approaches for how a manager can act in a rational way. We need broader, more complex ways of thinking about planning, deciding, managing, and organizing that do not depend on pre-existing specific goals." Since the essence of Simon's model had depended on the centrality of management-set goals, such conclusions were leading empirical researchers into quite different pastures.

PLANNING AND PARTICIPATORY APPROACHES TO DECISION-MAKING

Planning in the tradition of scientific management and participation in the tradition of human relations are two of the great themes of public management. Like other great ideas, they are not easily killed. Although the attack on both schools by Simon and others was severe, although it made academics and practitioners alike aware of the limits of facile planning or participatory remedies, the attack did not prevent continuing interest in both types of solutions to organizational decision-making problems.

There were many reasons for the continued salience to and even growth of planning approaches to public administration. First, there were many areas in which calculable solutions *did* exist, where both ends and means *could* be agreed upon: traffic engineering, defense procurement, allocation decisions in service delivery. Second, even where ends and means were not consensual, planning tools often were sought out because officials desired the increased coordination they afforded: case management in social services, management by objectives in federal agencies, program budgeting in state and local government. Third, the advent of modern computer technology and accompanying software (e.g., linear programming, input-output models, econometrics) enabled decision-makers to handle far more information in a rational manner than officials in Simon's early days dreamed possible.

At a deeper level, the self-interested actions of organizations in a political environment lead to the necessity for planning. This was the theme of another influential work, James Thompson's *Organizations in Action* (1967). His theories were based on the same assumptions about self-interested conflict that the incrementalists had emphasized, but Thompson was led in an almost opposite direction, one which favored planning approaches to decision-making.

Thompson acknowledged that Simon was correct in describing decision-making in terms of bounded rationality, satisficing, and limited searches of alternatives. Thompson, however, criticized Simon's analysis as static, failing to adequately appreciate how searching behavior leads to organizational learning over time. Specifically, Thompson posited four areas which typically characterized this learning process:

1. *Buffering*: Organizations learn to protect themselves from their environments by surrounding their technical cores by input-output structures.
2. *Leveling*: Organizations learn to smooth input-output transactions to reduce fluctuations in activity levels.
3. *Adaptation*: Organizations learn to anticipate changes that cannot be levelled or buffered.

4. *Rationing*: If these three strategies fail to protect the organization's technical core from threat, the organization learns to restrict input or output. (Eg., a mental hospital may substitute
drug treatment for more time-intensive psychoanalytic treatment).

Planning is the inevitable vehicle for pursuit of these four strategies.

Planning, Thompson noted, involves an intrinsic drive for power. Power is
needed to control the environment and thereby reduce uncertainty about resources,
inputs, markets, clientele, regulations, and the like. Power is manifested in many
common organizational strategies. These include vertical integration (the drive to
gain jurisdiction over earlier and later phases of production or service, as in TVA's
drive toward involvement in all phases of rural development, not just electrifica-
tion); geographical integration (the drive toward administration through more in-
clusive jurisdictions, as in the tendency for welfare functions to shift from locality
to state to federal levels); and input incorporation (the drive to incorporate input-
side personnel into agency affairs, as in the tendency of universities to seek to become "total institutions" providing all services needed by students, not just classroom instruction).

The strategies and drives noted by Thompson account for the long-term tendency toward organizational complexity and growth. Complexity in turn requires
structure. Increase in interdependence is handled through hierarchies and depart-
mentalization and, if that doesn't suffice, through task forces and other more
flexible forms. The working of these forms of organization is political. Internal
relations in the complex organization are power relations. The organization becomes governed by power coalitions in a constantly shifting flux of bargaining
relationships. This is particularly so in public management, where the task environment is dynamic and means-ends knowledge is rarely perfected. These characteristics increase the range of organizational options for change. This in turn increases
both potential opportunities and threats for various coalitions within the complex
organization.

In summary, Thompson argued that coping with uncertainty was the essence
of administration. It led to striving for power vis-a-vis the environment, including
other organizations. It led to a variety of strategies, all involving increased levels of
complexity and planning. Along with this, particularly in organizations of the type
often found in the public sector, came the formation of coalitions of power within the organization.

Participatory management theories address the question of how to organize
the politics of complex organizations. It is wrong to think of planning and participation as opposites even though their respective roots in the conflicting scientific
management and human relations schools might suggest that. If Thompson is correct, the politics of planning, however "scientific" that planning may be, requires
human relations skills (Garson and Brenneman, 1981a; 1981b). The strength of
participatory approaches, explored in Chapter 7, is the general consensus among

researchers that participation in the decision process increases commitment to the decision. Conversely, exclusion heightens alienation from formal channels of decision-making and encourages those excluded to resort to informal organizations (e.g., power coalitions) which may be at odds with organizational goals. For these reasons, interest in participatory management flows directly from Thompson's analysis of organizations in action.

Because participation is analyzed at length in the next chapter, little will be said about it here except to note that it is of special importance in public administration compared to business administration. Using national data, Smith and Nock (1980) have shown that government white collar workers are significantly less positive about social and intrinsic aspects of their work than are their business counterparts. Correspondingly, they are more alienated from superiors and peers in spite of satisfaction with material job rewards. Smith and Nock concluded that work redesign increasing the decision-making authority of white-collar governmental workers is an appropriate policy based on these findings.

Much of the impetus toward participatory management in public administration came in the early 1970's, when the field—like many others—was buffeted by the social turmoil of the late 1960's and early 1970's. Symbolizing the new concerns of public administrationists in a period of change was a conference of younger scholars convened by Dwight Waldo, editor of the *Public Administration Review*. The proceedings of this conference were edited by Frank Marini (1971) in a volume titled *Toward a New Public Administration*. This "Minnowbrook perspective," referring to the location of the conference, was a focal point for those interested in participatory approaches to decision-making in government.

The Minnowbrook conference reflected diverse viewpoints which can be summarized only by resort to a certain amount of simplification. In general, the analysis was this. Industrial complexity is increasingly shifting political matters into the bureaucratic arena. This was reflected not only in the civil rights movement and other social movements, but also in trends toward a younger, more affluent population. The Minnowbrook writers anticipated what Smith and Nock later found: a new type of employee interested in sharing in decisions and making work relationships more authentic. Tendencies in this direction were also caused by the increasing necessity, in an era of rapid change, of making normative judgments about which people disagree. Rather than make these inevitable judgments through the force of experts and authorities it was better to seek a different decision-making model.

The participatory decision-making model associated with "the new public administration" was not the traditional concept of representative democracy. It was not the idea that more decisions should be made by union or other offical employee representatives or by referenda among agency employees. What was being advocated might be described as a problem-solving team approach. It involved organization development around improvement of change skills like listening, inquiring, clarifying, networking, and constructive utilization of organization conflict. The participatory organization of the "new public administration" was to be one marked by noncompetitive trusting relationships, client-centered services, flexible project team organization, impermanent hierarchies, and tolerance for conflict.

This approach to decision-making called for cooperation and consensus, not competition and majority rule. As empirical research by Tjosvold and Deemer (1980) later showed, a competitive approach to solving work problems was associated with insecurity, closed-mindedness, knowledge but not acceptance of the position of others, and failure to reach agreement. Cooperative approaches were shown to be associated with security, openness, positive expectations, heightened interest, positive orientation toward others, and ability to reach compromise decisions. As one public administrationist recently concluded, "if we want to learn how to make democratic and participative decisions, we should abandon the methods usually labeled 'democratic' (voting and parliamentary procedure)" in favor of group consensus methods (Thayer, 1980).

RESEARCH ON GROUP DECISION-MAKING

A concern for participatory methods of decision-making thus led public administrationists into an area that had formerly been the preserve of social psychologists and behavioral scientists—research on group behavior. Here empirical evidence was found on such questions as "Under what conditions is group consensus most likely?" and "What are the effects of participation on group decision-making?" Evidence was also available on more applied questions like "What is the best size for decision-making groups?" and "How should groups be seated for maximum effectiveness?" It is to questions of this type that we now turn.

As noted in our earlier discussion of communication, much research has found that group decision-making is superior to individual decision-making in certain respects. In general, groups tend to make slower decisions than individuals, but those decisions are of higher quality. There are five reasons for this: 1) groups have a broader fund of knowledge and are in a better position to formulate objectives; 2) groups generate a broader search for alternatives; 3) groups subject alternatives to more critical investigation; 4) groups are more willing to take risks since potential blame is shared; and 5) because groups are inherently participative, group decisions are more likely to be accepted than individual decisions (on advantages of group decision-making, see Shaw, 1932; Lorge, Fox, Davitz, Brenner, 1958; Hall, 1971; on risk-taking, see Bem, Wallach and Kogan, 1955; Dion, Baron, and Miller, 1970; Clark, 1971; Fisher, 1974).

This is not to say that administrators should invariably opt for group decision-making. Individual decision-making is not only faster, it may have other advantages in some situations. Individual decision-making, for example, may lead to more ideas generated per individual and to more unique ideas, if the individual would be inhibited in making suggestions before a group (see Taylor, Berry and

Block, 1958; Dunnette, Campbell, and Jaastad, 1963). In extreme cases a form of "groupthink" may emerge, whereby group members isolate themselves from negative feedback and, indeed, reality (Janis, 1972). Because of these problems in group decision-making, some managers have preferred methods discussed below such as the nominal group technique, which combines aspects of individual and group decision-making.

Clearly, the advantages of group versus individual decision-making depend partly upon *who* the decision-makers are. The identity of the decision-makers is the first of several "contingency factors"—situational variables which affect the appropriateness of group decision-making. Participants who are nonsocial, solitary, and independent in personality orientation, for instance, are poor choices for membership in decision-making groups (Gurnee, 1937). Individuals with a capacity for abstract thinking (often a function of education and experience), in contrast, are more effective in group decision-making (Hendrick, 1979). Likewise, younger and lower-level organizational members are often more effective in utilizing group processes (Webber, 1974).

Group *composition* is also a contingency factor. Groups that are heterogenous in composition are generally superior in effectiveness compared to homogenous groups (Laughlin, Branch, and Johnson, 1969; Hoffman and Maier, 1961). Presumably this is because heterogeneity brings a broader range of information, resources, and skills to bear upon the problems discussed. On the other hand, there is some evidence that homogenous groups are more task-oriented and heterogenous groups more social relations-oriented (Reitan and Shaw, 1964). Homogenous groups, therefore, may be superior when group process is unnecessary to identify goals and tasks.

Group *size* is a third contingency factor. In general, the larger the group, the less the participation in the decision-making process. Large groups (over fifteen members) tend to generate fewer ideas per member and reach lower quality decisions. Moreover, such large groups tend to factionalize into smaller subgroups (see Collins and Guetzkow, 1964; Davis, 1969). Very small groups (under five) are consensual, but also reach lower quality decisions (Hare, 1972). Most analysts recommend medium sized decision-making groups of five to twelve members because groups of this size make higher quality decisions on the basis of more ideas generated per person (Ziller, 1957; Thomas and Fink, 1963; Manners, 1975). Of this class of more effective-size groups, those in the medium-small end tend to be the most satisfying to participants (Slater, 1958; Hackman and Vidmar, 1970).

Finally, group *process* is a fourth set of contingency factors. Research suggests, for example, that consensus decision-making is better than methods which reach decisions through leader choice or majority vote (Asch, 1856; Vroom, Grant, and Cotten, 1969). But as we noted in discussing organizational communication (Chapter 4), communication network designs can influence behavior of individual group members. For example it seems to be helpful if groups are seated in a democratic manner, as in a circle, rather than in a square, triangle, or other shape placing some individuals in prominence (Hall, 1971). Side-by-side seating leads to less conflict than across-table seating. In general, group process facilitates decision-making when it incorporates participation, openness, equality of status, and security (see Sherif, White, and Harvey, 1955).

Group decision-making depends not only upon these four contingency domains but also upon other considerations. Groups function best when the decision task has demonstrable "answers," when they do not require a complex, multistage process over a long period of time (Shaw, 1971). Although often superior in general, group decision-making is rarely of as high quality as the decisions of the organization's most proficient member (Shaw, 1971). The nominal group technique and the delphi method are approaches to decision-making which have been developed to take advantage of the benefits of both group and individual aspects.

The Delphi Method and the Nominal Group Technique

The Rand Corporation, a private policy research organization, pioneered the Delphi method of decision-making as a format for achieving group consensus without such problems of group decision-making as the danger of domination by a single aggressive individual, the possible neglect of shyer members, and the tendency for decisions at the end of meetings to be unduly rushed because of time pressure. The Delphi method was simply a systematic approach to the traditional device of polling experts, whether outside professionals or the organization's own members.

In the Delphi method decision-making concerns are translated into a written questionnaire which is administered, usually by mail, to a panel of individuals thought to be knowledgeable. Among the most common uses is to achieve group consensus on anticipated changes for forecasting purposes. Rand, for example, has used Delphi to develop forecasts of trends in population growth, weapons systems development, and automation. It can also be used to project political trends, for organizational goal-setting, or for educational curriculum development.

The technique was developed by Rand analysts Norman Dalkey and Olaf Helmer in the 1950's. Delphi, Helmer wrote, "replaces direct debate by a carefully designed program of sequential individual interrogations interspersed with information and opinion feedback derived from a computed consensus from the earlier parts of the program" (Helmer and Rischer, 1959). It normally involves six steps:

1. Identification of a group of experts
2. Administration of a questionnaire; typically four dimensions are examined:
   a. Direction: e.g., will use of Organization Development (OD) techniques in public administration increase or decrease?
   b. Degree: e.g., how great will be the change in terms of some standard (for example, ratio of OD-related person-hours to total person-hours of all agency functions)?

      c. Time Frame: e.g., when will the event occur? (for example, when will 90 percent of all agency employees be involved in at least 20 hours of OD-related functions annually?)

      d. Likelihood: e.g., what degree of confidence does the respondant attach to each of the judgments above?

3. Questionnaire results are statistically aggregated and a second-round questionnaire is administered after the panel of experts receives first-round feedback.

4. The process is repeated until the last round does not increase panel consensus further.

5. Sometimes panelists may be brought together for face-to-face meetings to provide the analysts with further insight.

6. The decision resulting from the Delphi process is reached by the analyst on the basis of group consensus.

Since its development by Rand, the Delphi method has received hundreds of applications in public management, including the prediction of teacher education developments in Canada (Clark and Coutts, 1971), the forecasting of vocational training needs in California (Brooks, 1972), and the projection of developments in public administration as a discipline (Wald, 1973).

Delphi does help avoid group decision-making biases such as the tendency toward group conformity and deference to the views of the highest-status individual. It has not been without its critics, however. Sackman (1975), among others, has noted the following problems of Delphi: bias resulting for the common problem of drop-outs from panels of experts; frequently vague and ambiguous wording of items in Delphi's questionnairs; and the danger that Delphi's very anonymity may encourage panelists to respond in superficial, irresponsible ways. It is also biased toward decision-forcing, encouraging panelists to give *some* prediction even though the real consensus is that prediction on a reliable basis is impossible.

In spite of these problems, validation studies of the Delphi technique have shown that it leads to more reliable forecasts than can be obtained through group-based approaches. Campbell (1966), for example, found that business students could predict the performance of leading economic indicators better using this method than others. Dalkey and Helmer have likewise found experimentally that Delphi is superior to majority vote and leader decision methods of decision-making (Dalkey and Helmer, 1963; Dalkey, 1968). Dalkey (1969) has also found it better than face-to-face consensual methods, as have Breinholt and Webber (1972).

Delphi is clearly a promising decision-making technique. Nonetheless there is some evidence that even higher quality decisions can be attained through such methods as the nominal group technique (NGT), which combine Delphi procedures with the face-to-face aspects of conventional group decision-making. NGT is also a six-step process:

1. A group of 7 to 10 experts or organizational members are selected and meet face-to-face, whereupon they are presented

    by the analyst with a problem which is to be the focus of de-
cision-making.

2. After individually and silently listing pertinent ideas on paper
   (e.g., suggestions for solving an organizational problem), each
   person reveals one of these ideas at a time as the analyst lists
   them on flip-charts; the analyst continues around the group until all suggestions are listed.
3. After all ideas are listed without comment, the analyst asks for
   statements of clarification, agreement, or disagreement with
   each.
4. Using anonymous balloting, group members then tentatively
   rank the suggestions and the analyst lists by rank order all the
   suggestions that have received serious consideration.
5. The analyst then leads further discussion aimed at further clarification as well as elimination of duplicate ideas or ideas which
   are of low priority.
6. As a final step, group members rate all the remaining ideas
   anonymously. The idea with the highest average rank becomes
   the NGT decision outcome.

The NGT approach, developed by Van de Van and Delbecq (1975) in the
1960's, has been found by its originators to be superior to Delphi in eliciting the
generation of ideas and in securing task involvement (Van de Ven and Delbecq,
1974). Their colleague, Gustafson (1973), has come to similar conclusions in other
research. More recently, Burton and Pathak (1978) have found further advantages
in the NGT method. These researchers found NGT required only easily-attainable
skills, counteracted typical group-problem-solving biases such as dominance by
strong personalities, encouraged tolerance for nonconforming ideas and conflicting views, equalized participation to a greater degree than other methods, and promoted a sense of participation and ownership in decisions reached. Burton and
Pathak found NGT to be especially valuable for decision-making when agency participants were often inner-directed in personality rather than individuals with
strong other-directed social skills. Another contingency of NGT was discovered by
White, Dittrich, and Lang (1980), who found that NGT produced significantly
better rates of decision-implementation than decision-making through conventional
groups, but only for simple to moderately complex situations. These research efforts suggest that outgoing people making complex decisions may well find NGT
procedures an unnecessary waste of time. For a wide range of decision-making
situations, however, NGT will often lead to more participant satisfaction, higher
quality decisions, and more likelihood of decision implementation (on governmental applications, see Mercer and Woolston, 1980).

MANAGING DECISIONS: A CONCLUSION

The management of decision-making is in many ways the culmination of the management of organizational behavior in general. Like other behavioral areas in public administration, management of this aspect of agency life is not reducible to simple formulas. It is specifically not reducible to either centralized planning and econometric modelling on the one hand nor to blind faith in incrementalism and "muddling through" on the other. Because the management of decision-making is contingent upon so many factors and because a contingency theory of decision-making is in its infancy, the discretion of the manager is rather great. Correspondingly, the ability of the textbook-writer to prescribe solutions is rather limited! Nonetheless, a few generalizations may be made for those seeking to apply organizational theories of decision-making to the practical level of day-to-day management of decisions.

Louis Gawthrop (1971) is among those who have categorized the management of decisions as falling in three types: the planning mode, the incrementalist mode, and the synergistic mode. These represent alternative styles for organizing decision-making. The planning mode is a prescriptive model under which the manager seeks to generate as many alternatives as possible, assesses the costs and benefits of each, and chooses the optimal solution. Though it allows for consultation, it is typical of what Schein (1969) terms the authority method of decision-making under which power mainly resides in the hands of the manager and his or her expert advisors. The incrementalist mode is characterized by marginal changes in existing budgets and practices. In Schein's terms, it is often the result of the "plop" method (decision-making by default), minority decision-making (presenting the organization with *faits accompli*), or majority decision-making (based on compromise).

The synergistic mode, in contrast, is a combination of planning and incrementalist models. It is also a participatory approach. In Schein's terms, it is decision-making by consensus. Sometimes the synergistic mode is taken to be merely decision-making by participation of the human relations type. As Tushman (1977) as well as Gawthrop have noted, however, the participatory mode of decision-making often advocated in organizational behavior literature has severe problems, particularly in public management. It neglects a political approach to organizations, makes false assumptions about the extent of openness and trust, and fails to take account of how power differentials affect organizational communication. A synergistic method of decision-making, by comparison, rejects the notion of dichotomizing politics and administration.

The political aspects of the public management of decision-making are manifested in many ways. Kipnis and Schmidt (1980) have shown that for a wide variety of organizations, communications patterns and influence tactics are dependent upon the differential statuses of those involved. Rationality (planning) tactics and approaches increase, for example, as statuses increase in the organization. Decision-making influence tactics also vary simply because some are more effective than others. Harari, Mohr, and Hosey (1980) have documented, for example, the greater effectiveness of certain tactics in a public university setting. Specifically, these authors found that the most effective tactic was asking for large changes and settling for moderate ones (as opposed the foot-in-the-door strategy or the rational-moderate request strategy). Political aspects of decision-making are also inherent in the factionalization apparent in informal organization (discussed in Chapter 4), in differential perceptions of organizational and self-interest, and in career-related motivations leading managers to take credit for success and distance themselves from failure.

Because of the political aspects of administration, successful change cannot be a matter of decision-making by a blueprint imposed from the top. Efforts must be made to involve lower echelons as a prerequisite for effective delegation and implementation in later stages. Often it is necessary to develop policy-making skills and teamwork experiences as part of organizational development prior to the main agenda of major organizational change. (On such skill-building for city management, see Becker, 1979; Saunders, 1979). The synergistic mode advocated by Gawthrop must also be conceived as a broad organization development effort, not technical problem solving. Managing decisions is a process, not a technique—though techniques like the nominal group approach may be useful.

In general, the management of decisions starts with the identification of the problem. This sounds obvious but administrators are prone to skip over this step. In the public sector problems are often complex and solutions not obvious. In a health care setting, for example, administrators may leap to the assumption that the problem is lack of resources when the real problem might be conceived as too much in-patient rather than out-patient care. Problem identification may be undertaken by analysts using multivariate analytic techniques, of course. Such staff preparation for decision-making meetings is appropriate. Nonetheless, the participative brainstorming of what's right or wrong in the organization is the first step of the group process of decision-making.

The second step is analysis of problem causes in terms of prioritizing problems by three criteria: magnitude of the problem in terms of the value of improvements which could be made; susceptibility of the variables involved to manipulation by the agency; and urgency of the problem in terms of time frame. Brainstorming, prioritizing through paired comparison rankings, nominal group and a variety of other techniques may be used at this point. In the actual group meetings at this step the manager often plays the role of clarifier or summarizer of progress toward consensus.

As in the management of all meetings, certain group process characteristics are desirable. Sometimes an outside change agent can elicit these characteristics better than the perhaps-intimidating presence of the manager. What are these characteristics? They are many: to avoid premature closure, to seek openness and consensus rather than majority vote, to be descriptive rather than evaluative (to reduce defensiveness), to use humor, to be concrete, to focus on the actionable, to avoid stigmatizing "far-out" ideas, to encourage participation of reticent members, to utilize repetition and summaries, to accept conflict, to be generally ego-supportive.

As consensus on a decision emerges, typical approaches move toward establishment of task forces or matrix organizations. More broadly, decision implementation should be conceived as a sociotechnical process, not just a technical one (see Davis, 1979). Moreover, it is important to explicitly assign tasks to people for motivational reasons. Mossholder (1980) has found, for instance, that assigning specific challenging tasks to individuals increases performance levels compared to methods in which the task is assigned without goals.

The fourth step of managing decisions is evaluation and feedback. In this phase the manager is charged with developing evaluative measures. These measures will become motivational goals and must be carefully designed and implemented to avoid neglect of performance on unmeasured criteria. Participation in evaluation and feedback increases employee commitment to the change effort and involvement in decision-making.

The topic of management decision-making eventually leads back to situational factors associated with leadership, motivation, socialization, change, participation, and other organizational behavior topics treated in other chapters. If decision-making could be reduced to a specific series of steps or techniques then much of the justification for having managers at all would disappear. The objective of this chapter has been to familiarize the reader with the range of orientations toward decision-making as a managerial and organizational activity in the public sector. The three broad traditions of planning, incrementalism, and participation-synergy each come to bear on decision-making in contemporary agencies. The student of organization behavior can state with confidence that any one approach alone is inadequate. It can also be said that there are some typical techniques which have been found to be particularly effective in managing decisions. Ultimately, however, a contingency theory of decision-making is only in its infancy and needs much development before one can expect widespread impact on practitioners in the public sector. Of all the aspects of decision-making contingencies, however, the ones most studied have to do with the contingencies under which a participative approach to decision-making is most effective. This topic is treated in the next chapter.

REFERENCES

Argyris, Chris (1973a)   Some limits of rational man organizational theory. *Public Administration Review*, Vol. 33, No. 2 (May/June):pp. 253-267.
_____(1973b)   Organizational man: rational and self-actualizing. *Public Administration Review*, Vol. 33, No. 4 (July/August):pp. 354-357.

Asch, Solomon (1956) Studies of independence and conformity. *Psychological Monographs* (1956):pp. 68-70.

Becker, Christine (1979) Getting elected is just the beginning. *Public Management* (July):pp. 10-14.

Breinholt, R. and R. A. Webber (1972) Comparing Delphi groups, uninstructed and instructed face-to-face groups. cited in D. R. Hampton, C. E. Summer, and R. A. Webber *Organizational Behavior and the Practice of Management* Third Edition. Glenview, Illinois: Scott, Foresman (1978):p. 257.

Brooks, E. C. and L. M. Brooks (1933) Five years of 'planning' literature. *Social Forces*, Vol. 11, No. 2 (March):pp. 430-465.

_____(1934) A decade of 'planning' literature. *Social Forces*, Vol. 12, No. 2 (March):pp. 427-459.

Brooks, W. (1972) *North California Research Group Educational Study*. Sacramento, California: Office of the Chancellor, California Community Colleges.

Bunce, V. (1980) Changing leaders and changing policies: the impact of elite successes on budgetary practices in democratic countries. *American Journal of Political Science*, Vol. 24, No. 3 (August):pp. 373-395.

Burton, Gene E. and Dev S. Pathak (1978) Social character and group decision-making. *Advanced Management Journal* (Summer):pp. 12-21.

Campbell, R. M. (1966) *A Methodological Study of the Utilization of Experts in Business Forecasting*. Los Angeles: University of California at Los Angeles, doctoral dissertation.

Catlin, George E. G. (1932) Review of C. A. Beard, ed., *America Faces the Future* (1932), H. Laidler, *The Road Ahead* (1932), and G. Soule, *A Planned Society* (1932), in *American Political Science Review*, Vol. 26, No. 4 (August):pp. 730-733.

Clark, R. D., III (1971) Group-induced shift toward risk. *Psychological Bulletin*, Vol. 76:pp. 251-271.

Clark, S. C. and H. T. Coutts (1971) The future of teacher education. *Journal of Teacher Education*, Vol. 22, No. 4:pp. 508-516.

Cohen, Michael D., James C. March, and Johan D. Olsen (1972) A garbage can model of organizational choice. *American Sociological Review*, Vol. 17, No. 1 (March):pp. 1-25.

Collins, B. E. and H. Guetzkow (1964) *A Social Psychology of Group Processes for Decision-Making*, New York: Wiley.

Corwin, Edward (1932) Social planning under the Constitution. *American Political Science Review*, Vol. 26, No. 1 (February):pp. 1-27.

Dalkey, N. C. (1968) *Experiments in Group Prediction*. Santa Monica, California: Rand Corporation.

_____(1969) *The Delphi Method*. Santa Monica, California: Rand Corporation Memo RM 5888-PR (June).

_____and Olaf Helmer (1963) An experimental application of the Delphi Method to use of experts. *Management Science* (April):pp. 458-467.

Davis, J. H. (1969) *Group Performance*. Reading, Massachusetts: Addison-Wesley.

Davis, Louis E. (1979) Optimizing organizational-plant design: a complementary structure for technical and social systems. *Organizational Dynamics*, Vol. 8, No. 2 (Autumn):pp. 2-15.

Delbecq, Andre et al. (1975) *Group Techniques for Program Planning*. Glenview, Ill.: Scott, Foresman.

Dennison, Henry S. (1932) The need for development of political science engineering. *American Political Science Review*, Vol. 26, No. 2 (April):pp. 241-255.

Dion, K. L., R. S. Baron and N. Miller (1970) Group decision-making under risk of adverse consequences. *Journal of Personality and Social Psychology*, Vol. 1:pp. 453-460.

Dunnette, M. D., J. D. Campbell, and K. Jaastad (1963) The effect of group participation on brainstorming effectiveness for two industrial samples. *Journal of Applied Psychology*, Vol. 47:pp. 30-37.

Etzioni, Amitai (1967) Mixed scanning: a 'third' approach to decision-making. *Public Administration Review*, Vol. 27, No. 6 (December):pp. 385-392.

Fisher, G. Aubrey (1974) *Small Group Decision-Making: Communication and Group Process*. New York: McGraw-Hill.

Friedman, Milton (1962) *Capitalism and Freedom*. Chicago: University of Chicago Press.

Garson, G. David and D. S. Brenneman (1981a) Resource rationing in state agencies: the management and political challenge of productivity improvement. *Public Productivity Review*. (September):pp. 231-248.

_____(1981b) Incentive systems and goal displacement in personnel resource management. *Review of Public Personnel Administration*, Vol. 1, No. 2 (April):pp. 1-12.

Gawthrop, Louis (1971) *Administrative Politics and Social Change*. New York: St. Martin's Press.

Greiner, L. (1967) Patterns of organizational change. *Harvard Business Review*, Vol. 45, No. 3 (May/June):pp. 119-130.

Guerreiro-Ramos, Alberto (1980) A substantive approach to organizations. Ch. 7 in C. J. Bellone, ed., *Organization Theory and the New Public Administration*. Boston: Allyn and Bacon.

Gurnee, H. (1937) A comparison of collective and individual judgments of facts. *Journal of Experimental Psychology*, vol. 21.

Gustafson, D. H. (1973) A comparative study of differences in subjective likelihood estimates made by individuals, interacting groups, Delphi groups and nominal groups. *Organizational Behavior and Human Performance*, Vol. 9: pp. 280-291.

Hackman, R. and N. Vidmar (1970) Effects of size and task type on group performance and member reaction. *Sociometry*, Vol. 33:pp. 37-54.

Hall, J. (1971) Decisions. *Psychology Today* (November):51 ff.

Harari, Herbert, Deborah Mohr, Karen Hosey (1980)　Faculty helpfulness to students: a comparison of compliance techniques. *Personality and Social Psychology Bulletin*, Vol. 6, No. 3 (September):pp. 573-577.

Hare, A. P. (1972)　Interaction and consensus in different sized groups. *American Sociological Review*, Vol. 17:pp. 261-267.

Hayek, F. A. (1935) *Collectivist Economic Planning*. London: Routledge.

_____(1944) *The Road to Serfdom*. Chicago: University of Chicago Press.

Helmer, C. and N. Rischer (1959)　On the epistemology of inexact sciences. *Management Science*, Vol. 6:pp. 25-52.

Hendrick, Hal. W. (1979)　Differences in group problem-solving behavior and effectiveness as a function of abstractness. *Journal of Applied Psychology* Vol. 61, No. 5 (October):pp. 518-525.

Hoffman, L. R. and M. R. Maier (1961)　Quality and acceptance of problem solutions by members of homogenous and heterogenous groups. *Journal of Abnormal and Social Psychology*, Vol. 62:pp. 401-407.

Janis, Irving L. (1972) *Victims of Groupthink*. Boston: Houghton Mifflin.

Kipnis, David and Stuart M. Schmidt (1980)　Intraorganizational influence tactics: exploration in getting one's own way. *Journal of Applied Psychology*, Vol. 65, No. 4 (August):pp. 440-452.

Laidler, Harry (1932) *Socialist Planning and a Socialist Program*. New York: Falcon.

Laughlin, P. R., L. G. Branch, and H. H. Johnson (1969)　Individual versus triadic personality on a unidimensional completion task as a function of initial ability level. *Journal of Personality and Social Psychology*. Vol. 12:pp. 144-150.

Lindblom, Charles E. (1959)　The science of 'muddling through.' *Public Administration Review*, Vol. 19 (Spring):pp. 79-88.

Lorge, I. and D. Fox, J. Davitz, and M. Brenner (1958)　A survey of studies contrasting the quality of group performance and individual performance, 1920-1957. *Psychological Bulletin*, Vol. 55.

Lorwin, L. L. (1931) *Advisory Economic Councils*. Washington: Brookings Institution.

Manners, G. E., Jr. (1975)　Another look at group size, group problem-solving, and member consensus. *Academy of Management Journal*, Vol. 18, No. 4: pp. 715-724.

Mannheim, Karl (1950) *Freedom, Power and Democratic Planning*. New York: Oxford University Press.

March, James C. and Johan P. Olsen (1976) *Ambiguity and Choice in Organizations*. Bergen, Norway: Universitetsforlaget.

March, James G. and Herbert A. Simon (1960) *Organizations*. New York: Wiley.

Marini, Frank, ed. (1971) *Toward a New Public Administration: The Minnowbrook Perspective*. Scranton, Pa.: Chandler.

McCaskey, Michael B. (1979)　The management of ambiguity. *Organizational Dynamics*, Vol. 7, No. 4 (Spring):pp. 31-35.

Mercer, J. L. and Susan W. Woolston (1980) Setting priorities: three techniques for better decision-making. *Management Information Service*. International City Management Association, Vol. 12, No. 9 (September):pp. 1-9.

Meyer, John W. and Brian Rowan (1977) Institutionalized organizations: formal structure as myth and ceremony. *American Journal of Sociology*, Vol. 83, No. 2 (September):pp. 340-363.

Moore, O. K. and S. B. Anderson (1954) Search behavior in individual and group problem solving. *American Sociological Review*, Vol. 19.

Mossholder, Kevin W. (1980) Effects of externally mediated goal setting on intrinsic motivation: a lab experiment. *Journal of Applied Psychology*, Vol. 65, No. 2 (April):pp. 202-210.

Myrdal, Gunnar (1960) *Beyond the Welfare State*. New Haven: Yale University Press.

Nalbandian, John and Donald E. Klinger (1980) Integrating context and decision strategy: a contingency theory approach to public personnel administration. *Administration and Society*, Vol. 12, No. 2 (August):pp. 178-202.

Perrow, Charles (1972) *Complex Organizations*. Glenview, Ill.: Scott, Foresman.

_____(1978) Demystifying organizations. in R. Sauri and Y. Hasenfeld, eds., *The Management of Human Services*. New York: Columbia.

Peters, Thomas J. (1979) Leadership: sad facts and silver linings. *Harvard Business Review*, Vol. 57, No. 6 (November/December):pp. 164-172.

Polanyi, Michael (1951) *The Logic of Liberty*. Chicago: University of Chicago Press.

Reitan, H. I. and M. E. Shaw (1964) Group membership, sex composition of the group, and conformity behavior. *Journal of Social Psychology*, Vol. 64:pp. 45-51.

Sackman, Harold (1975) *Delphi Critique: Expert Opinion, Forecasting, and Group Process*. Lexington, Massachusetts: D. C. Heath and Company.

Saunders, Robert J. (1979) Improving policy-making skills. *Public Management* (July):pp. 2-5.

Schein, Edgar (1969) *Process Consultation: Its Role in Organizational Development*. Reading, Massachusetts: Addison Wesley Company.

Schull, Fremont, Andre Delbecq, and L. L. Cummings (1970) *Organizational Decision-Making*. New York: McGraw-Hill.

Shaw, M. E. (1932) A comparison of individuals and small groups in the rational solution of complex problems. *American Journal of Psychology*, Vol. 44.

_____(1971) *Group Dynamics: The Psychology of Small Group Behavior*. New York: McGraw-Hill.

Sherif, Muzafer, B. J. White and O. J. Harvey (1955) Status in experimentally produced groups. *American Journal of Sociology*, Vol. 60:pp. 370-379.

Simon, Herbert A. (1945) *Administrative Behavior*. New York: MacMillan.

_____(1957) *Models of Man*. New York: Wiley.

Simon, Herbert A. (1973)   Organizational man: rational or self-actualizing? *Public Administration Review*, Vol. 33, No. 4 (July/August):pp. 346-353.

_____, Harold Guetzkow, George Kozmetsky, and Gordon Tyndall (1954) *Centralization vs. Decentralization in Organizing the Controller's Department.* New York: Controllership Foundation, Inc.

Skok, J. E. (1980)   Budgetary politics and decision-making. *Administration and Society*, Vol. 11, No. 4 (February):pp. 445-460.

Slater, P. E. (1958)   Contrasting correlates of group size. *Sociometry*, Vol. 21: pp. 129-179.

Smith, Michael P. and Steven L. Nock (1980)   Social class and the quality of work life in public and private organizations. *Journal of Social Issues*, Vol. 36, No. 4:pp. 59-75.

Staats, E. B. (1980)   Why isn't policy research used by more decision-makers? *GAO Review*, Vol. 15, No. 1 (Winter):pp. 21-25.

Taylor, D., P. C. Berry, and C. H. Block (1958)   Does group participation when using brainstorming facilitate or inhibit creative thinking? *Administrative Science Quarterly*, Vol. 23:pp. 23-47.

Thayer, Frederick C. (1980)   Organization theory as epistemology: transcending hierarchy and objectivity. Ch. 6 in C. J. Bellone, ed., *Organization Theory and the New Public Administration.* Boston: Allyn and Bacon.

Thomas, E. J. and L. F. Fink (1963)   Effects of group size. *Psychological Bulletin*, Vol. 60:pp. 371-384.

Thompson, James D. (1967) *Organizations in Action.* New York: McGraw-Hill.

Tjosvald, Dean and Deborah K. Deemer (1980)   Effects of controversy within a cooperative or competitive context on organizational decision-making. *Journal of Applied Psychology*, Vol. 65, No. 5 (October):pp. 590-595.

Tugwell, Rexford (1933) *Industrial Discipline and the Governmental Arts.* New York: Columbia University Press.

Tushman, Michael (1977)   A political approach to organizations: a review and rationale. *Academy of Management Review*, Vol. 2, No. 2 (April):pp. 206-216.

Van de Van, A. H. and A. F. Delbecq (1974)   The effectiveness of nominal, Delphi, and interacting group decision-making processes. *Academy of Management Journal*, Vol. 17, No. 4:pp. 605-621.

Vasu, Michael L. (1979) *Politics and Planning: A National Study of Planners.* Chapel Hill, N.C.: University of North Carolina Press.

Vroom, Victor, Lester Grant, and Timothy Cotten (1969)   The consequences of social interaction in group problem-solving. *Organizational Behavior and Human Performance* (February):pp. 77-95.

Wald, Emanuel (1973)   Toward a paradigm of future public administration. *Public Administration Review*, Vol. 33, No. 4 (July/August):pp. 368-372.

Webber, R. A. (1974)   The relation of group performance to the age of members in homogenous groups. *Academy of Management Journal*, Vol. 17, No. 3 (September):pp. 570-574.

Weiss, Carol H. (1980), *Social Science Research in Decision Making*. New York: Columbia University Press.

White, Sam E., J. E. Dittrich, and J. R. Lang (1980)   The effects of group decision-making process and problem-solving situation complexity on implementation attempts. *Administrative Science Quarterly*, Vol. 25, No. 3 (September):pp. 428-440.

Zeitz, Gerald (1980)   Hierarchical authority and decision-making in professional organizations. *Administration and Society*, Vol. 12, No. 3 (November):pp. 277-300.

Ziller, R. C. (1957)   Group size: a determinant of the quality and stability of group decisions. *Sociometry*, Vol. 20:pp. 165-173.

PARTICIPATION

Participation is perhaps the single most common theme in the discussion of organization behavior in public administration. Participatory management was at the heart of the human behavioral attack on classical approaches to organizational behavior, and specifically on scientific management. It figured prominently in the "New Public Administration" movement of the 1960's and 1970's, and is a mainstay of current work in the new field of organization development. Participation is a critical concept in the study of motivation since it is a key to organizational commitment and acceptance of change. Participation is also a central theme in the study of decision-making, outlined in the previous chapter, because of its role in broadening the process of choice and selection. Yet in spite of these and many other evidences of the importance of participation in public management, most public organizations retain an essentially hierarchical structure and operate through relatively centralized, nonparticipatory processes. How can this contradiction be explained? This question is the focus of the present chapter.

Participatory management poses unique problems for *public* administration. On the one hand a considerable body of evidence based in the human behavioral literature suggests that participatory forms of administration are more effective in many of the contexts in which government operates. Moreover, there is a long tradition of government emulating the managerial developments in the business sector, where one now increasingly encounters participatory reforms. (In the next section we will examine many of the forces pushing public administration in a participatory direction.) On the other hand formidable forces unique to the public sector tend to prevent the spread of participatory management.

How is public management different? That it *is* different is now widely recognized even in the business community (see Fottler, 1981; Whorton and

Worthley, 1981; Curtis, 1980). Although many differences exist, three major ones impede participatory management in the public sector:

1. *Accountability*: The public sector is more accountable. Almost any issue can become politicized. Whereas secrecy in business is a legally-protected right, freedom-of-information acts prohibit secrecy in most government operations. Moreover, business is results-oriented whereas government is accountable in process as well as outcomes. That is, due process of law—not just efficient delivery of services—is a major requirement of good public administration.

   What happens to a public manager who is faced with accountability for his or her procedures and results, whose records may be open to public view, and who knows that at any moment public interest groups, investigative journalists, minority representatives, legislative committees, or executive overseers may choose to make almost anything into a political issue? What happens in such a high-accountability setting is conservative management. The manager is inclined to protect the agency by "going by the book," avoiding risks, and not delegating decision-making powers to those who may be less accountable. The need for tight accountability has a pervasive centralizing effect which often undermines forces for lower-level discretion which participatory approaches require.

2. *Performance measurement*: The public sector lacks a clear criterion like profitability by which agency performance can be measured. This fact compounds the dilemma outlined above. Large private-sector organizations often attempt to improve effectiveness by decentralizing operations to smaller profit centers—units held accountable for profitability but not required to follow centralized procedures on personnel, production, or other administrative matters. Because means-ends knowledge is imperfect in areas government deals with, it is typically not possible for government to do the same. It cannot ordinarily allow decentralized units to operate autonomously because there is no profit-like measure of performance by which the central office can maintain effective control.

   By the same token, it is very difficult to measure the performance of many government employees. Such employees often provide services addressed to problems (e.g., eliminating welfare dependency) which are little understood. For example, it is difficult to argue that a social worker who handles twice as many welfare cases as another is more effective. Indeed, that

social worker may be attaining speed by such superficial and ar-
bitrary case treatment that more harm is being done than good.
Because it is hard to measure individual performance, public
agencies typically prefer the simpler route of holding employees
to certain standard operating procedures established centrally
for everyone.

The counterargument that "If you'd allow me and my team
to decide things autonomously we'd be able to deliver more
profit" doesn't apply. Performance measurement in public service is so difficult that public administrators usually could not
document gains that might come from a participatory approach.
Ironically, compared to business, public organizations are more
accountable but their employees are less accountable! The result
is organizations that rely heavily on centralized standard operating procedures that are the antithesis of participatory management.

3. *Political legitimacy*: The most basic public-private difference
   that impedes participatory approaches is the representative
   theory of democracy itself. Employees are not supposed to participate in decision-making or have autonomy in traditional
   democratic theory. That theory holds that the people elect leg-
   islatures which make policy and chief executives who implement policy through appointed officials. These officials' role is
   to carry out day-to-day implementation, not influence policy.
   Though political scientists have found that the politics-admini-
   stration dichotomy that this suggests is untenable in practice,
   the more important fact remains that in a society based on the
   ideology of representative democracy, little public legitimacy
   exists for nonelected bureaucrats to engage in participatory
   decision-making.

   The democratic political system thwarts participation in
   other ways too. The system leads to a two-layer public service
   composed of an upper crust of politically-appointed chiefs and
   middle and lower layers of civil service careerists. This bifurcated
   management composition leads to centralization. On the one
   hand the political chiefs, who serve relatively short terms, distrust the long-term civil servants and ordinarily seek to central-
   ize departmental control at the top, not delegate participatory
   powers to career civil servants. On the other hand, the civil servants fear the whims of the political chiefs and form powerful
   employee organizations which support a strong civil service system which protects their jobs. That system, however, is invariably centralized and a severe obstacle to participatory approaches

to management. Thus democratic ideology itself leads to an
agency interest group structure which is opposed to organizational democracy!

The forces of resistance to participatory approaches to management in the
public sector are many. The success of these forces are evidenced in the spread of
budgetary and other management control systems, in the centralizing effects of
public unionism, and the unabated upgrading of civil service professional requirements (nonparticipatory trends in American public administration are treated more
extensively in Garson and Williams (1982).

The foregoing discussion might bring into question the relevance of participation to public management, but the obstacles are not the whole story. Below we
will outline the forces *favoring* participatory management in public administration,
followed by a look at some comparative and domestic models which also provide
evidence in favor of participative management. Participation has been more successful in some settings than others, and after examining these models we will look at
the contingencies under which participation is most likely to succeed in the public
sector. The conclusion will present a summary of practical administrative considerations in the management of participation in public-sector agencies.

FORCES FAVORING PARTICIPATION IN MANAGEMENT

The argument that participatory management is on the ascent in American public
administration rests on four major assumptions. The first assumption is that the
values of our democratic heritage point to organizational democratization as a goal
for social development. A second assumption posits that changes in the public
workforce are leading to increased employee demands for participation. Third, it
is argued that the technological environment of public administration favors participatory management. Finally, it is contended that participatory management is
more efficient and that, as public administration enters an era of austerity, it will
be forced by economic necessity to seek out more democratic forms or organization. These four assumptions are examined below.

Culture

Functionalist sociologists have long argued that all social systems change through
an evolutionary pattern of normative upgrading and specification (cf. Parsons,
1965). Given cultural values which uphold the norms of equality and democracy
this theory predicts that over time organizational life will adapt to better and
better specify these norms. Just as upgrading the norms pertaining to the value of
equality have gradually led to the inclusion of more groups into full citizenship
rights, so one would expect that the social dynamic upgrading the norms pertaining to democracy would gradually lead to fuller and fuller implementation of

participatory norms in more and more settings. This should be specially true of *public* administration because of the symbolic role of government in sanctioning cultural values.

There is support for the idea that participatory values are dominant in American organizational life, at least at an abstract level. A 1973 report to the Department of Health, Education, and Welfare, for example, cited a national survey of 1,533 American workers at all occupational levels. These workers ranked such job aspects as interesting work, resources to do the job well, and adequate authority to do the job as more important than pay (Special Task Force, 1973). The HEW report interpreted these data as supportive of recognition of the need for a participatory work environment which would provide delegation of authority and the challenge of responsibility for work, recognizing that authority and responsibility involve organizational democratization in some form.

More recently, in 1979 the U.S. Office of Personnel Management conducted the first government-wide attitude survey of federal employees (USOPM News, 1979). This random survey of 14,000 federal employees found that federal bureaucrats, like workers surveyed earlier, rated challenging work responsibilities as more important than salary. More significant, large numbers reported their organizational settings to be conducive to participation. Some 47 percent said their supervisors encouraged them to participate in important decisions, and 73 percent said their supervisor asked their opinion on work problems. Seven out of ten respondents in the Senior Executive Service felt they had enough authority to carry out their work effectively. These findings suggest a widespread if not universal pattern of delegation of authority and participation in decision-making in American public administration at the federal level.

Not only is a form of participatory environment relatively widespread in government, the values supporting such an environment are now finding codification in the professional standards of public administrators. This process of value specification and normative upgrading is exactly the type of development predicted by functionalist sociology, cited earlier. *Professional Standards and Ethics*, a workbook issued by the Professional Standards and Ethics Committee of the American Society for Public Administration in 1979, contains many provisions implying a participatory environment.

For example, the *Professional Standards and Ethics* document does not specify solutions to moral dilemmas but does strongly imply the following:

- that bureaucrats should be informed about the work of regulatory agencies, legislative committees, and courts affecting their programs
- that the bureaucrat should deal in some way with inequities, omissions, and contradictions in laws affecting his/her work
- that they should feel a responsibility for the performance of their agencies, not just of their jobs

- that opposing views on sensitive issues should be solicited
- that administrators should respond to the "right to know" and "need to know" requirements of appropriate parties
- that public managers should have sufficient knowledge of individual motivation, group dynamics, and alternative modes of leadership

The Professional Standards and Ethics Committee stops short of equating participatory management with ethical administrative style but it is difficult to avoid the implication that the norms of public administration are pushing in this direction. A participatory orientation flows from the ethic of responsibility, which the Committee clearly endorses.

The value of responsibility means that public administrators are called on to avoid the "I am just following orders" syndrome. Public administrators implement professional ethics by continually questioning the propriety of standard operating procedures that have arisen through convenience, expediency, pressure, impulse, or inertia (Professional Standards and Ethics Committee, 1979). There is a strong presumption that this questioning process will involve others, soliciting opposing views, wrestling jointly with moral issues, deciding on some basis involving participatory input if not collective decision-making. ASPA's sanctioning of responsibility as a primary professional ethic for public administrators implies affirmatively dealing with moral issues which inherently cannot be resolved through rational analysis of a quantitative problem-solving type. If one acknowledges that expert analysis or benevolent authoritarianism are not appropriate responses to the posited ethic of responsibility, it is almost inevitable that professionalism in public administration come to be associated with some degree of participatory management.

Workforce

The changing nature of the public work force reinforces the cultural impetus behind participation in governmental management. Among the changes are trends in education, age, and sex of the public work force. Each trend can be cited in support of the assumption that there will be increased employee demands for participation in the future.

Considering the 34,000 federal workers in top managerial positions (GS 15 through 18), there has been a striking increase in educational level. By 1977, 63 percent held master's degrees or higher, up ten percent from a decade earlier. Compared to the approximately 35 percent of the general population with at least some college education, the entire federal work force rate is 55 percent (*U.S. News and World Report*, 1980). Some 70 percent of federal civilian jobs are white-collar (CPM, 1980). More significant, professionalization of governmental occupations has proceeded rapidly. Following WWII, social workers, law enforcement officers, planners, and many other occupations have become dominated by individuals with professional credentials. Professional schools for master's degree candidates in public administration and related fields have also grown rapidly. Of 79 leading programs in public administration surveyed recently by the National Association of Schools of Public Affairs and Administration, only 18 percent had been in existence prior to 1960. Some 48 percent have begun since 1970! (Stokes, 1981.)

The consequence of this educational revolution has been that federal jobs have become much more competitive, even prior to the Reagan administration cutbacks. In 1978 the federal government was receiving 76 inquiries and 12 applicants for each position listed—the highest rate in the history of the competitive civil service (Campbell, 1978). During the 1980's public-sector jobs, while still rising in absolute terms, have slowed relative to the rate of population increase and, more specifically, the rate at which college-trained individuals seek governmental employment (Barabba, 1980). Increasingly, the few who survive the competition for federal jobs are likely to perceive themselves as having undergone a rigorous selection process designed to produce an elite corps of public managers.

How does this relate to participation? In spite of increasing educational levels, the ratio of responsible, policy-making, managerial jobs to other public jobs is not increasing. The age of computerization creates ten keypunchers for every data analyst. Graduates in public administration fields often find their career expectations greatly frustrated. Lower managerial levels become increasingly staffed by "overeducated" individuals who feel their capacities far exceed the minimal responsibilities of their jobs. The solution often proposed to this dilemma is participation. Team management, project organization, participative goal-setting and many other democratic reforms are advanced to improve the quality of working life of the overeducated, underchallenged public worker. While such reforms are at present relatively sparse (Kanter and Stein, 1981), the increasing education of public workers is undoubtedly a force for participation in management that must be reckoned with.

Although educational trends are foremost among the workforce factors favoring participatory management, age and sex also are contributing factors. During the 1980's and 1990's, top management jobs will be occupied by the bulge of civil servants representing the post-WWII "baby boom" (Barabba, 1980). This generation was college age during the social ferment of the 1960's and was a prime causal factor in the student demands of that era for participatory democracy. While only a minority were radicals of that era, it can be argued that a cultural imprint is borne disproportionately by this age cohort and that their democratic values may find greater expression as they come into higher positions of managerial control. Likewise it can be argued that the democratic values of the women's movement will find disproportionate expression in public administration since women are more highly represented in the public sector than the private (Barabba, 1980); this argument is made by Kanter and Stein, 1980).

Technology

In addition to cultural and workforce factors it is often contended that technological considerations point toward the ascendance of participation in public administration. Many studies of technology and work organization suggest that the
type of work performed by public organizations is conducive to participatory
management:

1. *Public Management as Craft.* Nearly two decades ago, Blauner
   found that craft industries were more conducive to participatory consciousness than were assembly-line industries (Blauner,
   1964). As George Berkley's well-known text, *The Craft of Public Administration* (1981), suggests, public management more
   nearly falls in the former category.
2. *Public Management and Interdependence.* Taylor (1971) studied
   organizational change processes and found highly interdependent contexts to require more intensive interaction and inter-
   communication of the type afforded by participatory management. Public organizations are more highly interdependent than
   most business organizations for a number of reasons: political
   accountability, common revenue base, social nature of the task,
   and geographic jurisdiction.
3. *Public Management and Innovation.* As Clayton (1980) has
   noted, technological change results in stress, accommodation of
   which often requires intervention of governmental agencies
   which mandate new social technologies. Both stress reduction
   and acceptance of change are goals for which participatory
   styles of management are highly appropriate. The more processes are innovative and non-routine, the less feasible are traditional mechanistic, hierarchical management approaches (see
   Perrow, 1967). The sociotechnical approach to organization design is based on this principle, using participatory approaches
   to accommodate the social impact of technological change (see
   Trist and Bamforth, 1951; Emery and Trist, 1959; Davis and
   Trist, 1972; Susman, 1976).

In general, technology is a factor in professionalization of the public service.
The upgraded competency levels involved in professionalization bring expectations
of decision-making roles and participation in the work process. Because public
management is a craft devoted to facilitating the social adaptation of an interdependent world to increasingly rapid change, participatory approaches may be of
special importance in the government sector.

Efficiency

Participatory management, it is argued, is on the ascendant because it is efficient, not just because it responds to cultural values, reflects the needs of a changing public workforce, or is adaptive to technological forces. This assertion is difficult to prove, however. The literature on participation has been summarized by some as showing participation has no correlation with organizational efficiency, while others assert it is a virtual panacea for agency ills. Much of the confusion in the literature is based on three methodological problems.

First, very little literature exists specific to *public* administration. Given gross differences in public and private administration (e.g., political effects, lack of profit criterion or market controls, civil service constraints, task ambiguity) this deficiency in the literature itself almost prevents generalization about participation and efficiency in government.

In addition, a second methodological problem exists in that the dependent variable, efficiency, is notoriously difficult to measure in public administration. Consequently, even if an agency has an experiment in participatory management, it is unlikely to have in place a means of measuring its effect on productivity. If it does have such a measurement system, the researcher must often question its meaningfulness (e.g., is a manpower program to be rated high because of a high placement rate, even if there is no effect on the unemployment rate? is a school productive just because its students test well?). The causes of public policy variables are usually only dimly known, complex in nature, and difficult to measure.

A third obstacle in the literature is a corresponding imprecision in the independent variable, participation. Unfortunately, social scientists have frequently made sweeping generalizations about "participation" on the assumption that one type can be equated with another. One author may be discussing full-blown worker self-management of a socialist sort, however, while another may use "participation" merely to refer to the situation in which a traditional hierarchy deigns to ask employees' opinions on some matter. The determinants and effects of different forms of participation may vary and cannot be aggregated meaningfully in some pronouncement that "participation is efficient" (or not efficient).

Summary

Is participatory management in the cards for public administration because, being more efficient, it will help governments face the problems of fiscal austerity of the 1980's? This assumption about the forces for participation is not proved by existing social science literature. We can find instances where it contributes to efficiency, but we can also find the reverse. Various types of participation are effective in different situations. Before discussing the contingencies on which successful participative management depends, however, it is appropriate to first survey briefly models

of participatory management found in other countries and here in the United
States. It is these real-life models rather than social science research which provides the strongest impetus toward participatory management. In addition, this
survey will contribute toward understanding the range of types of participation
and the circumstances under which these types have been found to be feasible.

COMPARATIVE MODELS OF PARTICIPATION

In spite of its strong democratic heritage, participatory management has not developed as extensively in America as in a number of other countries. Because of
this advocates of organizational democratization in the United States have often
seen in other countries' practice models which our own country might emulate.
Prime among these comparative models are the Swedish model of industrial
democracy, West Germany's system of codetermination, the Japanese model of
quality circles, the Israeli kibbutz model, and the Yugoslav system of worker self-
management. Each has been held up as a successful illustration of the use of participation in management. Since virtually every discussion of participative management draws on one or more of these models either explicitly or implicitly, it is
helpful to review each here.

Swedish Industrial Democracy

Sweden's experiments with participation have had peculiar appeal to Americans.
It was this model which was emphasized in the HEW report on work organization,
cited earlier (Special Task Force, 1973). The Volvo efforts have often been cited
as prime examples of how participative management should work (*Economic and
Industrial Democracy*, 1980). Volvo has been a world leader in attempts to improve the quality of working life through a renewed emphasis on craftmanship.
This emphasis assumes a participative approach which gives the worker greater
control over his or her craft. In some Swedish industries industrial democracy is
taken quite far, abolishing the first two lines of supervision. Thus, in these factories,
workers may control their own work from receipt of orders to final inspection
and shipment. In addition, many Swedish firms allow worker representatives on
corporate boards in addition to the two required by law since 1972. In 1976 new
legislation guaranteed Swedish unions the right to bargain collectively for additional rights to participation in management decision-making. Currently there is a
movement to use worker pension plans or other funding to allow employees to
gain ownership control of Swedish enterprises. If allowed, this reform could place
most Swedish industry under worker ownership and ultimate control by the year
2000 (Thimm, 1979). The popularity of these proposals is in no small part rooted
in the successful performance of Swedish industrial democracy, a success which
has led to a higher standard of living than exists in the United States.

West German Codetermination

A joint labor-management administrative system called *mitbestimmung* (codetermination) was established in post-WWII West Germany as part of Allied efforts at denazification. Under this system near-parity labor-management representation was created on coal and steel industry boards in 1951. In 1952 this representation was extended to all industry, but with only one-third labor representation. An amendment a quarter-century later increased this to near-parity, as in coal and steel, effective by 1978. In addition to board representation, work councils were established throughout West German industry in the 1950's. These councils were given significant veto powers with regard to hours, shifts, rest periods, leave plans, pensions, regulation of piece work, and discipline. They also had co-decision powers with regard to shutdowns, mergers, relocations, basic technology changes and, since expansion of powers in 1972, to training programs, remuneration systems, and personnel surveys.

After their establishment, the codetermination reforms came to be seen as a major cause of West German prosperity. Chancellor Schmidt, for example, referred to codetermination as "that which has accounted for the competitive economic advantage we have enjoyed internationally thus far" (Raskin, 1976). When a delegation from Britain seeking solutions for the sluggish English economy visited West Germany, Schmidt told them that the key to his country's "post-war economic miracle was its sophisticated system of worker participation" (*The Economist*, 1976). Although critics have noted the tendency of codetermination structures to become bureaucratic over time, their continuation and expansion has been a strong priority of West German unions, which find codetermination a useful device (see Garson, ed., 1977). The savings of codetermination in terms of averted strikes and labor-management harmony is itself a powerful appeal to Britain, the United States, and other Western nations with comparatively high rates of labor unrest (on the European model, see Strauss, 1979; Bass, Shackleton, and Rosenstein, 1980; and Thimm, 1980).

Japanese Quality Circles

Quality circles, known in Japan as quality control circles, are the newest of the participatory models to attract strong American interest. Partly this interest is based on Japan's high productivity, which contrasts with America's chronic productivity problems. Perhaps interest in the Japanese model is also based on the fact that quality circles are a rather conservative type of participation, focusing on daily work processes rather than on management questions. The promise of dramatic gains in efficiency combined with the nonthreatening nature of the proposed reform makes the quality circle the most-discussed participatory innovation of the 1980's.

A quality circle is a group of about eight workers who meet during company time (but without extra pay) to discuss and make proposals concerning improvement of quality, improvement of cost reduction efforts, safety reforms, and similar on-the-job matters. Though participation is voluntary, the extremely strong corporate team ethos of Japanese culture assures that, when sanctioned by management, participation is high. One quarter of all Japanese hourly workers are members of some 100,000 quality circles in Japan (Yager, 1980). Participants receive limited training in problem-solving, communication, and leadership skills. Managers tend to see the quality circles as useful feedback devices which are a secondary but integral part of Japanese management process and one of the many determinants of Japan's productivity success.

Critics of the Japanese model argue that it is sold by American consulting firms as "salvation in a box" (Zemke, 1981). In fact, it is argued, quality circles are successful only when top management is committed. Harvard Business School Professor Robert Hayes investigated six Japanese companies, for instance, and found quality as high in companies without quality circles as those with. Other companies had suspended quality circles or otherwise assigned them only a nominal/symbolic role within the organization. What is often presented as "Theory Z," Japan's answer to Theory X or Theory Y, may be indistinguishable from the latter (see Cessaris, 1981; Theories X and Y were terms used by Douglas McGregor, 1980, to describe the scientific management and human relations orientations discussed in chapters 1 and 2). Semke (1981) reports, for example, that quality circles are now part of and used interchangeably with such Theory Y based movements as organization development and quality of work life efforts in the United States. Indeed, quality circles bear a striking resemblance to the long-practiced group approach to suggestion systems, such as the Scanlon Plan companies (see Moore and Ross, 1978), but without the direct rewards to the workers—and, so far, without as persuasive documented effect.

Israeli Kibbutzim

The Swedish, German, and Japanese models of participatory management are all private-sector based. While governmental organizations occasionally experiment with autonomous work groups like Sweden (e.g., Toronto's system for park maintenance crews), like Germany (e.g., teacher representation on numerous Office of Education boards), or like Japan (e.g., Wake County, N.C.'s quality circle program), such experiments are relatively rare. In no small part this is because of the obstacles to participation which are unique to *public* administration, discussed earlier. Indeed, these same obstacles have been effective in preventing large-scale spread of autonomous work groups in Swedish government, of codetermination in West German agencies, or even of quality circles in Japanese public administration. In contrast, the Israeli kibbutz and Yugoslavia's self-management systems represent models which have been applied extensively in public administration in their own countries. Both rest on political and cultural environments which are radically different from the American context.

The kibbutz sector of the Israeli economy is primarily agricultural, though it accounts for about 6 percent of Israeli industrial production as well. The kibbutz is a self-governing community operating on a communal, egalitarian basis. As such it provides a model of radical democracy in local government, including democratizations of associated work organizations. Worker assemblies in community-owned metal-working, plastics, woodworking, and other light industry decide on production and investment plans, work arrangements, choice of candidates for training, and nomination and election of certain officials. The worker assembly is not autonomous, however, since the kibbutz assembly (of which the workers are members, along with other kibbutz citizens) must approve the enterprise investment plan and elect the plant manager and management team. Management is characterized by a fully egalitarian pay structure, rotation of top management and line supervisors, settlement of grievances by general workers' meetings, and abolition of the distinction between public and private administration. Work norms dealing with shifts, breaks, meals, and so on, for example, are recommended by a factory board composed of top management of the enterprise, top management of the kibbutz, rank-and-file worker representatives, and a youth representative.

The kibbutz system represents a commitment to a radically egalitarian and communal system of governance integrating community and enterprise administration (Fine, 1973). Though it is associated with high productivity and growth, few if any American communities would find this model applicable. It is pertinent, however, to the rapidly proliferating instances of American communities collaborating with workers of a failing enterprise to rescue the local tax base through refinancing such firms under worker and community investments (see Conference on Alternative State and Local Public Policies, 1977). Such communities may find the Israeli model of enterprise representation and community representation an interesting one, even if the general model of egalitarian communalism is rejected (see Yodin, 1975).

Yugoslav Self-Management

Yugoslavia, also a country with a tradition of agrarian communal democracy, is a second and more important model of radical organizational democracy in both public and private sectors. Worker self-management of economic enterprises was introduced by law in Yugoslavia in 1950 and was central to the Constitutional Law of 1953, the Constitution of 1963, and the Workers' Amendment of 1971. These laws established a system in which workers' councils are formed to elect enterprise managers, vote on enterprise plans, oversee the grievance process, and carry on all aspects of the enterprise's business.

Evaluation of this model is complex (see Garson, 1974) but several observations are relatively uncontested: 1) most work organizations implement workers' councils, involving widespread participation (about half of eligible workers serve on the councils at one time or another—20 percent of the population); 2) the councils do exercise significant powers, including removal of enterprise heads; 3) the council system leads to a somewhat more egalitarian pay structure and to greater expenditures on social items (e.g., housing, recreation, health); 4) the councils are often bureaucratic, dominated by the manager, by technocrats, by the League of Communists, or the unions; 5) the council system has not prevented (but may have reduced) strikes and other work problems; and 6) the self-management system is at least a corollary and perhaps a cause of Yugoslavia's extremely high rate of growth and productivity during the postwar period. This last fact has made Yugoslavia a leading model for Third World countries seeking development models and ideas (see Abrahamsson, 1977).

From the 1950's through the early 1970's, self-management in the public sector followed a similar course, but with inclusion of community and interest representatives. For example, a public school would be governed by a workers' council which would elect the principal (an administrative head) and a pedagogue (an academic head) as well as decide on other matters. But the council would also include representation from the school's maintenance staff, from the secretarial staff, from parents, and from the community. Likewise a public hospital would be governed by a workers' council, but would include community and interest representation. In addition, public-sector workers' councils, like all workers' councils, must operate within the laws and constraints laid down by communal, republic, and national governmental bodies.

By the 1970's Yugoslav leadership had become aware of numerous problems, the most pressing being the tendency of work organization workers' assemblies to operate autonomously from communal assemblies, to be too centralized and bureaucratic, and to lack decision-making discretion due to the indebtedness of enterprises to (and hence decision-making subservience to) banking institutions. The last problem is in some ways the most difficult and is only now being addressed (see Vlaskalic, 1981). The other two, however, were addressed in major reforms introduced in the Constitution of 1974 and the Law on Associated Labor of 1976.

This legislation sought to accomplish two objectives: 1) to radically decentralize decision-making powers to smaller units within public and private organizations, units called basic organizations of associated labor (BOAL's); and 2) to merge workers' representatives and communal representatives in new "delegate assemblies" reminiscent of the Israeli model. While it is still too early to assess these reforms, the current direction of Yugoslav leadership is to extend and strengthen the BOAL's and the delegate assemblies, particularly the latter (*Socialist Thought and Practice*, 1981). During the last elections some two and a half million Yugoslavs were elected members of delegations, representing BOAL's and worker councils, committees, self-management interest groups, and sociopolitical organizations. The delegations are increasingly called on to heighten their role in decision-making pertinent to distribution of that portion of the enterprise surplus dedicated to social purposes. At the same time, during the last decade Yugoslavia's self-managed economy has increased the per-capita social product by 50 percent and raised living standards by two thirds—in sharp contrast to the relative inertia or even stagnation of many hierarchically-organized Western economies. This performance alone assures continued world-wide interest in the Yugoslav system.

Summary

Comparative models of participatory management range from the mild reforms of Japanese quality circles to the radical egalitarianism of Israeli kibbutz assemblies. Each of the five countries cited has taken its own unique approach to participatory management. Each is a political economic system with an exceptional productivity record. Each cites participation as the critical element of its success. It is these "mega-experiments" rather than the studies of particular organizations so emphasized in organization theory literature which have given the greatest impetus to the movement for participatory approaches to management.

In seeking to apply comparative experience to American public administration, the manager faces a dilemma. The reforms which are easiest to adapt (e.g., quality circles) may be the least effective. On the other hand, more extensive reforms presuppose rather radical changes in political processes which are beyond the discretion of the manager. Nonetheless, each of the five models has elements which are reflected in participatory reforms undertaken by public organizations in America: autonomous work groups as in the Social Security Administration's experiments with modularization (McKenna, 1977); the Metropolitan Atlanta Rapid Transit Authority's experiments with team decision-making (Golembiewski, 1977). the quality circles experiments of the Norfolk Naval Shipyard and settings reported in the *Quality Circles Journal*; joint administration-teacher-community decision-making in educational settings (see Ends and Mullen, 1973); or San Francisco's contracting of sanitation functions to worker self-managed enterprises (Young, 1972).

AMERICAN MODELS OF PARTICIPATION IN PUBLIC MANAGEMENT

While one can cite instances of public-sector participatory approaches such as those above, most American models of participation in management come from the private sector. Business-sector examples cover a full range of models (see Table 7). These range from profit-sharing plans, in which participation is only nominal, to medium-participation modes like job enrichment, to high-participation models like experiments in work group autonomy.

When the 1973 Special Task Force to HEW reported on work organization, nearly all the models surveyed were from the private sector (see Special Task Force,

TABLE 7.

Degrees of Participatory Intervention in Management

	Profit Sharing
	Suggestion Systems
	Job Enlargement
More Participation ↓	Job Enrichment
	Co-Decision-Making
	Work Group Autonomy
	Self-Management

1973). These included profit sharing at Donnelly Mirrors of Holland, Michigan, under which workers determine their annual salaries and receive productivity bonuses which, to be paid, require workers to find new, more productive work systems. Also surveyed was the suggestion system at J. P. Hood and Sons of Boston, under which a cash award system for suggestions led to numerous worker-supervisor teamwork efforts. Job enlargement was exemplified by P. P. G. Industries of Lexington, N.C., where one job category was abolished so workers in another job category could do both functions, thereby broadening their jobs. Job enrichment was illustrated by an experiment at Monsanto Chemical of Pensacola, Florida, where employee task forces were established to restructure certain jobs. Codecision-making was illustrated at Kaiser Aluminum Corporation of Ravenswood, W.Va., where the time clocks were removed, supervision virtually eliminated, and workers were freed to decide what maintenance jobs needed to be done and in what priority. Work group autonomy was exemplified by the Pet Foods Division of General Foods, Topeka, Kansas. Here workers were organized into autonomous work groups each responsible for a production process, with pay based on the number of jobs an employee trained himself to perform. Finally, the Special Task Force cited certain Yugoslav firms as examples of self-management models. In each case the HEW report concluded that participation had led to higher morale and usually increased productivity as well.

Do the considerations which led some private-sector organizations to adopt participatory methods also apply in the public sector? For example, many of the oldest and most successful participatory experiments in America are associated with the cooperative movement (cf. Berman, 1967; Brower, 1976). Laudable as this movement is, it is difficult to imagine public agencies operating on the worker ownership and profit-sharing assumptions of the cooperative model. Likewise, many private-sector experiments in worker participation have originated in companies which had been failing and were rescued by an injection of union and public funds which entailed heightened levels of participation of workers and/or citizens in management, as at the Rath Packing Company of Waterloo, Iowa (Newsweek, 1981). Many Scanlon Plan participation efforts likewise started when companies, faced by financial problems, adopted participative management as a productivity resort (Moore and Ross, 1978). This, too, is not a likely scenario for the public manager.

When the private sector manager thinks of participation, what comes to mind is employee participation, not customer participation in management. In contrast, the public sector manager quickly thinks of citizen participation but finds the idea of worker participation more problematic for reasons outlined at the start of this chapter. Citizen participation is a long-established aspect of public administration. It is a familiar model rooted in the pioneering work of the TVA and the Agricultural Department in the Depression era (see Lilienthal, 1944). Citizen participation was institutionalized in the Administrative Procedures Act of 1946 (e.g., the hearings requirement). During the social turmoil of the 1960's it became a popular cause (cf. Waldo, 1968). Although the popularity of citizen participation is now mitigated with a greater appreciation of its frustrations and problems (cf. Moynihan, 1969; Aron, 1979), it is now a well-established part of the repertoire of skills and orientations of modern public managers, particularly in forms allowing for systematic feedback on citizens' reactions to public policies (cf. Stipak, 1980; Fitzgerald and Durant, 1980; Gormley, 1981).

The legitimacy of the citizens' participation model in public administration does not transfer easily to the concept of employees' participation. As discussed at the outset, the ethos of representative democracy confers the right of access and participation on citizens but not on public employees. Moreover, the citizen participation models most in use, such as citizen survey feedback, are not models of direct face-to-face democratization and do not challenge managerial decision-making prerogatives to the extent employee participation seems to threaten.

In spite of obstacles, however, participatory models of public administration do exist in the United States. Organization development, an approach to agency change which typically involves participative goal-setting efforts, is becoming increasingly common (see Golembiewski, ed., 1980). Often public sector illustrations fall on the low end of the participation spectrum represented in Table 7, as, for example, the ubiquitous suggestion system schemes. Somewhat more advanced are the quality-of-work-life efforts such as that at the World Bank (Simmons, 1980), in which staff participate in group meetings which set objectives and outline critical next steps.

A more formal arrangement is the increasingly popular labor-management committee in which representatives of management and usually organized employees meet regularly to achieve common goals. Goals typically include 1) improving labor relations; 2) improving quality of working life; 3) improving productivity; 4) giving employees a say over workplace issues; 5) dealing with personnel issues; and 6) promoting harmony between employee groups. (Clark, 1980.) A particularly successful labor-management committee experience has been reported in New York City's Department of Sanitation, Bureau of Motor Equipment. (Contino and Lorusso, 1982.) Other successful experiments in participative group decision-making regarding work planning and process have been reported for welfare agencies (Davis, 1979) and for public schools (Duke, Showers, and Imber, 1980). Experiments in the public sector include not only participation of bank officials, social workers, or teachers, but of blue collar government workers as well, as in the Ohio Department of Highways (Powell and Schlacter, 1971). Nonetheless, on balance the student of organizations would have to conclude that these experiments, while largely successful in terms of productivity improvement, are less common in the public sector than the private. This raises the question of what contingencies in the public sector most favor successful experimentation in participatory management.

CONTINGENCIES OF PARTICIPATION

Successful implementation of participatory management depends on three types of contingencies: structure, orientation, and process. That is, the probability of success will increase if the agency displays certain favorable characteristics in terms of the way it is organizationally structured, in terms of the orientation of its managers and employees, and in terms of the actual participatory process and related decision-making processes to be implemented. Each of these three types of contingencies may be discussed in turn.

Structure

The most obvious of the structural variables is size. Smaller agencies typically are more successful in implementing participatory management (Abrahammson, 1977). In smaller units face-to-face contact is more feasible, relationships are more personal, decision-making can be more immediately responsible, and coordination is easier. Correspondingly, in large units participation must be more structured and remote, though a "linking-pin" chain of small groups (c.f. the quality circles) at each ascending organizational level is an approach to this obstacle. In the public sector, however, large departments have rarely implemented such complex link-pin chains of participative groups. On the contrary, the general trend seems to be toward centralization of executive command at the level of the department head and his or her policy planning staff. Moreover, as in large businesses with standard personnel policies, the civil service system in government tends to institutionalize a large-scale, centralized structure which is not favorable to participation (see Driscoll, 1979).

Technology and work process also affect the nature of organizational participation. As Loveridge (1980) has pointed out, this includes four major contingencies. First, participation is favored when the work process brings people together in face-to-face units rather than disperses them (as some service delivery agencies do). Second, participation is favored when the internal power structure of the organization is not autocratic (in this aspect civil service protections of employees reduce autocratic power and create needs for cooperation, cooptation, or participation). Third, participation is favored to the extent that work flow is not dictated by urgent deadlines for goods or services developed to specifications set by others (thus education provides a more favorable environment than does the Postal Service). Fourth, participation is favored when the work process can be disaggregated without needs for compensating by a burdensome coordination process. For example, oil refineries in the private sector and internal revenue agencies in the public sector illustrate units unfavorable to participation because in each, task elements are highly systematized and constrained—by technological parameters in the former case and by legal systems in the latter.

Orientation

Favorable structure is not enough for participatory management to succeed. The agency's members must be oriented in a favorable direction as well. This highlights the fact that participation is not merely a rational management tool—it is also social process. Like all social processes its outcomes are very much dependent on the prior attitudes of the participants. Here the public sector differs from the private. Various surveys of government and business have shown that public and private sector workers perceive and evaluate their jobs in substantially different ways (Smith and Nock, 1980). In particular, blue collar government employees are more satisfied than their private sector counterparts, but white collar public employees are less positive about social aspects of their work and about intrinsic job aspects. White collar government employees, therefore, may be more motivated toward participatory management than their colleagues in the business world.

Many other orientations and predispositions have been shown to affect the success of participatory management:

- managerial support: like nearly all organizational change efforts, participation typically requires top-level support
- managerial style: managerial style should be participative; not all managers can effect this style and some are threatened by participation
- participants should not be highly authoritarian nor low in need for independence
- subordinates must display toleration toward ambiguity, identify with organizational goals, and wish to share in decision-making

In addition to findings such as these (see Tannenbaum and Schmidt, 1973; Steers, 1975; Vroom, 1960; French, Key and Meyer, 1966), other studies tend to confirm that participation is not favored when employees are off-the-job-oriented (Hulin and Blood, 1968). Also, numerous studies show a nonparticipative, even threatening management climate can be more motivating to some employees than is democratic management (e.g., Dorsett, Latham, and Mitchell, 1979).

Process

As with structure, so favorable orientations do not assure success of participatory management. The third critical set of contingencies concerns the decision-making process itself. Sometimes obvious organizational process requirements, such as secrecy, virtually preclude participation in decision-making. Given the increase in privacy legislation and the sensitivity of government agencies to it, this in itself can be a serious obstacle. Participation is favored when the process is not reducible to rational problems best solved by experts, when task ambiguity is neither so great as to prevent consensus not so low as to obviate the need for discussion, and when path-goal clarity is present (see Evans, 1970, 1974; House and Mitchell, 1974; Vroom and Yetton, 1973). Path-goal clarity means that management has provided valued rewards for participation (on the importance of rewards, see Neider, 1980), when performance is seen as leading to rewards (Vroom, 1960), and when effort is perceived to lead to performance (on the importance of challenging yet reachable goals, see Latham and Locke, 1979).

A survey of world-wide participation models by Bernstein (1976) has led to six process-related prerequisites being identified for organizational democratization: 1) participation in decision-making (lesser forms of participation, like suggestion systems and profit sharing, tend to ossify or become viewed as manipulative); 2) frequent feedback on results (employees need to know the investment of energy is having an effect); 3) full sharing by the participants of managerial information needed for decision-making (refusal to share information quickly becomes confrontative and sabotages participatory management); 4) guaranteed individual rights (the power of the participatory decision-making group should be clearly circumscribed at the outset); 5) independent appeal in cases of disputes (the decision-making group should not simultaneously serve an adjudicative function, since this leads to conflicts of interest; and 6) presence of democratic predispositions, as discussed above. Although drawn from national examples of participatory management (the "mega-experiments" outlined in a previous section), Bernstein's conclusions seem to be generalizations which would apply to American public administration as well.

In summary, participatory management is contingent on a large host of factors. No one factor is determinant. Technology, for example, even of the assembly-line type, does not absolutely preclude a participatory approach. The manager is faced with a wide variety of options and the challenge of administering a complex sociotechnical process with structural, attitudinal, and process variables. How does the manager organize for participatory interventions in the agency given this complexity?

PARTICIPATION AND MANAGEMENT PLANNING

If the manager has examined the contingencies of participation and has concluded that prospects warrant establishment of a participatory program, many obstacles immediately become apparent. Introduction of a participatory management effort is time consuming and, often, threatening to management. This particularly likely to be so of lower-middle management since participatory schemes often involve devolution of the powers of this class of managers onto the employees themselves. Even higher management is often not sympathetic to participation (see Haire, Ghiselli, and Porter, 1966). Among employees, too, some individuals will not respond, others will seek to use participatory forums to set unchallenging goals, or to work for objectives different from those of the organization. The result can be demoralization and productivity decline rather than the intended effect.

On the positive side, the manager can usually count on participation increasing employee satisfaction and, if not directly leading to higher productivity, at least helping to reduce turnover and absenteeism. Participation has strong tendencies to mobilize group enforcement of norms. In a democratic society, norms in agency settings are apt to be democratic even when prior practice has been autocratic. Participation tends to bring latent democratic norms to the forefront and to lead to resocialization of employees and management. Participation also increases the flow of information, providing better performance feedback for employees and greater ultimate capacity for higher management to understand and influence the sociotechnical processes of the agency.

Public administrationists have seen both the obstacles and the promises of participation in management. Nearly a decade ago Dwight Waldo, then editor of the *Public Administration Review*, forecast two possible alternatives for American bureaucracy—one hierarchic, based on the imperatives of technology, and the other democratic, based on social needs for participation (Waldo, 1974). The democratic path, which he favored, was an eclectic one. It encompassed such concepts as collegial decision-making, flexible organizational structures, the mixing of public and private sectors, and emphasis on the manager's role as a coordinator of fluid agency subsystems.

The democratic alternative for public administration was much emphasized in the late 1960's and early 1970's. In this period Frederick Mosher, another former editor of the *Public Administration Review*, wrote, "Over the past three decades there has been a substantial movement in the direction of bringing into the managerial processes and decisions of large organizations the ideals and techniques of democracy through greater participation by the officers and employees themselves in reaching organizational decisions (Mosher, 1968). Mosher went on to list many of the developments cited by Waldo, including the rise of organizational development, management by objectives, and decentralization as well as direct participation in decision-making. These and other calls for democratization in the public sector (see Smith, 1969; Waldo, 1969; Pateman, 1970; Berkley, 1971; Marini, 1971) have now, a decade later, receded in intensity.

In the 1980's, faced with cutback management forced by economic retrenchment, it is hardly surprising that participation has lost some of its appeal. There are several reasons why participation figures less prominently in management planning under austerity than it does under conditions of growth. These reasons have to do with changes in the structural, attitudinal, and process contingencies of participation discussed above.

Structurally, retrenchment conditions are centralizing. Austerity emphasizes control functions residing in the overhead agencies of personnel and budget (in contrast, growth conditions emphasize the more decentralized structures of program delivery). Austerity also transforms the internal bureaucratic struggle over resources into more of a zero-sum game and this, too, tends to force decision-making to structurally higher levels less favorable to participatory management. *Attitudinally*, there is less employee effective demand for participation. Job security issues become paramount and, in Maslow's terms, austerity pushes the workforce back down the needs hierarchy of value concerns, away from self-actualization and participation. Most important, in terms of *process*, conditions of retrenchment undermine path-goal relationships crucial to the success of participatory management. The decline in availability of rewards weakens both the performance-reward and the effort-performance linkages necessary to motivation in path-goal terms. Not only does the employee become uncertain or even skeptical that adequate rewards exist to be allocated for performance under productivity-related participation plans, but also cutbacks often determine the translation of effort into performance. That is, retrenchment frequently means the employee will have fewer organizational resources to deal with agency service demands which are changing and often intensified by an adverse economic environment. The undermining of these linkages means that the path-goal relationships necessary for motivation are weakened.

Participation efforts in particular suffer because of this change in process contingencies because participation innovations must prove their merit through reinforcement of the participants. Research clearly suggests reward and other path-goal linkages must be operative for successful implementation of participation plans (cf. Neider, 1980; Lawler, 1974). In fact, even prior to introducing a participation effort management should seek to anticipate types of decision outcomes. Planning of this type enables management to identify possible positive responses to participatively-set decisions. The object is not to predetermine outcomes and manipulate participation but rather the manager seeks to have in ready abeyance at least some positive changes which can be implemented quickly as reinforcements for change.

If participation is started with fanfare and then management is too immobilized to respond to the process, the critical formative employee attitudes toward the participation plan are apt to be ones of frustration and cynicism. All participatory plans raise expectations of change. To plan for participation but not for change is to puncture rising expectations. The frustration of raised expectations routinely leads to such negative organizational behaviors as withdrawal, turnover, resistance, aggression, and even sabotage (cf. Buss, 1961; Dollard, 1964; Gurr, 1968).

It is better for management to avoid participative interventions altogether than to fail to plan early responsiveness to the change forces such efforts set in motion.

The many other aspects of management planning for participation include such factors as planning orientation sessions for top management to foster participative concepts; scheduling of participation meetings during agency time; planning of feedback mechanisms on participation processes; planning integration of the participative process with the reward system; the training system, and the information system; and establishment of review and evaluation procedures for the experiment (see also Bourdon, 1980).

The core of managerial planning for participation, however, remains not the mechanics but rather the establishment and maintenance of path-goal linkages on which the entire effort must rest. It is in this pivotal aspect that the most carefully managed efforts in participatory management are closely integrated with career planning and development for the individual employee. Ultimately each employee must see the relationship among the many elements of a participative management system: training and management development, performance and its appraisal, group decision-making and feedback, and rewards and career advancement. Tying together all the complex elements of a shift toward participation in an agency requires managers to have a firm understanding of the nature of organizational change, a topic to which we turn in the next chapter.

REFERENCES

Abrahamsson, Bengt (1977). *Bureaucracy or Participation: The Logic of Organization* (Beverly Hills, CA: Sage).

Adizes, Ichak and E. M. Borgese, eds. (1975). *Self-Management: New Dimensions to Democracy* (Santa Barbara, CA: ABC-Clio).

Barabba, Vincent P. (1980). Demographic Change and the Public Work Force, paper, Second Public Management Research Conference, Brookings Institution, November, 1980.

Bass, Bernard M., V. J. Shackleton, and E. Rosenstein (1979). "Industrial Democracy and Participative Management: What's the Difference?", *International Review of Applied Psychology*, Vol. 28, No. 2 (Oct.):pp. 81-92.

Bellone, Carl J. (1980). *Organization Theory and the New Public Administration* (Boston: Allyn and Bacon).

Berkley, George (1971). *The Administrative Revolution* (Englewood Cliffs, N.J.: Prentice-Hall).

_____(1981). *The Craft of Public Administration*. 4th ed. (Boston: Allyn and Bacon).

Berman, Katrina (1967). *Worker-Owned Plywood Companies* (Pullman, Wash.: Washington State University Press).

Bernstein, Paul (1976). *Workplace Democratization: Its Internal Dynamics* (Kent, Ohio: Kent State University Press).

Blauner, Robert (1964). *Alienation and Freedom* (Chicago: University of Chicago Press).

Bourdon, Roger D. (1980). A Basic Model for Employee Participation, *Training and Development Journal*, Vol. 34, No. 4 (April, 1980):pp. 24-29.

Brower, Michael (1976). Experience with Self-Management and Participation in United States Industry, in Garson and Smith, eds. (1976):pp. 73-92.

Buss, A. (1961). *The Psychology of Aggression*. (N.Y.: Wiley).

Campbell, Alan K. (1978). Revitalizing the Civil Service, *National Civic Review*, Vol. 67, No. 2.

Cessaris, Ann C. (1981). A Soft Approach to Human Relations, *Training*, Vol. 18, No. 10 (Oct.):p. 64.

Clark, Susan G. (1980). Executive Report on A Guide to Labor-Management Committees in State and Local Government. U.S. Department of HUD and U.S. O.P.M. under contract NP-7ACO19.

Clayton, Ross (1980). Technology and Values: Implications for Administrative Practice, in C. J. Bellone, ed. (1980): ch. 4.

Conference on Alternative State and Local Public Policies (1977). *New Directions in State and Local Public Policy* (Washington: Conference on Alternative States and Local Public Policies).

Contino, Ronald and Robert M. Lorusso (1982). The Theory Z Turnaround of a Public Agency. *Public Administration Review* (January/February):pp. 66-71.

Curtis, Donald A. (1980). Management in the Public Sector: It Really Is Harder. *Management Review*, Vol. 69, No. 10 (Oct.):pp. 70-74.

Davis, L. E. and E. L. Trist (1972). Improving the Quality of Work Life: the Sociotechnical Approach, (Philadelphia: University of Pennsylvania Management and Behavioral Science Center).

Davis, T. R. V. (1979). OD in the Public Sector: Intervening in Ambiguous Performance Environments, *Group and Organization Studies*, Vol. 4, No. 3 (Sept.):pp. 352-365.

Dolanc, Stane (1981). An Instrument of Working Class Rule, *Socialist Thought and Practice*, Vol. 21, Nos. 6-7 (June-July):pp. 50-69.

Dollard, John et al. (1964). *Frustration and Aggression* (New Haven: Yale).

Dorsett, Dennis L., G. P. Latham and T. R. Mitchell (1979). Effects of Assigned versus Participatively Set Goals, Knowledge of Results, and Individual Differences in Employee Behavior When Goal Difficulty is Held Constant, *Journal of Applied Psychology*, Vol. 64, No. 3 (June):pp. 291-298.

Driscoll, James W. (1979). Working Creatively with a Union: Lessons from the Scanlon Plan. *Organizational Dynamics*, Vol. 8, No. 1 (Summer):pp. 61-80.

Duke, D., B. K. Showers, and M. Imber (1980). Teachers and Shared Decision-Making, *Education Administration Quarterly*, Vol. 16, No. 1:pp. 93-106.

Scandinavian and Swedish Work Research: A Symposium, Economic and Industrial Democracy, Vol. 1, No. 2 (May).

The Economist (1976). The Germans Know How, Sept. 4, p. 80.

Emery, F. and E. L. Trist (1959). Sociotechnical System, paper, Institute of Management Sciences, annual meeting, Paris.

Ends, A. Walden and D. J. Mullen (1973). Organization Development in a Public School Setting. pp. 226-247 in J. J. Partin, ed. (1973).

Evans, M. G. (1970). The Effects of Supervisory Behavior on the Path-Goal Relationship, *Organizational Behavior and Human Performance*, Vol. 5, (May): pp. 277-298.

_____(1974). Effects of Supervisory Behaviors on Extension of the Path-Goal Theory of Motivation, *Journal of Applied Psychology*, Vol. 59 (April):pp. 172-178.

Fiedler, Fred E. (1967). *A Theory of Leadership Effectiveness*. (N.Y.: McGraw-Hill).

Fine, Keitha S. (1973). Worker Participation in Israel, pp. 226-267 in G. Hunnius, G. D. Garson, and J. Case, eds. (1973).

Fitzgerald, Michael R. and R. F. Durant (1980). Citizen Evaluations and Urban Management: Service Delivery in an Era of Protest, *Public Administration Review*, Vol. 40, No. 6 (Nov./Dec.):pp. 385-394.

Fottler, Myron D. (1981). Is Management Really Generic? *The Academy of Management Review*, Vol. 6, No. 1 (Jan.):pp. 1-13.

French, J. R., E. Kay, and H. H. Meyer (1966). Participation and the Appraisal System, *Human Relations*, Vol. 19:pp. 3-19.

Garson, G. David (1974). *On Democratic Administration and Socialist Self-Management: A Comparative Survey Emphasizing Yugoslavia* (Beverly Hills, CA: Sage).

_____(1976). *Political Science Methods* (Boston: Holbrook).

_____ed. (1977). *Worker Self-Management in Industry: The West European Experience* (N.Y.: Praeger).

_____and M. P. Smith, eds. (1976). *Organizational Democracy* (Beverly Hills, CA.: Sage Publications).

Golembiewski, Robert T., ed. (1980). Symposium on Perspectives on Public Sector OD. *Southern Review of Public Administration*, Vol. 4, No. 2 (Sept.).

Gormley, William T. (1981). Statewide Remedies for Public Underrepresentation in Regulatory Proceedings, *Public Administration Review*, Vol. 41, No. 4 (July/Aug.):pp. 454-462.

Greene, Charles N. (1972). The Satisfaction-Performance Controversy, in K. O. Magnusen, ed. (1977), *Organizational Development Design and Behavior* (Glenview, DE: Scott, Foresman):pp. 166-179.

Gurr, Ted (1968). Psychological Factors in Civil Violence. *World Politics*, Vol. 20 (Jan.):pp. 245-278.

Haire, M., E. Ghiselli, and L. Porter (1966). *Managerial Thinking* (N.Y.: Wiley).

House, Robert J. and T. R. Mitchell (1974). Path-Goal Theory of Leadership, *Journal of Contemporary Business* (Autumn):pp. 124-138.

Hulin, C. L. and M. R. Blood (1968). Job Enlargement, Individual Differences and Worker Response, *Psychological Bulletin*, Vol. 69.

Hunnius, Gerry, G. D. Garson, and John Case, eds. (1973). *Workers' Control* (N.Y.: Random House).

Latham, Gary P. and E. A. Locke (1979). Goal-Setting: A Motivational Technique That Works. *Organizational Dynamics*, Vol. 8, No. 2 (Autumn):pp. 68-80.

Lawler, E. E. III (1974). For a More Effective Organization, Match the Job to the Man, *Organizational Dynamics*, Vol. 3, No. 1 (Summer):pp. 21, 22.

Lewin, Kurt (1947). Frontiers in Group Dynamics: Concept, Method and Reality in Social Science, *Human Relations*, Vol. 1:pp. 5-42.

Lilienthal, David E. (1944). *TVA: Democracy on the March* (N.Y.: Harper and Row).

Loveridge, Ray (1980). What is Participation?: A Review of the Literature and Some Methodological Problems, *British Journal of Industrial Relations*, Vol. 18, No. 3 (Nov.):pp. 297-317.

Magnusen, Karl O. (1977). *Organization Design, Development, and Behavior: A Situational View* (Glenview, IL: Scott, Foresman).

Marini, Frank, ed. (1971). *Toward a New Public Administration: The Minnow-brook Perspective* (Scranton, PA: Chandler).

McGregor, Douglas. *Human Side of Enterprise*, (N.Y.: McGraw-Hill, 1960).

McKenna, H. F. (1977). Managing Change in Government. *Civil Service Journal*, Vol. 17, No. 4 (April-June):pp. 1-9.

Moore, Brian E. and T. L. Ross (1978). *The Scanlon Way to Improved Productivity* (N.Y.: Wiley-Interscience).

Mosher, Frederick (1968). *Democracy and the Public Service* (N.Y.: Oxford).

Moynihan, Daniel P. (1969). *Maximum Feasible Misunderstanding* (N.Y.: Free Press).

Neider, Linda L. (1980). An Experimental Field Investigation Utilizing an Expectancy View of Participation, *Organizational Behavior and Human Performance*, Vol. 26, No. 3 (Dec.):pp. 425-442.

Newsweek (1981). When Employees Take Over, *Newsweek*, 1 June: 74.

Parsons, Talcott (1965). Suggestions for a Sociological Approach to Organizations, *Administrative Science Quarterly*, Vol. 1.

Partin, J. J., ed. (1973). *Current Perspectives in Organization Development* (Reading, MA: Addison-Wesley).

Pateman, Carole (1970). *Participation and Democratic Theory* (London: Cambridge University Press).

Perrow, Charles (1967). A Framework for Comparative Analysis of Organizations, *American Sociological Review*, Vol. 32, No. 2 (April):pp. 194-208.

Powell, Reed M. and J. L. Schlacter (1971). Participative Management: A Panacea? *Academy of Management Journal*, June 1971, pp. 165-173.

Professional Standards and Ethics Committee (1979). *Professional Standards and Ethics: A Workbook for Public Administrators* (Washington, D.C.: American Society for Public Administration).

Raskin, A. H. (1976). The Workers' Voice in German Companies. *World of Work Report*, Vol. 1, No. 5 (July).

Reuter, Vincent G. (1977). Suggestion Systems: Utilization, Evaluation and Implementation, *California Management Review*, Vol. 19 (Spring):pp. 78-89.

Rhenman, Eric (1964). *Industrial Democracy and Industrial Management* (London: Tavistock, 1968).

Simmons, John (1980). Participative Management at the World Bank. *Training and Development Journal.* Vol. 34, No. 3 (March):pp. 50-54.

Smith, Michael P. (1969). Self-Fulfillment in a Bureaucratic Society. *Public Administration Review*, Vol. 29, No. 1 (Jan./Feb.): 30.

_____and S. L. Nock (1980). Social Class and the Quality of Work Life in Public and Private Organizations. *Journal of Social Issues*, Vol. 36, No. 4:pp. 59-75.

Socialist Thought and Practice (1981). Third Congress of Self-Managers of Yugoslavia: Symposium Issue, Vol. 21, Nos. 6-7 (June/July).

Special Task Force to the Secretary of HEW (1973). *Work in America* (Cambridge, MA: MIT Press).

Steers, R. M. (1975). Task-Goal Attributes, n-Achievement, and Supervisory Performance, *Organizational Behavior and Human Performance*, Vol. 13:pp. 392-403.

Stipak, Brian (1980). Local Governments' Use of Citizen Surveys. *Public Administration Review*, Vol. 40, No. 5 (Sept./Oct.):pp. 521-525.

Stokes, Donald (1981). Mellon Project Report, paper, National Association of Schools of Public Affairs and Administration, annual meeting, Lexington, KY, Oct., 1981.

Strauss, George (1979). Workers' Participation: Symposium Introduction. *Industrial Relations*, Vol. 18, No. 3 (Fall):pp. 247-261.

Susman, Gerald I. (1976). *Autonomy at Work: A Sociotechnical Analysis of Participative Management* (N.Y.: Praeger).

Tannenbaum, Robert and W. Schmidt (1973). How to Choose a Leadership Pattern. *Harvard Business Review* (May/June):pp. 162-180.

Taylor, James C. (1971). Some Effects of Technology on Organizational Change. *Human Relations*, Vol. 24.

Thimm, Alfred L. (1979). Union-Management 'Codetermination' in Sweden. *Journal of Social and Political Studies*, Vol. 4, No. 2 (Summer):pp. 147-173.

Thimm, Alfred L. (1980). The False Promise of Employee Codetermination. *Business and Society Review*, No. 32 (Winter, 1979-80):pp. 36-41.

Trist, L. and K. W. Bamforth (1951). Some Social and Psychological Consequences of the Longwall Method of Goal-Setting, *Human Relations*, Vol. 4:pp. 1-38.

U.S. News and World Report (1980). Profile of Federal Workers. August 4.

U.S.O.P.M. *News* (1979). OPM Releases Attitude Survey Results, *USOPM News*, Nov. 9, 1979 (entire issue).

U.S. Office of Personnel Management (1980). *Occupational Federal White Collar Workers* (Washington, D.C.: OPM, annual).

Vlaskalic, Tihomir (1981). A Key Link in the Spreading of Self-Management Practice. *Socialist Thought and Practice*, Vol. 21, Nos. 6, 7 (June/July):pp. 39-49.

Vroom, Victor (1960). *Some Personality Determinants of the Effects of Participation* (Englewood Cliffs, N.J.: Prentice-Hall).

_____(1964). *Work and Motivation* (N.Y.: Wiley).

_____and P. W. Yetton (1973). *Leadership and Decision-Making* (Pittsburgh: University of Pittsburgh Press).

Waldo, Dwight, ed. (1969). A Sumposium. *Public Administration Review*, Vol. 29, No. 1 (Jan./Feb.).

_____(1963). Public Administration in a Time of Revolution. *Public Administration Review*, Vol. 28, No. 4 (July/Aug.):pp. 362-368.

_____(1974) Reflections of Public Morality. *Administration and Society*, Vol. 6, No. 3 (Nov.):p. 277.

Whorton, Joseph W. and J. A. Worthley (1981). A Perspective on the Challenge of Public Management: Environmental Paradox and Organizational Culture, *The Academy of Management Review*, Vol. 6, No. 3 (July):pp. 357-362.

Yager, Ed. (1980). The Circle—A Tool for the 1980's, *Training and Development Journal*, Vol. 34, No. 8 (August):pp. 60-63.

Young, Dennis (1972). *How Shall We Collect the Garbage?* (Washington: Urban Institute).

Yudin, Yehuda (1975). Industrial Democracy as a Component in Social Change: The Israeli Approach and Experience, ch. 6 in Adizes and Borgese, eds. (1975).

Zemke, Ron (1981). What's Good for Japan Might Not Work for You, *Training*, Vol. 18, No. 10 (Oct.):pp. 62-65.

ORGANIZATIONAL CHANGE

Organizational change refers to any significant alteration of the behavior pattern of a large number of the individuals who constitute an organization (Dalton, 1978). But to understand the nature of organizational change managers need to look beyond human factors alone. (O'Toole, 1979.) Organizational culture and climate, as well as structure, technology and environment will all be represented in models guiding managers who successfully produce change. This chapter outlines the critical elements of this person-organization interface and proposes strategies which managers can employ to effect change within an organization. We proceed by defining each of the factors relevant to organizational change and then consider the actual change process, the type of organizational learning involved and the strategies managers may adopt to help organizations change.

ORGANIZATIONAL CULTURE

The culture of an organization is that set of beliefs and expectations shared by organization members which produce norms that shape behavior. Behavior takes the form of styles of action which typically reflect responses that have proven successful in the past. (Schwartz and Davis, 1981.) The culture of an organization binds it together and differentiates it from other groups. At the macro level, we can identify the broad outlines of the dominant organizational culture that public managers share.

The culture of public management is based on a set of values, referred to by Gerald Caiden as our "ideology of public service." The core of these values can be summarized in 7 points.

1. Public administration is a machine for the implementation of the general will, as conceived by the representatives of the people. Government is public trust to be used in the general interest and not for the benefit of a particular sectional interest.
2. Public officials are servants of the public, not vice versa.
3. Civil officials should be the embodiment of all public virtues - they should be hardworking, honest, impartial, wise, sincere, just, and trustworthy. Official conduct should be beyond reproach.
4. Public officials should obey their superior and subordinate their personal interests, unless objection is based on conscientious grounds whereupon they should leave public office before publicly declaring their opposition to governmental policy.
5. Civil servants should perform their duties efficiently and economically.
6. Appointment to public office should be on the basis of merit of person and not on the privilege of class.
7. Public officials should be subjected to the law in the same way as other people. (Caiden, 1981.)

Beyond these generalizations, differences among the cultures of agencies may exist. Differences might take the form of degree of stress given to these general values, or emerge as values represented in some agencies and absent in others. For example, a manager in the state auditor's office may adhere strictly to the rules and regulations for expenditure of public monies; while the managers of a program for severely handicapped children might have a flexible interpretation of expenditure rules because inclusion of children in the program is their first concern. The culture of each organization distinguishes the values of the handicapped-services agency from those of the auditor's office. These differences in culture stem from the task or technology of each agency and the environment within which each operates—factors we discuss at length in a later section of this chapter.

Organizational culture does not always contribute to agency effectiveness. Elements of some organizational cultures may be dysfunctional in the long run as we can illustrate through our handicapped-services program example. While it may be understandable that program managers adhere to the norm of rule flexibility in determining eligibility, if this value is given free rein program clientele might multiply to the point that the most severely handicapped clients may be neglected because of case overload.

The dominant culture of public sector management is not monolithic. It has evolved through the years and is changing today. However, cultural change is never easy. One aspect of public management culture undergoing change today is the dicta which governs agency loyalty. Until now the only choices open to the manager who disagrees with the policy actions of supervisors have been to remain silent or to leave the organization. Albert O. Hirschman in *Exit, Voice and Loyalty* proposes a third option, "voice," a compromise between silence and resignation. Voice is ". . . an attempt to change things through articulation whether by your dissatisfaction to those in a position to make changes, or by grousing to anyone who will listen. . .voice is essentially an art, constantly evolving in creative new directions. In contrast to exit, voice implies a continuing (if shared) loyalty to the entity that is causing stress." (Hirschman, 1979.)

In the 1970's this option has been called whistleblowing. In recognition of the need to discourage values which inhibit disagreement within an organization, a Special Counsel's office, linked with the Merit System's Protection Board, has been established in the federal sector. The office handles whistleblowing by receiving and investigating charges of agency or employee misconduct and by providing some protection for anonymous complaints.

ORGANIZATIONAL CLIMATE

We have seen that in the 1970's organizational change is often motivated by changing norms or values outside the organization. Sometimes the motivation for change is introduced by changed values of the employees. But again, change does not come easily. Typically it is preceded by a serious problem in the climate of the organization.

Organizational climate is a concept closely related to but distinct from organizational culture. Climate measures whether people's expectations about what it should be like to work in an agency are met. (Schwartz and Davis, 1981.) The concepts of culture and climate can be distinguished from one another by reflecting on our discussions in chapters 2 and 3 of Douglas McGregor's Theory X, Theory Y. Theory X and Theory Y are expressions of different organizational *cultures*. Theory X, casting the employees as inherently lazy, leads to attitudes and behavior emphasizing tight control. Theory Y, believing employees to be positively disposed toward work and growth oriented, generates attitudes and behaviors emphasizing employees autonomy and self direction. *Climate* by contrast relates to the measure of employee acceptance of the prevailing culture. For example, if a particular agency has a prevailing Theory X culture and new employees enter the organization with Theory Y values, a climate problem will develop. Employees do not share the dominant organizational culture value.

An example of a climate problem familiar to many public sector managers, centers on criteria for selection in employment. A central element of the public management organizational culture noted above requires that, "appointments to positions should be based on the merit of the person." But the real world of politics often dictates selection on the basis of political affiliation and participation. While most managers acknowledge someplace for patronage appointments, debate centers on how many appointments should be political and how politics should weigh as against other factors. One state executive recently reported a climate problem he experienced as a result of patronage selection.

> *Learning to cope when ordered to hire political supporters of the incumbent administration [patronage] has been extremely difficult for me. I am strongly committed to the ethics embodied in our state personnel system setting out standards for hiring on merit, service, qualifications, ability, etc., including affirmative action. Political favoritism is not one of those publically acknowledged and justifiable considerations. In my view it violates the system. I do appreciate referrals of potential employees. However, when I am forced to hire with political considerations as the determining factor I experience severe conflict between my ethical commitments and my personal need for job security. For a long time I retained my sense of responsibility for each "decision" and suffered as a result. My adaptation has been to reduce my feelings of responsibility for this situation although I do not believe this is a good outcome for me personally or for the long term administrative and organizational integrity of my position.*

In governmental organizations climate problems emerge when employees perceive substantial deviation from the merit norm produced by the kind of patronage pressure described in this case.

Often organizational culture and climate are imperceptible to managers in the thicket of agency decision-making. Yet both climate and culture can either foster or impede change efforts. Sometimes managers turn to organizational development specialists to diagnose these subtle dimensions of an organization's readiness for change. Typically such consultants look for incongruence either between organizational culture and actual practices (a problem of climate), or between organizational culture and new agency goals. A lack of fit gives the organizational development consultant a starting point for developing a change plan. But culture and climate are not the only factors that shape change efforts. Organizational structure, technology and environment also come into play.

STRUCTURE, TECHNOLOGY, ENVIRONMENT

Literature which focus on the interaction of structure and technology to explain organizational behavior, is usually labelled structural analysis. Some structural analyses also incorporate the concept of organizational environment. Structure, technology, environment, and their interaction may influence the direction and limits of organizational change. Here we simply describe those concepts as they appear in the organizational literature.

Organizational structure refers to the coordinating system in an organization, including job descriptions, the policies and procedures for coordinating jobs, and the management roles charged with securing coordination. Technology refers to the network of tasks tied to the organizational goal. Those activities that have to be accomplished together with the equipment and people necessary to accomplish them constitute the technology of the agency. Agencies are founded on the need to serve some public purpose. This policy objective calls forth specific technology and structures fitting the agency mandate. Since public sector managers don't start with people and shape structure and technology to fit, rather vice versa, some elements of structure and technology need to be treated as control variables in any discussion of organizational change. However, managers should be cautious about treating structure and technology as absolutes. The organization theory literature helps put these factors in perspective.

The structural approach to organizational analysis makes the assumption that organizational roles characterize the types of people who should occupy them. Thus people in those roles exhibit the expected traits and behaviors. Kanter (1977) characterizes the implications of structural arrangement in this way: "Positions carry a particular structure of rewards. . . The structures of rewards, in turn, channel behavior, setting people on a course which ties them further into their roles, makes them even more a product of their situations." Five basic assumptions underlie the structural analysis model:

1. The nature of the total organization system is important in shaping the relationship of any employee to work.
2. Employees choices about how to behave in a particular organization is rational and adaptive. It reflects strategic decisions directed toward managing a situation.
3. The structure of an organization does not so much control as it limits in the sense of restricting the range of options and confronting the individual with a characteristic set of problems to solve.
4. The content of a job as reflected in the formal job description and its location in the organizational hierarchy has much to do with how people actually behave.
5. Formal task and formal location of position have much to do with an incumbent's ability to demonstrate competence in an organization. (Kanter, 1977.)

Structural analysis is often accompanied by a further analysis which sees technology as the determinant of structure and thus of behavior. Blair and his associates have shown, for example, how technology is associated with specialization, hierarchy, increase in supervisory ratios and increase in worker responsibility and skill levels. (Blair, Falbe, McKinley, and Tracy, 1976.) The thesis that organizations differ in their tasks and therefore in the way they are run (Perrow 1970) garnered some support in the empirical studies of Joan Woodward in the early 1950's. Her research on British manufacturing firms found an empirical relationship between technology or the nature of production systems, patterns or organization, and business success. (Woodward, 1958; Woodward, 1972.) Research conducted in other settings yielded similar findings (Trist and Bamforth, 1951; Walker and Guest, 1952; Burns and Slaker, 1961; Sayles, 1958.)

An organization's environment is another element often considered when assessing the impact of structure and technology on efforts toward change. Organizations, whether public or private are open systems which interact with the environment. Political, economic, technological, legal, and social dimensions of the environment shape the interaction by providing resources necessary to achieve organizational objectives. While some degree of firmness of organizational boundaries is necessary to maintain organizational identity, all organizations are vulnerable to environmental influences. Lawrence and Lorsch (1967) point to the accessibility of critical information in the manager's environment as the major factor in shaping how organizations are structured. Uncertainty in the environment reflects the gap between the information a manager needs to achieve organizational objectives and the information he holds at a particular point in time. From the managerial viewpoint the seriousness of the problem posed by environmental uncertainty depends on the rate at which information changes, the time span of feedback and the certainty of information gained at any particular point in time. All organizations do not face the same type of environment. In a classic article Emery and Trist (1965) use movement to differentiate environments. They describe environments as either political and random, placid and clustered, disturbed and reactive, or turbulent.

In the public sector there are many instances of managers attempting to manage their environments. When program directors develop and cultivate outside constituents, when public relations officers nurture good relationships with the press, and when managers succumb to pressures to promote a loyal party worker over a more worthy civil servant, we see examples of public servants engaged in exchange with critical forces in their environment.

Some literature in organizational analysis treats structure, technology, and environment as virtual determinants of organizational action, with debate centering principally on how these variables interact and what causes what. The most deterministic of this literature sees technology as the prime cause of most effects we observe in organizational life. But our review of this literature concludes that while there may be some independent effects of technology on an organizational structure, (Aldrich, 1972; Child, 1972, Child and Mansfield, 1972) and in turn on behavior, this impact does not justify the technological determinist view. Studies of Mohr (1971) and Melman (1971) for example support the conclusions that in relation to the employees participation dimension of organizational structure, technology is not a significant determinant. Mohan's review of the general impact of various context factors concludes that none of the causal connections we have been discussing are sufficient determinants in themselves. Rather in organizational change efforts, normatively committed organizational leadership is the key variable. (Mohan, 1972.) We turn now to considering how managers deal with these dimensions of organizational life to effect change.

ORGANIZATIONAL LEARNING AND ORGANIZATIONAL CHANGE

In order to effect change managers must understand the nature of organizational change. In our view opinion has been too much ruled by Toffler's *Future Shock* (1970), which tells us that ungoverned change dominates modern life. While we recognize that change is pervasive and rapid, we also must emphasize the exceptional nature of organizational change. Kaufman's *Are Government Organizations Immortal?* (1976) or Kastelic's (1974) discussion of how old forms are reissued under new labels are better guides than Toffler to the process of organizational change. Indeed from both the social policy left, as reflected in the environmental movement, and the social policy right, as expressed in the Christian fundamentalist movement, pessimism abounds about the very desirability of change because of its human costs and its destabilizing nature. Given the cautious response evoked by change of any kind, managers need to be schooled in the change process—or in how organizations learn. Thus, against this background, we consider specific strategies for change, the basic points on managing change, and finally structural possibilities for institutionalizing change.

Chris Argyris (1980) offers the most useful conceptualization of organizational change in the literature today. He adopts a learning metaphor to describe the alternative change modes. Organizational learning occurs whenever there is a match between organizational intentions and organizational results or whenever a mismatch is detected and corrected by an organization. The Argyris learning model is based upon a mental construct which sees an organization as a system. The basic assumptions of system theory are central to this analysis.

Systems theory sees an organization as a system which can be identified by some sort of boundary which differentiates the organization from its environment. Systems are processual in nature and can be conceptualized in terms of a basic model which stresses input, throughput, output, and feedback. Overall the systems operation can be explained in terms of striving to fulfill systems needs geared toward survival. Units within an organization can be viewed as subsystems with their own systemic characteristics. The operation of a system is empirically visible in the behavior of its constituent elements. Boundary transactions internally between subsystems and externally via the environment are critical features of organizational life. (Burrell and Morgan, 1979.) From the vantage point of organizational learning the critical concept is feedback. In systems theory feedback describes the process whereby information concerning the outputs or the process of the system is fed back as input into the system, perhaps leading to change in the throughput process and/or future outputs. The feedback loop is the path feedback follows from output to subsequent feedback and new input.

Adopting a systems framework Argyris outlines two types of learning occuring in organizations: single loop learning and double loop learning. Single loop learning is like a thermostat that senses it is too hot or too cold and adjusts the heat accordingly. (Argyris and Schon, 1978.) Single loop learning occurs when a match between intentions and results is produced or a mismatch is corrected without having to question the organizational assumptions and policies. For example, a new procedure for mailing social security benefit checks or for correcting errors in the way welfare payments are distributed illustrates single loop learning. Double loop learning occurs when a match is produced or a mismatch corrected and changes are made in the basic organizational policies or assumptions. Using the thermostat analogy, double loop learning would occur if one asked if the thermostat concept itself was appropriate. In the social security check example double loop learning would occur if the organization considered reformulating the entire social security program. Double loop learning is typically associated with the kind of inquiry which resolves incompatible organizational norms by setting new priorities and weighting of norms or by restructuring norms themselves (Argyris and Schon, 1978).

Single loop learning problems are the ones most typically encountered by public sector managers. Think about the manager of a unit charged with processing certification forms for participation in a supplemental income program for hearing disabled citizens. The manager observes that nearly a third of the employees are falling below the performance standard for the number of certification requests processed per month. This performance standard, of 20 applicant reviews per month, was established after a study preceeding the initial implementation of the entire disabled benefits program and was based upon the projected work load for each employee with certification responsibilities. When the manager of the unit responds to this feedback by counselling the employees that their performance level must be raised in order to meet the standard, without questioning the performance standards themselves or the quality of performance accomplished, we have a case of single loop learning. This case illustrates the strengths and weaknesses of the single loop mode. The minimum criterion of 20 forms per month served as a good performance measure in the past and was perhaps a fitting measure for most units involved in the program. Clearly some numerical measure is necessary in order to aggregate performance ratings across units for purposes of comparing relative productivity. In other words, important organizational purposes are served by maintaining this numerical indicator of performance. It is an important management information tool. But this very tool may inhibit double loop learning essential to effectiveness of the overall benefits program. Perhaps the applicant certification review process requires more time for the hearing disabled applicant who is the subject of this unit's program than does the review process for certification of other types of disabilities which are handled by other units in the department. Alternatively, it may be that the norm of 20 certification reviews per month is simply too high given the number of hearing impaired applicants or potential applicants in the population. In either case simply counselling the employees to certify more applicants inhibits learning about the real source of the problem.

However, there are significant potential disincentives for a manager of a unit engaging in double loop learning. If the truth is that the number of hearing impaired who were certifiable initially was overestimated and that the high early numbers were simply a function of backlog which has now been taken care of, finding out the truth would not serve the personal interest of the manager in charge of the hearing impaired program. It might mean reduction in staff and therefore reduction in organizational status. Another example in the affirmative action area illustrates the same point. A Deputy Secretary in the state agency is placed in charge of implementing a new Women in Management program. After hearing from the Governor's Council on the Status of Women of the need to place more women in management the Deputy sends out a memo and asks 5 division heads to submit the names of five women who might be eligible for advanced management training. Next, with the list of 25 names in hand, the Deputy invites all of these women to attend a state-sponsored executive development program. Much to his surprise he finds only two women willing to accept this offer of advancement. Following a single loop model the Deputy concludes: "Women do not want to advance in this organization. The need for affirmative action doesn't exist." The short term disincentives for engaging in double loop learning for this manager are clear. If the fault for lack of interest in advancement does not lie in the women, it might lie in the organization—a conclusion with personally and organizationally threatening consequences. Chris Argyris captures the essentials of this organizational change paradox illustrated in both examples above. "The difficulty is that in real life, truth is a good idea when it is not threatening. If truth is threatening, the appropriate tactics and games will be displayed to reduce the threat while covertly distorting the truth." (Argyris, 1980.)

This discussion of organizational learning illuminates the problem of organizational change. While change by accommodation and adjustment can occur within a single loop learning mode, conditions of modern public organizations call for a deeper capacity to change, or for double loop learning. While we are concerned with both types of learning we invite managers to focus particularly on ways that double loop learning might be enhanced by the following managerial change strategies.

MANAGERIAL CHANGE STRATEGIES

One thing that we know about the change phenomenon is that it has two parts corresponding to the concern for production and the concern for relationship dimensions discussed in Chapter 3. There is a technical part, the goal redefinition and/or reorganization that needs to be implemented and a social part, the feelings, values and attitudes of people involved in its implementation and impact. Strategies managers adopt should be sensitive to both parts of the change experience.

Kotter and Schlesinger (1979) outline four managerial approaches to change sensitive to both dimensions.

Education and communication

Change is effected through the force of information. This strategy assumes a fairly solid latent consensus which will easily emerge once information is provided and misinformation dispelled. Dissemination of studies and model regulations is an example of this type of strategy.

Participation and involvement

Change is effected on the basis of the commitment which results from participation in decision-making. This approach assumes that a large number of actors can reach a mutually acceptable compromise if they are allowed to interact on a face-to-face basis. Conferences with a working agenda are an example, as are many organization development strategies.

Negotiations

This is similar to participation, but only a few actors are involved. The approach assumes there are distinct points of view about the change in question and that powerful interests must be directly represented and reconciled. Retreats of top management may illustrate this strategy.

Authoritative determination

Change is effected by directives from the top. This strategy assumes that consensus is so obvious or, at the other extreme, so impossible, that participation and negotiation are inappropriate. This strategy suggests a plan involving efforts directed toward the top management levels, not toward the much larger numbers of users and affected parties.

Quite possibly managers would involve elements from each of these approaches developing a change strategy fitting to a particular case.

BASIC POINTS ABOUT MANAGING CHANGE

In thinking about a strategy for a broad change effort involving many actors, in many jurisdictions or subsystems, managers should consider the literature on organizational development [O.D.]. O.D. is the applied expression of organizational change theory which holds that change efforts involve distinct stages or phases. (See French, 1969.)

On the basis of a review of eighteen diverse change efforts, Greiner (1967) has usefully summarized six phases typical of such an O.D. effort:

1. Pressure and arousal: awareness of the problem at top levels of management; placing the problem as a priority agenda item; legitimation of lower levels treating the problem as a priority.
2. Intervention and reorientation: Call for reexamination and change, legitimated by top management but often facilitated by an outside newcomer as a catalyst (a consultant, a manager from another line division, a staff support professional, or a new agency head).
3. Diagnosis and recognition: A shared process of inventorying problems.
4. Invention and commitment: Search for alternatives on a collaborative basis.
5. Experimentation and search: Provisional decision-making and trial implementation.
6. Reinforcement and acceptance: Publicity for performance improvement, reward for improvement, integration of change with training and support systems.

The classic formulation of change through organizational development reduces the process to three stages. Kurt Lewin (1947, 1951) identifies these stages as: 1) unfreezing, by the introduction of new information or experiences which change old value priorities; 2) changing, by actual decision-making which sanctions new processes; and 3) refreezing, by reliance on training, rewards, and other means to perpetuate the new system. The thought is that managers must avoid the temtation to just do Stage 2, ignoring the need for laying the preliminary groundwork for later follow-up on decisions about change.

The first stage has certain typical features. As one researcher has shown (Huse, 1975), the first stage usually requires certain concrete efforts to "unfreeze" the situation by decreasing resistance to change. Examples of considerations here are the following: 1) have you communicated effectively evidence showing the change is helpful to those who must decide on change?; 2) have you considered how the change will threaten to diminish the prestige and authority of relevant actors?; 3) have you afforded relevant actors an opportunity to be part of the change process from the start?; 4) have you sought to legitimate the change by securing the support of the highest levels of management from the beginning?; 5) have you provided a means whereby actors can share their perceptions, thereby establishing peer reinforcement of new change-oriented attitudes? These may seem to be common sense rules, but many managers planning change efforts either forget them or assume they can safely ignore one or more of them. In most cases all five consideration are really necessary.

Change action begins with diagnosis, but managing change is a snowballing process. A vision of change starts at the center, others are involved in the vision refined, then a wider group is brought in and this changes goals further, until eventually all the actors are brought into then network and goals are crystallized in a decision. This is very different from "marketing," in which a preset product is sold without change to an audience. In managing change, the audience is progressively brought into the "production process."

In introducing a new affirmative action program, for example, the audience of potential users, higher level managers, etc., is brought progressively into the change effort. Ordinarily representatives of each type of actor are brought in at the outset, the more prestigious the representatives the better. What these representatives usually do at the outset is engage in diagnosis. Where are women, and minority group members now in the respective units? What have been the retention/advancement patterns regarding them in the past? What are the special problem areas?

There is an extensive literature on organizational diagnosis (cf. Levinson, 1972). However the core of diagnosis is simply engaging in some effort to find out 1) what the current situation is; 2) what people think the situation will be if nothing is done; 3) what people want the situation to be; and 4) what people perceive as the obstacles. An impressive array of techniques can be used in diagnosis ranging from brainstorming to survey research to Lewin's "force field analysis." Whatever the form taken, action begun in diagnosis provides feedback which is then the focus of the middle stage, the changing process.

Depending on the strategy adopted the changing process will involve a large or small number of people. A three-day working conference on equal employment opportunity involving a couple of hundred participants would be a participatory approach to an affirmative action program. The authoritative approach to the same program might be a retreat or planning session involving only a few key decision-makers. Regardless of the strategy, however, the middle stage—the changing process itself—has a few typical features.

First, the middle stage involves face-to-face decision-making meetings, and whether small meetings or large conferences, they demand substantial skill. Our communications chapter highlights the art of meeting management and points out aspects of non-verbal communication to which managers must be sensitive. It is worth noting that such decision-making meetings have a typical sequence whether they are stretched out over many meetings or condensed in one.

The recommended typical sequence is as follows: 1) legitimation of the change objective by the highest-ranking officials possible; 2) presentation of diagnostic findings by a representative planning team, documenting the need to change and widespread readiness to change; 3) introductory activities involving those attending in sharing perceptions on the subject; 4) brainstorming of what's good, what's wrong, what changes would help, what obstacles remain (often done in small groups which report back to the whole); 5) participative establishment of goals; 6) formation of task groups addressed to action steps and obstacles. Generally speaking, these steps are helpful whether the decision-makers are a large conference or a small set of key officials. The less the consensus and commitment of the decision-makers, the more each step is necessary.

The third stage of the change process is more or less important, depending on whether you are instituting a new procedure or eliminating a former problem. The follow-up or "refreezing" stage in managing change is less critical in an effort like deregulation, where the outcome is to be elimination rather than institution of activities. To the extent new activities are required by a change, as in the example of instituting a new AA program, it is necessary that they be reinforced by being built into reward systems, into performance appraisals, MBO reporting, and incorporated into professional association activities. In the case of deregulation, such as discontinuing an ongoing AA effort, most of this sort of unusual change consideration is irrelevant. Nonetheless, follow-up needs to reflect some effort to update training efforts. Follow-up should also provide for some system of evaluation of the change, with provisions for the decision-making group to review and refine the change at a later point.

PARALLEL ORGANIZATIONS

Our discussion of organizational change has focused on a theory of organizational change, conditions that inhibit change, and change strategies. The assumption of our analysis is that the basic structure of bureaucracy remains intact and that change efforts should not be premised on the withering away of the formal organization. Rather, these interventions are keyed to conventional bureaucratic structures.

One emerging approach to organizational change takes off from the assumption that the task of changing traditional bureaucratic structures is so overwhelming that the most effective strategy is to circumvent the problem by creating "parallel structures". There are alternatives to bureaucracy which can be fashioned parallel to conventional structures. The "parallel structures" concept assumes that there are some tasks and conditions for which line hierarchy is better suited than any alternative. (Stein and Kanter, 1980.) Particularly in public sector organization, clear lines of authority and responsibility drawn by conventional hierarchy facilitate achieving the important objective of official accountability. Parallel structures do not displace bureaucratic structures which continue to do what they do best, define job titles, pay grades, fixed reporting relationships, and related formal tasks. Rather this is an attempt simultaneously to introduce environmental responsiveness and thus change capability permanently into bureaucratic organizations through alternative formal structures. The "parallel organization" is defined by Stein and Kanter as "an attempt to institutionalize a set of externally and internally responsive, participatory, problem-solving structures alongside the conventional line organization that carries out such routine tasks". (1980.) It is not a new structure, such as the matrix organization which displaces the bureaucratic structure by institutionalizing new reporting relationships. Rather it is an additional, formal and permanent management structure. The main job of a parallel organization is to facilitate change by: providing continued re-examination of routines, exploration of new options, development of new processes, tools, procedures. As new routines prove themselves they are transferred from the parallel organization to the bureaucratic organization for full integration and maintenance.

These activities which are parallel to but independent of the hierarchy of an organization benefit both people and organizations by providing:

1. a chance for employees to gain experience that is not strictly job related
2. a chance to have an impact on the agency in ways other than through one's immediate job
3. a way to detour around bureaucratic structures that might not be working, to see and to solve problems
4. a mechanism for managing new activities that exist outside of people's jobs (Kanter and Stein, 1980).

Typically this type of structural intervention hinges on commitment from top management, but if executives at the top of public agencies become convinced of its merits it provides the vehicle for engaging in the double loop learning detailed by Argyris and Schon. Beyond the gains from a change perspective, parallel structures provide a vehicle for creating new ways of grouping people in an organization. Thus new possibilities for challenge, learning, growth, new access to resources and support are created for organizational members.

A good example of an effort to establish a parallel structure in a public agency is the affirmative action research project in North Carolina. This project used organizational change technology to advance minority and female employment opportunity in state government. Alternative organizational structures served as the vehicle for innovation.

The development and installation of the parallel structures in North Carolina state government proceeded through several overlapping stages, each representing a significant element in the project. First information gathering was conducted by a staff of internal and external consultants. Surveys measuring racism, sexism, organizational climate, supervisory and peer leadership, group process, and satisfaction were conducted in departments participating in the project. Next divisional affirmative action committees were formed, composed of at least 50 percent female and 50 percent minority members, with the division director, the EEO officer, personnel representatives, and eleven other members representing the hierarchical levels of the division. The committees were basically self directional, but received suggestions from the affirmative action consulting staff. Then the information gathered from the affirmative action survey and from the divisional affirmative action quarterly reports was analyzed and summarized by the consulting group and fed back to the committees for committee reflection and reaction. Based on this feedback experience the committees developed a plan of action which varied from division to division. Among the activities adopted by committees were to establish division affirmative action guidelines, to recommend sensitivity training to increase awareness of racist and sexist attitudes, to procure training in better management practices in order to lead to better problem solving on the job and to initiate interventions to improve the work climate generally. In the final stage, the committees presented their plans of action to management groups in the organization in an effort to integrate the proposed change into the bureaucratic processes and procedures and to diffuse results within the system.

Institutionalizing parallel organizations ic clearly not a panacea for organizational change, but anticipating problems helps to make the most of this intervention mode. In the parallel organization example cited above several typical forms of resistance were encountered. Resistance came from some personnel staff who felt that their organizational role in the bureaucratic structure was being subsumed by the work of this new parallel structure, the divisional affirmative action committee. In each of the committees concern was expressed over the fact that the committees had no line authority to implement policies that were developed. In those cases where committee membership was not voluntary, the coerced members diminished the overall effectiveness of the committee work. Although top management supported the committee work, some subordinate managers who were responsible for chairing the committees feared that the committees could become a gripe session or otherwise a waste of time. In the case of some divisions the very culture that the parallel organization was trying to change was an impediment to the committee's effectiveness. Existing organizational norms prescribed very narrow job responsibility, little upward information flow, and decision making restricted to top administrators. The very establishment of the parallel structure, the committee, was in direct conflict with these norms. Notwithstanding these predictable areas of resistance organizations will increasingly turn to the use of these structural interventions in order to facilitate change. Parallel structures provide an institutional capability to change when the environment demands new routines, new policies, and new thinking in an organization.

CONCLUSION

In discussing the context within which managers manage, we acknowledge that human factors alone fail to account for success or failure in an organization. An organization's culture and climate, and its structure, technology, and environment enter to shape the outcome of change efforts. Change in an organization is a process of learning which occurs in two forms: as a simple response to feedback, single-loop learning, or as a review of central features of the organizational context, double-loop learning. To initiate effective change efforts, managers need to be sensitive to the strengths and pitfalls of both types of organizational learning. Each chapter that follows discusses critical arenas for managerial intervention.

REFERENCES

Aldrich, Howard E. (1972) Technology and Organizational Structure: A Reexamination of the Findings of the Aston Group. *Administrative Science Quarterly.* 17 (March):pp. 26-43.

Argyris, Chris. (1980) Making the Undiscussable and its Undiscussability Discussable. *Public Administration Review* 5/6:pp. 205-211.

Argyris, Chris and Donald A. Schon. (1978) *Organizational Learning: A Theory of Action Perspective.* Addison-Wesley, Reading, Mass.

Blair, Peter M., Cecilia McHugh Falbe, William McKinley and Phelps R. Tracy. (1976) Technology and Organization in Manufacturing. *Administrative Science Quarterly.* 21 (March):pp. 20-40.

Burns, T. and G. M. Stalker (1961) *The Management of Innovation.* Tavistock Institute, London.

Burrell, Gibson and Gareth Morgan. (1979) *Sociological Paradigms and Organizational Analysis.* Heinemann, London.

Caiden, Gerald E. (1981) Ethics in the Public Service. *Public Personnel Management* 10:pp. 146-152.

Child, John. (1972) Organization Structure and Strategies of Control: A Replication of the Aston Study. *Administrative Science Quarterly* 17 (June):pp. 163-177.

Child, John and Roger Mansfield. (1972) Technology, Size and Organization Structure. *Sociology* 6 (September):pp. 369-393.

Dalton, Gene W. (1978) (Influence and Organizational Change. Organizational Development in Public Administration, edited by Robert T. Golembiewski and William B. Eddy. Marcel Dekker, Inc.: New York.

Emery, F. E. and E. L. Trist. (1965) The Causal Texture of Organizational Environments. *Human Relations* 18.

French, Wendell (1969) Organization Development: Objectives, Assumptions and Strategies, reprinted in Walter E. Natemeyer, ed. *Classics of Organizational Behavior.* More Publishing Company: Oak Park, Illinois.

Greiner, L. (1967) Patterns of Organizational Change. *Harvard Business Review.* Vol. 45, No. 3 (May/June):pp. 119-130.

Hirschman, Albert O. (1979) Exit, Voice, and Loyalty, in *The Culture of Bureaucracy* edited by Charles Peters and Michael Nelson. Holt, Reinhart, and Winston, New York:pp. 209-217.

Huse, Edgar F. (1975) *Organization Development and Change.* West Publishing Co., New York.

Kanter, Rosabeth M. (1977) *Men and Women of the Corporation.* Basic Books, New York.

Kastelic, Frank. (1974) Innovation, Involvement, and Contemporary Service Organizations. *Journal of Sociology and Social Welfare.* 1 (Summer), pp. 233-243.

Kaufman, Herbert. (1976) *Are Government Organizations Immortal?* Brookings Institution, Washington, D.C.

Kotter, John P. and Leonard A. Schlesinger. (1979) Choosing Strategies for Change. *Harvard Business Review.* (March-April):pp. 106-114.

Lawrence, Paul R. and J. W. Lorsch. (1967) Differentiation and Integration in Complex Organizations. *Administrative Science Quarterly.* 12:pp. 1-47.

Levinson, Harry. (1972) *Organizational Diagnosis.* Harvard University Press. Cambridge, Mass.

Lewin, Kurt. (1947) Frontiers in Group Dynamics. *Human Relations.* 1 (June): pp. 5-41.

_____(1951) *Field Theory in Social Science.* Harper and Bros., New York.

Melman, Seymour. (1971) Managerial versus Cooperative Decision Making in Israel. *Studies in Comparative International Development.* 6:pp. 47-58.

Mohan, Raj P. (1972) A Preliminary Model of Organizational Renewal. *Indian Journal of Social Research.* 13 (December):pp. 179-193.

Mohr, Lawrence. (1971) Organizational Technology and Organizational Structure. *Administrative Science Quarterley.* 16 (December):pp. 444-459.

O'Toole, James J. (1979) Corporate and Managerial Cultures. *Behavioral Problems in Organizations,* edited by Cary L. Cooper. Prentice-Hall, Englewood Cliffs, New Jersey.

Perrow, Charles B. (1970) *Organizational Analysis: A Sociological View.* Wadsworth Publishing Co., Belmont, CA.

Sayles, L. R. (1958) *Behavior in Industrial Work Groups: Prediction and Control.* John Wiley, New York.

Schwartz, Hoard and Stanley M. Davis. (1981) Matching Corporate Culture and Business Strategy. *Organizational Dynamics.* (Summer):pp. 30-48.

Stein, Barry A. and Rosabeth Moss Kanter. (1980) Building the Parallel Organization: Creating Mechanisms for Permanent Quality of Work Life. *Journal of Applied Behavioral Science.* 16:pp. 371-388.

Toffler, Alvin. (1970) *Future Shock.*

Trist, E. L. and K. W. Bamforth. (1951) Some Social and Psychological Consequences of the Longwald Method of Goal Setting. *Human Relations.* 4 (1): pp. 3-38.

Walker, J. and R. H. Guest. (1952) *The Man on the Assembly Line.* Harvard University Press, Cambridge, Mass.

Woodward, Joan. (1972) *Industrial Organization: Theory and Practice.* Oxford University Press, London.

_____(1958) *Management and Technology.* HMSO, London.

PART II
MANAGEMENT APPLICATIONS

MANAGEMENT SYSTEMS

In the last decade there has been a shift in public administration toward greater application of organizational behavior concepts to management. At the same time there has been a proliferation of management decision-making systems such as program planning and budgeting systems (PPBS), zero-base budgeting (ZBB), and management by objectives (MBO), to name a few. All these systems involve the systematic relating of organizational goals to personnel and budgetary data. As systematic, often quantitative techniques, the systems approaches are often seen as "hard" task-centered tools which contrast with the "soft" person-centered methods drawn from the study of human behavior. In spite of apparent tensions, however, the thesis of this chapter is that management systems and human behavioral approaches function best when they are seen as complementary.

The application of management systems to human resource questions goes back some way in American public administration, antedating John F. Kennedy's installation of program budgeting (PPBS) in the Department of Defense. Planning, programming, and budgeting systems (PPBS) was a system which required that budgets correspond to program categories (that is, to objectives). By grouping expenses by program category it was possible to build on PPBS to make judgments about the costs and benefits of one program compared to another. Zero-base budgeting (ZBB), popularized under President Carter, required agencies to submit three budgets rather than one; a cutback budget, a stand-pat budget, and an expansion budget. This, too, was intended to increase the decision-making powers of top management. Management by objectives (MBO), emphasized during the Nixon administration, focused on the coordination of individual work plans with organization goals, and these with the budget. All three systems, like most others, increased information available to top decision-makers, enabling top management to make more effective decisions.

Much recent literature suggests the strength of management systems concepts. Gremillion, McKenney, and Pyburn (1980), for instance, have recently reported on the benefits of PPBS in the U.S. Forest Service. Amid economic cutbacks, PPBS-type analyses may find increased applicability during the 1980's (McTighe, 1979). Moore's (1980) survey of American municipalities showed widespread support for ZBB as a means of budget control. Even at the federal level after the departure of the ZBB advocates of the Carter era, substantial elements of ZBB have been left in place (Draper and Pitsvada, 1981). For its part, MBO has been reinforced by its potential linkage with the rapid growth of management informations systems (MIS), as in hospital administration (see Spano, Kiresuk, and Lund, 1977; Granvold, 1978; McConkie, 1979; Moore and Staton, 1981). While it may be true that any given management system is transitory, cynicism toward the cyclical nature of management system emphases should not obscure the pervasive cumulative effect of management systems on organizational life for American public managers. As Thomas Peters (1980) has noted, "Management systems are a critical variable in reversing a decline or spurring a new level of achievement. Even a dramatic strategic move, for instance, is likely to perturb the enterprise only briefly unless the old systems residues are attacked and remolded in parallel."

The focus of this chapter is the need to integrate the implementation of such management systems with behavioral concerns and techniques of the sort discussed in this book. Our premise is that both must be integrated for effective realization of the objectives of either. The chapter begins with a discussion of human behavioral concerns in the design of management systems. The following section treats the question of evaluation and research design in implementation of management systems. A concluding section presents common managerial problems in applying (or not applying!) behavioral concepts to systems applications.

DESIGN CONCERNS IN MANAGEMENT CONTROL SYSTEMS

The introduction of a management system is commonly perceived as a relatively technical matter by most agency employees. It is seen as emphasizing forms, budgetary data, and analytic constructs somehow tied to "management planning" and perhaps (fear and trembling!) to job evaluation and merit pay. Thus the management system appears on the scene as something of an unknown and, like most unknowns, it elicits a certain automatic resistance to the changes it brings. Ironically, such management systems are usually created to improve communication, coordination, and feedback. In the absence of careful attention to behavioral design concerns, however, implementation of these systems can backfire easily.

There are three major design issues in implementing a management system which concern various ways management system implementation can fail in public agencies. These issues are influence differentiation, suboptimization, and goal displacement. *Influence differentiation* refers to problems associated with participation and control, or lack thereof, in management systems. *Suboptimization* refers to design failures in process integration in systems implementation. Finally, *goal displacement* refers to the potential behavior-distorting effects of the information/ tracking system established in conjunction with a management system. Each of these design issues is briefly outlined below.

Many management systems involve issues of power, influence, and control in an explicit way. Since a common major purpose of a management system is to facilitate the flow of information to top management for analysis and review, management systems appear to be centralizing in effect. Just as the introduction of human behavioral interventions like autonomous work groups may threaten the established influence structure from the point of view of management, so the introduction of management systems may seem to employees to be merely a further tightening of oversight and control. While the tightening of control by management can be productive for the agency, there are many circumstances (the opposite of the contingencies favoring participatory management discussed in Chapter 7) in which it can be harmful.

Problems arising from the failure to join human behavioral interventions with management system implementation is discussed in the "Central City" case later in this chapter. The point here, however, is simply to establish the concept that management system design must recognize the political (power) dimension of agency change. This is done through systems design which emphasize influence integration rather than influence differentiation.

Influence differentiation is the normal mode by which agency members perceive power in the organization. That is, influence is perceived to be differentiated by function and level. Higher organizational levels exert greater influence over more functions. Low-level employees exert less influence over fewer functions. The influence differentiation mode, however "natural," carries with it an internal tension. On the one hand, power in the agency tends to be viewed as zero-sum in nature: the more influence the employees have, the less management has and vice versa. On the other hand, the purpose of management systems is to motivate the employee to contribute more to broader functions of the agency normally reserved for higher levels. That is, the management system is an appeal to the employee to identify with such broader organizational concerns as productivity and achievement of agency goals. The influence differentiation mode, however, does little to legitimate such an appeal. On the contrary, it fosters an ambiguous push-pull mentality in which the employee is expected to be subordinate in influence level and functional domain but also expected to be integrated in the functional concerns of higher levels.

Influence differentiation is not an abstract theoretical construct for systems implementation. In fact, it is probably the single most common cause of widespread cynicism toward management systems, accounting for their often transitory or faddish nature in public administration. Influence differentiation is not an inevitable orientation toward the agency's power structure. As Tannenbaum has noted of organizations taking an influence integration approach, involving both systemic and human behavioral innovations, both managers and employees can come to understand that influence is neither one-way nor zero-sum. It can be true, as Tannenbaum found of the organization member, that "While he controls more, he is not controlled less" (Tannenbaum, 1962, in Natemeyer, 1978). In planning management systems like ZBB, PPBS, or MBO, participative approaches do more than overcome resistance to change and increase employee satisfaction. They encourage a team perspective oriented toward exchange of ideas and feedback rather than an hierarchical perspective rooted in command and acquiescence. By providing concrete experiences with two-way influence and illustrations of nonzero-sum decision-making, a participatory approach fosters the influence integration mode of perceiving management systems, a prerequisite for successful systems implementation.

Suboptimization is the second of the major design concerns in systems implementation. When large agencies are divided into divisions or units which have the design responsibility for implementing a management system, there is a possibility if not likelihood that suboptimization will occur. Suboptimization is the design of a management system to meet unit goals not coordinated with agency goals. For example, PPBS may operate effectively within a purchasing division of a state department, achieving all its goals of efficiency, documentation of costs and benefits, and so on—yet it may be impeding larger organizational goals like responsiveness (PPBS may slow other units down) or decentralization (PPBS may be based on specialized skills provided centrally).

Suboptimization is really part of the broader design problem of goal displacement. All management systems select certain information for decision-making purposes. These data gathered in a management control system are critical because they carry fundamental assumptions about the purpose of the system. If information and purpose are mismatched, several breakdowns occur:

1. Desired purposes cannot be served rationally.
2. Time and resources spent in data collection are wasted.
3. Employees will displace behaviors in favor of measured performances

It is not true that "some data are better than none" in the case of management systems. It is entirely possible to sabotage an otherwise satisfactory organizational process through imposition of an inappropriately designed management control system.

The fundamental problem is that employees will distort behavior to display improvement on measured indicators. This is, indeed, one of the key intended effects of management systems—but it assumes that the agency or individual performance measures required by the management system accurately reflect the full range of intended performances. A measure which taps produced units per person-days is a fine one for a management system only if efficiency in production is the only performance desired. Such an indicator would not measure quality, effectiveness, or other values. Either the management system must be designed to measure all significant performance areas *or* the management system must be supplemented by other broader behavior-assessing approaches (e.g., performance appraisals, program reviews) which are presumed to do so. Otherwise employees will devote their energies toward showing achievement solely on that which is measured by top management—efficiency, in this case.

The basic design choice is between simplicity and complexity. Simple management systems are easier to administer and are less costly. Complex management systems may involve less goal displacement but administrative burdens may become prohibitive. A simple management system in the Postal Service, for example, might focus on number of mail items delivered per postal worker-day. It might be, however, that this rate has been changing due to changes in transportation, population density, technology, and other factors. A more complex measure might be percent increase in number of items delivered per postal worker-day compared to the trend line. This productivity measure alone could encourage neglect of quality, however, so a more complex system might also track a measure of client satisfaction or of accuracy of delivery. Other potential measures might include damage control, employees health and safety, or range of philatelic services. By tracking all possible measures the Postal Service's management system might easily wind up with two or three dozen unit and individual performance measures. Even then the possibility would still exist that some important dimensions might be neglected.

Neglected areas typically are those at the periphery of the agency's role. In public agencies these might include issues such as whether the management system should track environmental impact concerns, whether it should track indirect social impacts of policies, or whether the system should seek to measure data on political ramifications of policies. Typically, management systems avoid such areas. Forcing such concerns into the rigid formats of management systems would only make matters more controversial. But if environmental, social, or political impacts are not part of the management system, the agency cannot afford to ignore such considerations. The inevitable conclusion is that the management system must be designed not to replace but only to augment a broader, less explicit decision-making process which does consider wider issues.

All measurements on which management systems are based are subject to controversy. Even long-standing, routinized measures like the consumer price index or the unemployment rate, by way of comparison, are subject to intense intra-bureaucratic debate and conflict. The same sort of intraorganizational conflict is inevitably part of the formal or informal processes of any agency which seeks to implement a management system.

In conclusion, designing a management control system is a complex process involving important value choices. Because value choices are involved, top management must participate in establishment of a management system. Management must be intimately associated with the system and must stand behind the development process. Agencies opting for the easier, less expensive simple management control systems must either have unusually simple configurations of outputs or must be prepared for strong dysfunctional goal displacement effects. On the other hand, agencies which opt for more complex measures must be capable of long-range planning. That is, the evolution of such measures involves trial and error to find an appropriate balance between overmeasurement leading to excessive burden on the one hand or undermeasurement leading to excessive goal displacement on the other.

This trial and error process cannot be accomplished in one or two years. Establishment of a management control system makes sense only if the agency can reasonably be hoped to be stable. Aside from external considerations (e.g., change in political administrations), such stability is typically based on agencies which through organization development or some indigenous approach to human behavioral methods have undergone a process of goal clarification, consensus-seeking, and commitment-making. Without that process, requiring the application of human behavioral skills, the management system will soon collapse due to poor design associated with the problems of influence differentiation, suboptimization, and goal displacement.

THE RELEVANCE OF RESEARCH DESIGN TO CONTROL SYSTEMS

Administration under a management control system is different from routine management and consequently data collected under a management system are rarely the same as information collected prior to system installation. In considering the redesign of information collection for a new management system decisions are made which will determine its success. Two common mistakes occur at this point:

1. Because of the heavy actual and psychological investment in the old data system there is strong pressure to make do with the old forms and procedures. Because new forms of data collection are expensive in time and energy there is also pressure to collect only the most readily available data, which is not necessarily what the management system may require.
2. For data which *is* available, there is a tendency to assume that the more, the better.

In contrast, the appropriate approach is to gather all the information actually required by the assumptions of the management system, and no more.

Knowing what data will fill the needs of a given management system is an issue dependent on the particular system and the particular agency. In general, however, the procedure is to develop a list of indicators through a trial-and-error process which seeks to minimize goal displacement and other problems discussed above. The indicators developed will ordinarily include elements in each of the major agency functions: personnel, budgeting, scheduling, service delivery, and so on. These indicators are then translated into reporting forms used in a research design.

You may be thinking, "Research designs are for academic study. I thought we were dealing with management control systems! Why do we need a research design at all?" Let's back up. What is it we are trying to get at in a management control system? In general we are trying to measure the relationship between the inputs we control and the outputs we want. Inputs include time, personnel, technology, and resources. Outputs include changes in clients, delivery of services, impacts on environments, and accomplishment of tasks. The relationships are sociotechnical. That is, they depend not only on a given means-ends technology (e.g., a structured job training program) but also on the social relationships among staff and clients.

It is true that research design is not needed in simple organizational environments in which the means-ends technology is both known fully and is fully determinant. By definition, in such simple systems we already know the input-output relationships that management control systems are intended to find out. For that matter, in such simple contexts there is no need for a management control system at all, only routine reporting of input and output levels. In simple settings, management control systems only serve to quantify and justify agency operations, but management decision-making is not improved by having such systems and their cost in effort and resources is not justified.

At the other extreme, there is no need for research designs or management control systems in hypercomplex administrative environments in which inputs and outputs are constantly changing, variables cannot be measured, or objectives are diffuse in nature. For example, the attempt to implement PPBS in the U.S. State Department was largely a failure. In extremely complex environments management control systems again become costly and unnecessary burdens. At best they may assist decision-making in some smaller, less complex subsystem of the agency.

Management control systems and the research designs that go with them are appropriate for organizations in a middle range of complexity of environment. Such middle-range organizations are too complex for mere common sense to be adequate on the one hand, but not so complex on the other hand that they are beyond the state of the art of management control systems. While control systems advocates and consulting firms often sell such systems as universal in applicability, they are not. The attempt to apply them in inappropriate contexts leads to organizational problems of the first magnitude.

How Research Design Fits In

A management control system tracks data on inputs and relates them to outputs. Note the two parts: tracking and relating. Tracking data on inputs and outputs is the most obvious part, typically embedded in PPBS budget forms, MBO objective reports, and so on. This is the traditional management part. While the reporting may be more systematic and well-designed, the tracking function is not different in kind from pre-control system information management in most agencies. What makes control systems different is the analytic part which identifies presumed relationships of inputs to outputs. This relating process requires a research design because tracking and relating are two different processes.

In installing a management control system like ZBB, managers tend to fixate on the tracking part. After all, this is the data on which they make decisions. The control system's monthly reports of input levels (e.g., person-hours, expenditures) and program outputs (e.g., cases processed, social impacts, downtime, and externalities) seems at first glance all the manager needs. It is perfectly possible to design a management system with tracking as the only function.

A management *control* system, in contrast, requires the addition of a relating or analytic function. *How* are inputs related to outputs? *How* are costs related to benefits? In organizations of medium complexity the answers to these questions are often not obvious. We may know that 100 person-hours will result in an average of 1,000 papers being processed, but we are unlikely to know how many client effects will result. We are even less likely to know why sometimes many effects result and at other times there are few effects. Likewise it would be nice to know why units in some geographic areas are more effective than other units within the agency, or why the cost-benefit ratio is changing over time for the agency. These are control questions which require a system which goes beyond simple tracking.

A management system tracks data systematically. A management control system provides systematic means-ends analysis of this data using control variables. That is, cause-effect relationships are presented not on the basis of mere correlations which stand out from the tracked data (e.g., the units with more personnel have more output) but also take into account other variables (control variables) which may be at work (e.g., controlling for education, larger units may have less output since the output of educated staff is proportionately higher but educated staff are concentrated in the larger units, making them seem to have more output merely because they are larger).

Management systems such as MBO, PPBS, or ZZB may be used with solely a tracking function, or they may be operated in a more complex and sophisticated manner as management control systems. The latter require reliance on a research design. These range from the inexpensive but error-prone to the expensive but scientific. The most expensive and sophisticated are *experimental* designs as in the New Jersey Maintenance Experiment on guaranteed minimum wages and their social effects. Experimental designs require both randomly-selected treatment (receiving the income maintenance payments) and control (not receiving) groups, as well as time series data both before and after the treatment. Quasi-experimental designs are far more common, relying on such methods as time series analysis, replication, or other forms of multivariate analysis. Nonexperimental designs include before-after studies and comparisons of the given program with national norms.

An Example: Tracking v. Analysis in the Law Enforcement Assistance Administration

During the 1970's the Law Enforcement Assistance Administration (LEAA) funded extensive efforts to develop management systems. These were primarily oriented toward what we have termed the tracking function. They documented the quantitative levels of inputs and outputs over time. Performance measurement and professional standards development were the key elements of this LEAA strategy.

Performance measurement set up a data collection system which gathered information on crime, criminals, and justice system responses to events. In addition conventional data on budgeting and personnel in the justice system were also collected. Through such data it was possible to surmise trends in law enforcement administration.

Professional standards were also developed, on the basis of expert panels and peer surveys. Through these methods a very large number of professional standards and objectives were identified. Using these it was possible to develop measures of goal achievement (e.g., on police response times).

Tracking performance measures in relation to professional standards did not constitute a complete management control system, the LEAA discovered. For example, the management system just outlined resulted in such information as data on the amount of time between arrest and trial. Professional standards could be applied to set an objective of X number of days maximum from arrest to trial. Nonetheless, this information could not explain the reasons for the gap between professional standards and actual performance measures. The management systems developed to that point told whether there was a problem, but not why there was a problem.

In 1973 the LEAA published a comprehensive set of criminal justice management standards. Within a few years, however, it became apparent that the data collected at so much expense was not being used widely. The reason was that everyone already knew what the problems were and didn't need an elaborate tracking system to tell them. What they didn't know, but needed, were answers to the "why" questions.

In 1978 LEAA switched to a new strategy. In our terms, they decided to move from management systems to management control systems. That is, they decided to add an analytic function to the existing tracking functions. The LEAA retained the title of "performance measurement" but adopted a different approach in a new $1.1 million planning study. The new approach incorporated two elements: 1) quasi-experimental research using statistical analysis to develop explana-

tions of performance variance (that is, hypotheses regarding cause-effect relationships were tested using quantitative data); and 2) experimental and quasi-experimental field tests of relationships identified by statistical analysis were funded.
While the LEAA efforts later failed to mature due to the advent of the Reagan
administration in 1980 and the new fiscal conservatism in Congress, it is still true
that LEAA's switch to a management *control* system represented what must be
done to help managers in the field understand the important questions about
input-output relationships (see Zedlewski, 1979).

In summary, the first two sections of this chapter have presented the argument
that management systems and human behavioral approaches not only can but must
be joined in attempts to establish management systems. The reasons for this have
to do with the contributions that organizational theory and human behavior literature have to make to processes which 1) start with questions about value clarification, as management system do; and 2) require in their implementation a lengthy
period of commitment-making and process refinement, as management systems
also do. In this section on research design we have sought to add the additional
point that the most important management control questions require a systems
approach which incorporates research into causal relationships. While this could
be done in an autocratic manner by an elite group of experts, it is probably best
done by thinking of the organization as a self-evaluating agency (see Wildavsky,
1972). That in turn requires a reliance on human behavioral concerns lest the
management system's implementation fall into one of the numerous pitfalls discussed in the next section.

THE IMPLEMENTATION OF MANAGEMENT SYSTEMS

Although usually thought of as a "hard" intervention technique, implementation
of a management system requires a full measure of attention to the so-called "soft"
details of human behavioral considerations. Increasingly, systems analysts, industrial engineers, and others oriented toward "hard" approaches are involved in human behavioral intervention techniques as well. Without them, implementation of
management systems often becomes unproductive. In this concluding section we
present a real-world public-sector case study of just such an unsuccessful attempt
to implement a management system. The pitfalls of implementation divorced
from human behavioral approaches are outlined, followed by a summary of other
managerial considerations in applying human behavioral concepts to management systems.

The Case of Performance Engineering Systems in Central City

The Performance Engineering System (PES) was installed on a pilot basis in Central City's Department of Administration. Amid considerable fanfare, Mayor

Thomas Brown, a banker who had campaigned "to put the city back on business management principles," announced that PES symbolized his administration's dedication to administrative reform. The system, he said, would soon spread throughout city government and lead to savings of hundreds of thousands of dollars. Secretary Nancy Smith, head of the Department of Administration and a close associate of the mayor, was equally commited to PES and saw it as an opportunity to demonstrate her professionalism in carrying out the mandates of the mayor.

Secretary Smith had learned of PES from the mayor of a neighboring city and had brought it to the attention of Mayor Brown. Both saw PES as a general management system which could be implemented quickly for immediate demonstrable payoffs. Its purpose was to raise employee productivity through improvement of performance standards, task processes, and limitation on the number of personnel assigned to tasks. Tasks would be measured and performance standards set, after which a routine performance tracking system would document employee performances, whether above or below standard. To minimize implementation problems, there was to be no attempt to interface PES with existing performance appraisal personnel, or budgeting systems—all of which continued as usual. To save money and time, PES omitted any organization development component.

While PES meant some extra work for the various department heads, Brown and Smith felt that the demonstration effect of the benefits in the Department of Administration would soon overcome resistance to change. In addition, there was the political fact that this was a key symbol in Brown's program and Brown, as a strong mayor, could command the allegiance of his department heads.

Smith slated the start-up of PES for fall, 1982, with the first phase to be completed in the three major agencies of the Department of Administration by June 30, 1983. The following time schedule was adopted:

1. September 1 to October 15—training of PES analysts by consultants
2. October 15 to November 1—orientation of agency employees to PES in general orientation sessions
3. November 1 to January 15—time and motion studies measuring task accomplishment for employees in lower organizational levels; measurement at higher levels accomplished through analogous but more flexible techniques
4. January 15 to April 15—matching of standard times (calculated on the basis of task measurement) with estimated manpower needs; calculation of projected agency workloads
5. November 1 to April 15—simultaneously, conducting of process consultation to make recommendations regarding more efficient procedures, needed equipment investments, or changes in scheduling and assignments of personnel
6. April 15 to May 15—formulation of recommended position

changes (cuts to be made through attrition) and process changes,
with opportunity for agency heads to respond
7. May 15 to June 1–final report to the mayor; recommendation
of reversion of net savings to the city council; preliminary negotiation of PES expansion plans

On September 1, 1982, some sixteen individuals gathered at the temporary
PES office within the Department of Administration. Delegated by their agencies
to receive PES training were a broad range of personnel, including civil engineers,
personnel analysts, and administrative assistants, even secretaries. Some had had
training in PPBS or other management systems, but others had not. Of those who
had had such exposure, the experiences were sometimes with failed systems. As a
group they were younger personnel, energetic and eager for an opportunity to expand their career horizons through new professional experiences. Although their
training was only six weeks in duration, it was intense and left the PES analysts
highly motivated.

Although few questions were raised by employees at the general orientation
sessions, when actual PES analysis began in November the analysts found considerable employee resistance to measurement. In some agencies resistance was greater
than in others. When position cut recommendations were made in April, these
problems came to a crisis point.

When that point was reached the mayor, preoccupied with other problems,
was presented with a difficult decision. The proposed cuts were opposed by his
agency heads, who felt the PES system was not taking all important considerations into account. When these agency heads appealed to the mayor to restore
their cut personnel, the mayor ruled in their favor, preferring to go with known
and trusted political allies rather than an uncertain new management system. The
PES office found itself unable to argue with the mayor or, for that matter, with
the city Personnel Office and Budget Office, both of which supported the agency
heads' argument that their original position justifications had been properly documented and approved–demonstrating need, PES notwithstanding.

Though PES was completed in the Department of Administration and considerable savings identified, other departments failed to adopt it. Identified savings reverted to the City Council which, while pleased, was preoccupied with other
matters. The PES analysts were eventually returned to the same positions from
which they had been borrowed. Their home-agency superiors showed little interest
in the PES project. In the end, some process changes were made and a number of
low-level clerical and service positions were eliminated. The distribution of these
cuts was not very different from that brought about by position freezes previous
mayors had imposed. Nonetheless, when a new productivity system was installed
two years later, some of the PES lessons were incorporated and the PES implementation attempt was, at a minimum, a useful, if not always appreciated learning
experience for city government.

Lessons of the Central City Case

What are the lessons of a case like PES in Central City, from a human behavioral point of view? There are many. For our purposes, however, ten can be identified for brief discussion.

1. Rational Systems Versus Human Systems

There is a common but mistaken belief that if a system works it will spread by the force of its own example. This argument equates the demonstration effect in the public sector with the effect of competitive advantage in the private marketplace. Unlike the business marketplace, however, in the public sector there is no force equivalent to the profit motive as tied to consumer choice. The mere demonstration that a particular innovation is worthy is rarely in itself a strong motivator for change when installation of a new management system has high costs in terms of personnel, resources, and opportunities. While it might be rational to expect change on the basis of demonstration that a management system is cost-effective, the reality is that human systems respond in a more complex manner requiring other motivators be built into the project design.

2. The Limits of Command

In Central City it was assumed that the mayor's political authority would suffice to effect whatever changes were not motivated by the demonstration effect. While this might be true in some circumstances, the PES planners did not realistically assess the limits of political authority. If political command is to be the central motivator in a management system implementation, it must be more than a mere initial blessing—it must be a strong, continuing direct involvement by the chief executive. Chief executives, however, can rarely devote adequate time to management system implementation. Policy matters seem more important, the management system seems technical and mystifying, and there is an assumption that administrative matters should be something subordinates take care of. Beyond publicising systems like PES as symbols ("Yes, we have one!") the chief executive will rarely find political advantage in associating with the details of management systems design and implementation. In fact, to the extent the system envisions personnel and program cuts, the chief executive may want to maintain considerable distance from these details so as to preserve his options.

3. Equity For Major Actors

Every successful system implementation rests on a self-reinforcing incentive structure. In Central City, all system benefits reverted to the city council (albeit with political status benefits accruing to the Mayor and Secretary of Administration). This has a certain rationale in public administration since the legislative branch is supposed to make allocative decisions. In reality, however, not much can be said in favor of a system which fails to distribute benefits among those whose support is necessary for system success. For example, it would have been a better design to revert part of savings back to agency heads for funding of new, approved projects using savings derived from productivity-related cuts brough about by PES. A willingness to design a system with incentives for all major actors requires a relatively high degree of managerial sophistication, sacrificing short-run gains for the top actor (e.g., the city council) in favor of greater long-run gains through greater system effectiveness based on an equitable incentive system.

4. Equity For Minor Actors

Most management systems impact lowest-level employees more adversely than managerial employees. Ironically, it is these employees who have the least to say about their tasks. To the extent they are performing tasks inefficiently or unnecessarily, it is often their superiors who are to blame. On the other hand, since personnel costs are a high percentage of total costs in public administration, and since lower-level personnel are the bulk of all personnel costs, it is inevitable that savings engendered by a management system will come heavily through position cuts at lower levels. These in turn bring demoralization and opposition (particularly in unionized jurisdictions). Although a policy of layoffs through attrition is a major remedy, it should be recognized that the implementation of management systems has major externalities in the form of social costs. Part of system benefits properly should be dedicated to these costs as, for example, through establishment of relocation and retraining funds.

5. Process Needs

It is tempting to treat human behavioral approaches as an unnecessary frill. Why not take the direct approach to implementing a system like PES? The direct approach, it is reasoned, would save considerable time and money. Human behavioral corollaries to management system implementation are necessary for three reasons, however: 1) because general orientation meetings are an inadequate way to overcome almost-inevitable employee resistance to change; 2) because participation in the system design process is necessary to invest managers and employees with a sense of ownership in the system; and 3) because the organization must be acculturated to better understanding of each actor's role and needs in the new system to be implemented. Goal-setting, team-building, and other thrusts of organization development and like human behavioral approaches are fundamental to achieving a design responsive to these three needs.

6. Time Frame

Organizational change is a process which requires a longer time frame than does a technical change requiring only a solution. If a chief executive forges ahead with management system installation in a short period—and one year is too short—adequate organization development programs, adequate training programs, and adequate negotiation of coordination of the new system with old arrangements cannot be undertaken in time. Without these, failure follows.

7. Staffing Needs

Central City staffing was inadequate because junior personnel were selected to become PES analysts. This role called for them to come into agencies as outsiders, evaluate management practices, and recommend budget cuts for senior agency heads. This sort of "whiz kid" strategy occasionally works, as when under President Kennedy, Secretary of Defense Robert McNamara installed PPBS using a junior staff. But in that case junior status was counterbalanced by prestigious professional credentials and a triumphant success record in private industry. Lacking both position and professional status, the Central City PES analysts lacked the credibility to effectively defend their recommendations. Affected managers rightly claimed equal or greater professionalism in their opposition to PES recommendations, arguing that a six-week training program could not produce analysts of high caliber. And in fact, the short training program was inadequate to establish analyst self-confidence, let alone credibility with skeptical superiors.

8. Career Development Needs

The Central City PES system lacked a career development program for its analysts (just as it was isolated from all other Personnel Office functions). Although seemingly small, this was a critical omission. A key incentive for participation as a PES analyst was the prospect of career development. In practice, returning analysts found that back in their home agencies their PES experience was ignored. Instead, they found they were now out of touch with agency plans and programs and had to catch up to reestablish themselves. Needless to say, this was demoralizing to the analyst staff and was a significant factor in the discrediting of the PES program.

9. Program Coordination Needs

Management control systems are often marked by a self-defeating faddishness. PPBS, ZBB, and other systems come and go in rapid succession. When a new system like PES is to be tried, it faces an expectation that it too will soon pass. Officials prepare to "hunker down" for a year while it blows over. The passing of each system makes implementation of the next more difficult. This is so not only because of the skepticism faddishness breeds but also because each successive system leaves lingering residues which compete with the new system. Although requiring a much longer time frame, ideally the new system would be thoroughly coordinated with existing procedures in personnel, budgeting, and other "overhead" functions.

10. Setting Expectations

Most management systems are oversold initially, setting the stage for later dis-illusionment and abolition. By presenting the PES system as appropriate for all aspects of tasks at any level, in any department, a commitment was made to im-plement PES even in complex settings where it was inappropriate. Task measure-ment for lower-level employees, for example, was universalized into performance measurement for all employees. Unfortunately, the failure of performance measure-ment for nonroutine higher-level jobs then becomes generalized as a judgment that all task measurement is invalid. Once this expectation is set, strong pressure exists to shift away from the rejected function toward other functions. In the case of PES at Central City the shift was toward process consulting (providing particular-istic advice about agency-specific tasks), a function which varied greatly from agency to agency. In essence, as PES failed to meet unduly high expectations re-garding its core technology (task measurement) it shifted toward peripheral func-tions. The setting of over-high expectations leads routinely toward goal displace-ment, often followed by fragmentation of the management system.

CONCLUSION

At almost every point the management of systems implementation involves human behavioral considerations treated in recent literature on administration (see Garson and Brenneman, 1981a, 1981b). For example, Britan (1981) studied a major pro-ductivity program in the U.S. Department of Commerce and found that the rela-tive failure of the program to achieve substantial results was understandable only through an emphasis on examination of personal understandings and relationships of the sort studied by students of organizational behavior. Wallach (1979) like-wise emphasizes the importance of training in system changes. With regard to hu-man behavioral approaches of the participatory type, the need for these is high-lighted in Draper and Pitsvada's study (1981) of ZBB, emphasizing investment in the system through participation. Likewise, participatory methods are viewed as critical in Gregg and Diegelman's (1979) study of productivity systems in the Law Enforcement Assistance Administration and by Simon (1978) in his study of man-agement information system development and the need for team approaches.

To the student of human behavior in organizations, many of the considera-tions outlined in this chapter will seem like common sense. Unfortunately, they are not! In the real world of public administration it is more common than not to find even the most elementary human behavioral approaches ignored in favor of "hard," "direct," and "rational" implementation of management systems. Often, when such methods later fail, the organization's members are faulted as being too uncooperative or too ignorant to implement the system. We hypothesize that in the vast majority of such instances the system in question displayed poor incentive system design, failure to utilize organization development approaches, omission of human resource planning (e.g., career development), and other failures to apply human behavioral approaches. What is needed is a reconceptualization of the role of the manager. The concept of the manager as the controller of technical systems must be abandoned in favor of the concept of the manager as designer of social as well as task systems for the agency.

REFERENCES

Britan, G. M. (1981). *Bureaucracy and Innovation: An Ethnography of Change* (Beverly Hills, Cal.: Sage Publishing Company).

Draper, Frank U. and B. T. Pitsvada (1981). ZBB-Looking Back After Ten Years, *Public Administration Reviews*, Volume 41, Number 1 (January/February): pp. 73-75.

Ford, Charles H. (1980), Manage by Decisions, Not by Objectives, *Business Horizons*, Volume 23, Number 1 (February):pp. 7-18.

Garson, G. David (1981). From Policy Science to Policy Analysis: A Quarter Century of Progress?, *Policy Studies Journal*, Volume 9, Number 4 (Special Issue L2):pp. 535-543.

Garson, G. David and D. S. Brenneman (1981a). Limits of the Rational Model of Resource Rationing, *Southern Review of Public Administration* Volume 5, Number 1 (Spring):pp. 5-21.

Garson, G. David and D. S. Brenneman (1981b). Incentive Systems and Goal Displacement in Personnel Resource Management, *Review of Public Administration* (Spring):pp. 1-12.

Granvold, D. K. (1978). Supervision by Objectives, *Administration in Social Work*, Volume 2, Number 2 (Summer):pp. 199-209.

Gregg, James M. and R. F. Diegelman (1979). Red Tape on Trial: Elements of a Successful Effort to Cut Burdensome Federal Reporting Requirements, *Public Administration Review*, Volume 39, Number 2 (March/April):pp. 171-175.

Gremillion, Lee L., J. L. McKenney, and P. J. Pyburn (1980). Program Planning in the National Forest Service, *Public Administration Review*, Volume 2, Number 3 (May/June):pp. 226-230.

Huse, Edgar A. (1980). *Organization Development and Change, 2nd Edition* (St. Paul, Minn.: West).

Landau, Martin and Russell Stout Jr. (1979). To Manage is Not To Control: Or the Folly of Type II Errors, *Public Administration Review*, Volume 39, Number 2 (March/April):pp. 148-156.

McConkie, Mark L. (1979). Classifying and Reviewing Empirical Work on MBO: Some Implications, *Group and Organization Studies*, Volume 4, Number 4 (December):pp. 461-475.

McTighe, John T. (1979). Management Strategies to Deal with Shrinking Resources, *Public Administration Review*, Volume 39, Number 1 (January/February):pp. 86-90.

Moore, Perry (1980). Zero-Base Budgeting in American Cities, *Public Administration Review*, Volume 40, Number 3 (May/June):pp. 253-258.

Moore, Perry D. and Ted Staton (1981). Management by Objectives in American Cities, *Public Personnel Management Journal*, Volume 10, Number 2 (Summer):pp. 223-232.

Natemeyer, Walter E., ed. (1978). *Classics Of Organizational Behavior* (Oak Park, Ill.: Moor Publishing Company).

Peters, Thomas J. (1980). Management Systems: The Language of Organizational Character and Competence, *Organizational Dynamics*, Volume 9, Number 1 (Summer):pp. 2-26.

Sauser, William I. Jr. (1980). Evaluating Employee Performance: Needs, Problems, Possible Solutions, *Public Personnel Management*, Volume 9, Number 1 (January/February):pp. 11-18.

Simon, Sidney H. (1978). Personnel's Role in Developing an Information System, *Personnel Journal*, Volume 57, Number 11 (November):pp. 622-625.

Spano, R. M., T. J. Kiresuk, and S. H. Lund (1977). An Operational Model to Achieve Accountability in Social Work in Health Care, *Social Work in Health Care*, Volume 3, Number 2 (Winter):pp. 123-141.

Tannenbaum, Arnold S. (1962). Control in Organizations: Individual Adjustment and Organizational Performance, *Public Administration Review*, Volume 7, Number 2 (September):pp. 236-257.

Wallach, Arthur E. (1979). System Changes Begin in the Training Department, *Personnel Journal*, Volume 58, Number 12 (December):pp. 846-848 ff.

Wildavsky, Aaron (1972). The Self-Evaluating Organization, *Public Administration Review*, Volume 32, Number 5 (September/October):pp. 509-520.

Zedlewski, Edwin W. (1979). Performance Measurement in Public Agencies: The Law Enforcement Evolution, *Public Administration Review*, Volume 39, Number 5 (September/October):pp. 488-492.

PERFORMANCE APPRAISAL

In a summary of literature on organizational design and systems analysis published in 1965, Haberstroh drew two broad conclusions from his review of performance measurement research: "First, performance reporting is omnipresent and necessarily so. Second, almost every individual instance of performance reporting has something wrong with it" (Haberstroh, 1965). Performance appraisal remains omnipresent in the 1980's. While every instance may continue to have its drawbacks, employee and public tolerance for weaknesses in performance appraisal is less than ever before and pressures for greater validity and reliability are building.

In this chapter we will review the performance appraisal process by first addressing the needs of the organization regarding performance appraisal and the context within which those needs unfold. Then we explore alternative approaches for achieving performance assessment objectives and specify criteria to be considered in a model system. Finally we discuss the very specific managerial skills required in the assessment interview.

ORGANIZATIONAL NEEDS: WHY EVALUATE PERFORMANCE?

Performance appraisal has been defined as "simply an attempt to think clearly about each person's current performance and future prospects against the background of the total work situation" (Mayfield, 1960). With human resources representing the largest and most valuable factor of production in the public sector, organizational capacity for "clear thinking" on performance appraisal has always been important. Now, however, three new factors in the environment of human resource management place more stringent demands on performance appraisal systems.

First, the reluctance of the public to pay higher taxes, the continuing demand for public services, and the spiraling costs of producing and delivering existing goods and services, has placed extraordinary productivity demands on government. Well-constructed and implemented performance appraisal is often relied on as a panacea for meeting this challenge. While effective performance can't reduce these conflicting environmental pressures, it may provide the basis for a more rational managerial response to the legislative official alert to "bureaucratic waste."

Second, increased demand for equitable treatment of employees has challenged performance appraisal systems. Valid and reliable performance appraisal instruments can demonstrate equity to groups protected under various equal employment opportunity (EEO) laws and regulations. Because performance appraisals are used in making a variety of selection decisions including promotion, merit raise, training, and transfer, they must meet the standards promulgated by the various EEO enforcement agencies in the document, Uniform Guidelines for Employees Selection Procedures (See Chapter 11). In other words, performance appraisal is a selection procedure and as such may be the grounds for a charge of discrimination.

Dena Schneier reports that the courts have found the use of performance ratings to be discriminatory when:

- They are based on subjective and ill-defined criteria.
- They might be affected by sexual and/or racial bias.
- They are not collected and scored under standardized conditions, thus affecting their reliability and validity.
- The content of the rating instrument is not based on a careful job analysis.
- They are not shown to be job related through proper validation studies. (Schneier, 1978, see also Beacham, 1979).

Performance appraisals lacking validity and reliability can indict the selection decisions of public managers.

Third, with the ascent of public sector unions, performance appraisal systems have been targeted as an important subject in public sector arbitration. In the federal work force this trend has been accelerated by the required consultation with labor organizations in federal agency design of performance appraisal programs. (Federal Personnel Manual, Chapter 430.) Though performance standards are not subject to collective bargaining negotiations presently, union pressure for negotiation of standards will rise as pay becomes linked to the appraisal process. William Holley's recent analysis of arbitration decisions focusing on the performance appraisal component of collective bargaining agreements provides guidance to public sector managers (Holley, 1978). Typical examples of actions where arbitrators rule in favor of the grievant include:

1. When the employee has been denied the right to review performance appraisal records.
2. When performance appraisal systems are altered without consultation with union officials.
3. When appraisals are administered at improper times.
4. When a performance appraisal form doesn't meet the requirements and specifications of the collective agreement.
5. When employees are not made aware of performance standards that will be used in appraisals.

In taking adverse action against employees, there is one point managers shouldn't ignore. When an employee is discharged on the basis of negative performance appraisal, the burden of proof rests on the employer to justify the discharge. Arbitrators have also required employers to demonstrate that performance standards are in fact attainable. As a strategy for blunting endless challenges to management decisions, Holley advises public sector managers to anticipate increasing union interest in performance appraisal by designing performance appraisal programs that are sensitive to the thinking of union representatives.

Typically performance appraisal systems are adopted in order to serve one or more of the following objectives:

1. Management development—to provide a framework for developing employees by identifying and preparing individuals for enlarged responsibilities.
2. Performance measurement—evaluating individual employee accomplishments and measuring the relative value of an employee's contribution to the overall task of the organization.
3. Performance improvement—identifying areas of individual weakness and devising strategies for strengthening employees accordingly.
4. Compensation—determining salary and merit pay based upon performance.
5. Identifying potential—targeting candidates for promotion or transfer within the organization.
6. Feedback—discussing actual performance level against the organization's performance standards for an employee.
7. Manpower planning—evaluating the present supply of human resources for replacement planning.
8. Communications—providing a setting for open exchange between supervisors and subordinates. (Lazer and Wikstrom, 1977.)

Most performance appraisal systems cannot meet all these objectives simultaneously. One survey which asked 25 private sector human resource managers to list problems encountered with performance appraisal found the first item listed to be the conflicting and multiple uses of performance appraisal. Though the practical advantage of a multipurpose appraisal system is clear, its pitfalls should be acknowledged. We can illustrate this point by analyzing four broad kinds of performance appraisal: development planning, work review, compensation review and human resource allocation planning.

In *development planning*, which exists to improve the individual's skills and motivate individuals to take initiative for their own development, the manager is the consultant. As such he or she helps, supports, and evaluates the employee. The employee is the initiator, risk taker, creator, and definer of the situation. By contrast, in the *work review*, which is supposed to improve short-range productivity, the manager assumes the role of boss, director, controller, and evaluator. In this context the employee is a subordinate, responding to direction, although perhaps suggesting ideas. In the *compensation* review, where the purpose is to motivate effort to improve productivity, the manager is clearly an appraiser who evaluates the employee and judges his or her comparative value. Here the employee becomes his or her own advocate, evaluating and negotiating with the manager. Finally, in the *human resource planning* situation, when performance appraisal is used to assure long range productivity and organizational effectiveness, the manager evaluates and recommends. The employee is basically a salesperson promoting him or herself in light of the organization's long-range plans. Clearly, each of these appraisal situations gives rise not only to different, even compatible, roles, but also calls for different managerial skills, occasions different processes, and stimulates different problems. (Lazer and Wikstrom, 1977.)

Critical to effective performance appraisal is the manager's firm grasp of the purpose of each review. To the extent that purposes may be in conflict, effective management of the system demands awareness of the tension points. Organizations and managers must clearly define what they want performance appraisal to do for them. With criteria established and roughly ranked, organizations and managers can be prepared to explore alternative forms of performance appraisal technique. Before turning to specific appraisal techniques, however, general characteristics of an effective performance appraisal system should be addressed.

In promulgating its performance appraisal system for a federal employee, the U.S. Office of Personnel Management suggests the following list of characteristics as providing a frame of reference for effective performance appraisal systems:

1. Performance is measured against established comprehensive standards which are written in a clear and explicit style and communicated to the employee at entry on the job and at the beginning of the appraisal period.
2. Performance appraisal information is used for specific purposes, e.g., to determine developmental needs, awards, and retention and not for vague abstract reasons, such as appraisal for promotion potential unrelated to a particular type of job.

3. Appraisal criteria and techniques are appropriate to the specific purposes for which the appraisal is being done.
4. The information produced is useful for work-related decisions.
5. Data are as objective, reliable, and valid as possible.
6. Instruments for performance review and appraisal are easy for the participants to understand and use.
7. Supervisors are appraised in terms of how competently they perform their supervisory duties.
8. Employees are kept informed about methods and purposes of appraisals.
9. A process exists which allows for impartial resolution of complaints and review.
10. Employees are promptly notified in writing and preferably orally, too, of the results of their performance appraisal. To prevent misunderstanding about whether the appraisal was given or what the appraisal contained each employee is asked to indicate by signature and date, the receipt of the appraisal, not agreement with it.
11. Employees' performance appraisals are kept current.
12. There is no attempt to satisfy all the management purposes of the appraisal at a single annual discussion of performance. Systems provide additional opportunity for supervisors and employees to discuss, improve, and plan for job performance.
13. Employees are informed about the steps the agency will follow in using appraisal information to make decisions to reward, promote, reassign, train, retain in RIF, or demote employees." (Levinson, 1980.)

CONTEXT FACTORS AFFECTING PERFORMANCE APPRAISAL

Both task characteristics and organizational arrangement need to be taken into account in designing a performance appraisal system. (Dornbush and Scott, 1975.) Task, complexity, goal clarity, and predictability all bear on the appraisal process.

If a task if highly complex, such as provision of human services by public agencies, evaluation criteria need to be established for all parts of the process and costs in time and effort need to be weighed in order to learn the level of measurement for subtask achievement. Also, when goals are highly diffuse, as in the public sector, they do not allow for clear specification of performance properties. Efforts to impose specificity may result in goal transformation or goal displacement. (Dornbush and Scott, 1975.) Haberstroh warns that "performance measures should reflect real goals, for they surely will become operational goals in the day-to-day work patterns of affected personnel." (Haberstroh, 1965.) Finally if a task outcome is unpredictable, assessment of performance on the basis of results may yield inaccurate information. Outcomes may be unpredictable when factors other than the skill of the employee control performance. Potential controlling factors could include budget contingencies, client cooperativeness, and inept policy-making.

Organizational arrangements such as visibility of task performance also affect performance appraisal options. Many types of performance are difficult to observe because of the nature of the job, because of resistance of employees to observation, or because of prohibitive costs. Also, many employers may be conducting evaluations within a complex authority system, thus producing increased opportunity for miscommunication. For example, studies indicate that appraisals might be skewed by an appraiser's awareness, while evaluating subordinates, that he or she is also being evaluated by a superior. (McGuire, 1980.) Next, task interdependence is a feature of organizational life with important implications for performance appraisal. Often, particularly in public sector organizations, single outcomes cannot be traced to the contributions of individual employees. Typically it takes a contribution from a number of functional sources to produce a desired result. When operating within the context of high task interdependence the organization might try to segment the units in which the service is produced so links can be made between individual performances and outcomes.

The distribution of power in the organization will also be reflected in the evaluation process and is a principal factor in shaping the design of performance appraisal systems. Disagreement between evaluator and employee in terms of what and how to evaluate is resolved in both the public and private sector according to the distribution of power. This explains both the pressure on the part of the appraisee, who is often represented by a union, to gain influence on the appraisal process, and the capacity of the management to escape appraisal in many organizations. When appraisers either have little input into setting the criteria for appraisal, or when they are powerless in their own positions, evaluation will suffer, no matter the design. (Dorn Bush and Scott, 1975.)

Rosabeth Moss Kanter suggests that the reliability of formal performance measures tends to be greatest when the following conditions prevail in an organization.

1. The purpose of the appraisal is clear;
2. Tasks are simple;
3. Goals for the task are clear;
4. Outcomes are predictable;
5. Tasks are relatively independent;
6. Task performance is observable;
7. Criteria for performance are set by those later assessing performance;

8. Appraisers feel secure in their own jobs and have no personal stake in hurting the performer.

However when complexity, interdependence, power concerns, and multiple appraisal purposes increase, then so must flexibility of the appraisal system and sensitivity to its limitations. (Brinkerhoff and Kanter, 1980.)

PERFORMANCE APPRAISAL TECHNIQUES: A SURVEY

In this section we will survey eight performance appraisal techniques and explore two promising appraisal methods in depth.

Essay Appraisal

This technique asks appraisers to write a short statement covering a particular employee's strengths, weaknesses, areas for improvement, potential and so on. The method is often used in the selection of employees when written recommendations are solicited from former employers, supervisors, or teachers. Supervisors are free to rate performance without being constrained to rate specific attributes or responsibilities. The major disadvantage with essay appraisal is its variability in standards applied. This free form method invites supervisors to comment on different aspects of an employee's performance. While useful as part of an employee development and promotability assessment, essay appraisals are difficult to combine and compare and thus provide little assistance in salary or merit pay administration.

Graphic Rating Scale

A typical graphic rating scale assesses a person on quality and quantity of his or her work and on a variety of other factors that vary with specific jobs. Often included are personal traits such as flexibility, cooperation, level of motivation, and organizational ability. But quality and quantity of work, job knowledge, planning ability, are also rated. The predetermined scale allows the supervisor to assess employees, whether they are outstanding, superior, above average, average, below average, unsatisfactory. Such checklists typically allow supervisors wide latitude in interpreting terms. This, in conjunction with heavy personal trait focus, produces varying standards of comparison used across raters. The graphic scale does produce more consistent quantifiable data than the essay appraisal, and thus lends itself more to compensation decision-making.

Some combination of essay and graphic rating scale is the most common form of performance appraisal for state and local government. One recent study of major cities in the U.S. reports that 68 percent (N=30) appraise employees through graphic rating scales with some scope for essay type comments. (Lacho, et. al. 1979.)

Field Review

This type of appraisal is used as a check on reliability of the standards used among raters. A member of the personnel or central administrative staff meets with a small group of raters from each supervisory unit to go over ratings for each employee and to identify areas of dispute and to arrive at a usable standard. This group judgment technique tends to be more fair and valid than individual ratings. Though it is considerably more time consuming, when the principal individual assessment method is an essay, or graphic rating scale, the field review provides critical information on rater variation. This is especially necessary if performance appraisal is to be used in salary administration.

Forced-Choice Rating

There are many variations of this method, but the most common version asks raters to choose from among groups of statements, those which best fit the person being evaluated, and those which least fit. The statements are then weighted and scored in much the same way psychological tests are scored. The theory behind this type of appraisal is that since the rater does not know what the scoring weight for each statement is, he or she cannot play favorites. A member of the personnel staff applies the scoring weight to determine the rating. Though this approach does aim for fairness, it rankles managers who feel they don't need to be "tricked" into making honest appraisals. Obviously the usefulness of this appraisal is highest for making salary determinations and is lowest as a counseling or planning instrument in the appraisal review.

Critical Incident Appraisal

Supervisors are asked to keep a record on each employee and to record actual incidents of positive and negative behavior. This method is beneficial in that it deals with actual behavior rather than abstractions and thus provides factual incidents to discuss with an employee. But on the negative side it is time consuming for the supervisor and it share the free-form problem with essay appraisals. It is susceptible to varying standards of comparison and thus has limited use in salary administration.

Management By Objectives (MBO)

In this approach employees are asked to set, or help set, their own performance goals. Objectives are usually described in terms of performance standards or results, but employee development objectives are often included. Periodically employees and supervisors monitor progress against objectives and at the end of an appraisal period employees and supervisors assess performance against each objective. MBO has considerable merit in its involvement of the individual in setting standards by which he or she will be judged and its emphasis on results rather than on abstract personality characteristics. The disadvantage of MBO is in its susceptibility to the use of varying standards to establish performance objectives. Proper administration of MBO requires considerable time and skill. It is most appropriate for senior level positions that require individual goal setting. Moving down the organization it is important to recognize the manipulative potential of MBO in which pseudo-participation substitutes for genuine employee involvement. If management intends to impose work standards and objectives on lower level employees it should be done openly and explicitly.

Work-Standards

This approach provides for the organization to explicitly lay down work standards instead of asking employees to set goals and objectives. The work standards technique establishes work and staffing targets aimed at increasing productivity. Under work standards the organization develops or alters position descriptions for each position to reflect all the major responsibilities and standards of performance. When realistically used and when standards are fair and visible it can be an effective type of performance appraisal. The most serious problem is that of comparability. With different standards for different people, it is difficult to make comparisons for purposes of promotion.

Ranking Methods

For purposes of comparing people in different units, the best approach appears to be a ranking technique involving pooled judgment. The two most effective ranking methods include alteration-ranking and paired-comparison ranking. Both of these methods ask the supervisor to select "most valuable" employees (Oberg, 1972). While some variant of a ranking method is among the best available for developing valid ranking for salary administration, its usefulness in employee counselling and development may be negative. Thompson and Dalton report that contrary to the intention of the comparative method, inspiring employees to work harder, in fact it reduces employee self esteem and therefore performance. (Thompson ans Dalton, 1970.)

Assessment Centers

Assessment centers are gaining popularity for the prediction and assessment of future potential. Typically, individuals from different areas are brought together to spend two or three days working on individual and group assignments. The pooled judgment of observers leads to an order of merit ranking of participants. The greatest drawback of this system is its time and cost. But its substantial advantage is its potential impact on equal employment opportunity. It may give people currently invisible and imbedded deep in the organization a chance to demonstrate their potential to higher management in an organization. (Oberg, 1972.)

Given these eight basic performance appraisal techniques, what is the pattern of use in the public sector? At the federal level a new performance appraisal system, characterized as the "cornerstone" of the Civil Service Reform Act of 1978, is now in place. It represents a combination of several methods above and includes identifying critical elements of an employee's position, developing objectives, job related performance standards for those elements, periodic progress reviews and a direct relationship between appraisal of performance and pay (Brown, 1982).

Various types of performance appraisal systems are found in state and local government and survey data reporting current practices across these units of government suggest substantial variation in practices within jurisdictions. An Urban Institute study of fifty states, twenty-five counties, and twenty-five cities, conducted in the late 1970's, reported the following. Fifty of the hundred governments used systems that involved supervisor ratings of individual employees—either essay appraisals or rating instruments with non-specific performance factors. Sixteen jurisdictions used systems in which employees were appraised on the basis of their achievement of performance targets. In the remaining governments, individual departments determined their own appraisal systems (Greiner, et al. 1981.) Two performance appraisal methods receiving most attention in the literature, management by objectives (MBO) and behaviorally-anchored rating scales (BARS), are not widely used in government, according to the Urban Institute Survey. Only 15 of the governments responding used MBO and only one used behaviorally-based checklists. Nonetheless, MBO and BARS systems offer attractive alternatives to public managers.

MANAGEMENT BY OBJECTIVES

MBO is a basic management and control system that can be used directly in individual performance appraisal. As a management system, objectives or goals are established for the organization, each unit, each manager within each unit, and each employee within a work area. The focus in this goal setting phase is not on the behavior of the employee but on the effectiveness of the employee's contribution to organizational goals. Introduced by Peter Drucker in 1954, management by objectives is based upon a theory of motivation that assumes employees will be more productive if they participate in setting their work objectives. While there are many variants of MBO, three steps are common to most.

Mutual Goal Setting

Supervisors and subordinates meet to establish results employees will achieve. Objectives established should meet the following criteria:

1. They should be linked to the important objectives of the supervisor.
2. They should represent the employee's most significant responsibilities.
3. They should be achievable with reasonable effort and within existing resource limitations.
4. They should include for supervisors managing aspects such as planning and staff development.
5. They should be stated precisely enough so that there is little change of misinterpretation or disagreement over meaning. (Allen and Rosenberg, 1978.)

Coaching: Working Toward Goals

After objectives are set employees typically enjoy substantial freedom in achieving them. But in some adaptations of MBO, coaching on the part of supervisors is strongly encouraged both to guide and to lend support to employees. The supervisor may intervene to take stock of where the work stands relative to expected results, to exchange any new relevant information, or to jointly take a look at anticipated problems. Calhoun and Jerdee describe this coaching intervention as possibly the most important and challenging part of supervision. "Like a good athletic coach, a good supervisory coach observes his team members, knows them well, helps them to help themselves, and brings out the best in them. . . coaching is directly related to your subordinates doing a good job. They want your approval and to be able to come to you for help. Coaching skills help you capitalize on these needs of employees. Subordinates can and do change through coaching help from the superior." (Calhoun and Jerdee, 1976.)

Reviewing Performance

In this third step within MBO, performance is appraised in terms of goal attainment. The performance review is carried out in the form of a formal discussion between the supervisor and the subordinate at the end of a work period. The purpose is to reach agreement on what was done well and what improvements are needed. In performance review it is important to keep in mind extraneous factors that may have influenced the objective levels of accomplishment such as recision of legislation, budgetary uncertainty, and the whole network of other factors we have discussed.

The potential pitfalls of MBO have been catalogued in the literature (Schneier and Beatty, 1977) and focus primarily on the goal setting step. In mutual goal setting MBO may falter because of:

1. Overemphasis on objectives to the neglect of means.
2. Tendency to focus on short term results.

3. Temptation to include results already achieved.
4. Tendency to name results easily attainable.
5. Objectives established not in the control of the employee.
6. Significant conditions under which objectives are to be achieved are ignored such as decreasing cost by 15 percent without decreasing services.
7. Too many objectives may be stated, not distinguishing important objectives from unimportant objectives.

While goal setting is an especially delicate part of the MBO process, this appraisal system may falter because of a manager's neglect at the "working toward goals" or "performance review" stages. Failure of MBO may be attributed to a lack of coaching skill and willingness to apply it, or to inattention to performance review. With even the most finely-honed goals statement MBO as a performance appraisal device will prove inadequate to the task when the second and third steps of the process are neglected.

BEHAVIORALLY-ANCHORED RATING SCALES

While MBO focuses on employee effectiveness, behaviorally-anchored rating scales (BARS) focuses on employee behavior. Also concerned with getting results, BARS identifies with the critical areas of a job and describes more or less effective job behaviors in getting results. Combining two of the approaches to performance appraisal discussed above, performance standards and critical incident, BARS appraisal instruments are based on characteristics of a job or job family. BARS appraisal instruments are constructed through the following steps:

1. Jobs to be appraised are identified.
2. Job incumbents, their managers, or both identify dimensions of the job critical to results, and write several statements describing behavior that is especially effective and especially ineffective in gaining results. Then several statements are written describing neither especially effective or ineffective behavior.
3. Statements are grouped into performance dimensions by scale designers, discarding statements that are not job specific, not observable or do not fall within one of the job dimensions. Statements assigned to a job category by at least 75 percent of the job incumbents or managers are retained.
4. Each statement is evaluated by each scale designer. Statements are assigned a scale value from 1 (very ineffective performance) to 7 or 9 (very effective performance). Within the performance dimension the mean and standard deviation are calculated for all statements. The mean rating provides the scaled level of effectiveness for each statement. The degree of agreement among

raters on the scale values indicated by the standard deviation, with a statement typically retained if its standard deviation is less the 1.5. (Goodale, 1977.)

Specific measures which attempt to define performance dimensions and scale values in behavioral terms have been recommended by numerous researchers. (Barrett, 1966; Campbell, Dunnette, Lawler, Week, 1970)

BARS is a particularly useful technique if the manager gives high priority to feedback. By removing the ambiguity of performance appraisal, it helps reduce employee anxiety and provides the employer with very specific direction in advising the employee on performance improvement. In terms of a critical performance appraisal consideration, EEO, BARS may point the way toward less subjective and ultimately more valid performance appraisal. As well because BARS is a quantitative technique, appraisal scores can be tied to salary structure and ranges of scores on BARS can be tied to different level of merit raises. (Beatty and Schneier, 1977).

We have described MBO as a broad management and control system that could have individual appraisal applications. BARS, by contrast, is an individual appraisal device with potential to catalyze an entire organization. The spinoff effects of BARS may touch the whole human resource management area. BARS may identify behavioral criteria on which to make decisions and design selection tests; it may identify specific behavioral training objectives; and it may highlight areas of poor performance in the organization where special reward structures may be installed (Beatty and Schneier, 1977).

In terms of performance appraisal alone managers turn to BARS because it addresses several major problems in performance appraisal feedback. Kearney (1978) identifies four compelling advantages to the BARS system:

1. Clarification of differences between behavior, performance and results;
2. Emphasis of appraisal based on observed and measurable job specific behaviors;
3. Improved observation and evaluation skills of managers through their participation in scale construction;
4. Participation of job incumbents in identifying performance dimensions and identifying and scaling job behavior thus reducing disagreement over what constitutes satisfactory performance.

Disadvantages of BARS however are also evident:

1. The jobs of those to be appraised must be relatively stable in content;
2. There must be several people performing a job to spread the cost of scale development;
3. Managers must be able to observe subordinates on a systematic basis;

4. Since pooled judgments are used, enough managers and job in-
    cumbents must be available to construct the scale. (Kearney,
    1978.)

Both MBO and BARS appraisal systems rest on the assumption that the quality of appraisal is a dynamic process, not a yearly event. Both techniques trade on
a high level of participation by persons ultimately using the appraisal system. MBO,
with its effectiveness emphasis, fits best where managers and employees make
direct and measurable contributions to the task. In contrast, BARS may be more
appropriate where individual contributions to overall effectiveness may be hard
to trace. Often this breaks down into an argument for MBO applying to middle-
level positions and BARS to executives. Schneier and Beatty propose that organizations consider integrating MBO and BARS systems by asking employees:

1. What (i.e., results) are you to contribute to this organization in
    measurable terms?
2. How (i.e., behaviorally) do you expect to make this contribu-
    tion or accomplish this objective? (Schneier and Beatty, 1979.)

Traditional MBO would be used to answer the first question and BARS would be
used to deal with the second. (Beatty and Schneier, 1977.) Table 8 provides a
sample form illustrating the use of this MBO/BARS integration.

In this illustration the Unit Supervisor of the Personnel Action Processing
Section is able to set performance expectations which are measured against quali-
fiable measures of effectiveness, such as percent errors causing returns of forms.
But in addition that supervisor can point out to his manager desired behavior which
he exhibited, even though it may not have contributed directly to the numerically
stated goal. Raters can also identify deficiencies which help in counseling and
training decisions for employees.

THE APPRAISAL INTERVIEW

The appraisal interview, part of whatever appraisal system is in use, may be the
most difficult aspect of the process for most managers. Behavioral science research
on the characteristics of effective employee performance and development interviewing is growing steadily. (Maier, 1958; Meyer, et al. 1965, French, et al. 1966;
Kay, 1965.) Increasingly, evidence suggests that knowledge of interviewing skills
and practicing their use strengthens the effectiveness of the session. (Burke and
Burke, 1970.)

Maier has argued that there are both skills and methods requiring attention in
performance appraisal. "This differentiation between skill and method is important
because the goal of the interview determines which method should be used to
achieve it; and once we have clarified the goals. . .the problem of developing the
necessary skill is greatly simplified." (Maier, 1958.) Maier distinguishes between
three methods of interviewing: The "tell and sell" interview, which aims to let the

TABLE 8. An Integrated MBO/BARS Performance Appraisal

Job Title: *Unit Supervisor of Personnel Action Processing Section*
Job Objective: *Ensure prompt accurate processing of all personnel action forms*
Method of Measurement: *Quantity*

Processed Forms in Unit	Present	Date	Target	Date	Actual
% errors causing returns					
% forms processed by day following receipt					

INSTRUCTIONS: Please indicate what you believe to be the typical behavior of this unit supervisor based on your observation of his/her performance.

CHECK ONE

_____ Excellent:	Supervises total clerical processing of all personnel action forms. Maintains up to date knowledge of procedures and rules related to processing. Assist employees in proper processing methods and trains new employees. Attends all staff meetings involving procedures for processing forms to offer technical assistance on processing. Offers suggestions to forms development supervisor on form improvement.
_____ Very Good:	Stresses the importance of immediate form processing. Has good knowledge of processes and procedures. Communicates knowledge to employees. Trains new employees and offers technical assistance to staff when requested to do so. Asks employees to be timely in form processing.
_____ Good:	Is able to answer questions from subordinates and staff on form processes and procedures. Once a year holds update session on new developments in form processes and procedures.
_____ Average:	Gives information to subordinates on form processes and procedures but fails to stress the importance of timeliness in form processing.
_____ Below Average:	Does not actively supervise the processing of personnel action forms. Answers questions of subordinates on procedures but responses are not always accurate.
_____ Poor:	Gives wrong information on response queries about proper processing of personnel action forms.
_____ Unfavorable:	Fails to plan form processing work. Doesn't get forms processed in time to facilitate line manager's needs.

How could this manager improve his/her performance in the area of percent of correct personnel forms processed that is not included in the above description?

employee know how he or she is doing and to encourage compliance with an improvement plan; the "tell and listen" interview, which aims to communicate evaluation and provide for the release of defensive feelings; and the "problem solving" interview, where the principal aim is to stimulate growth and development in the employee.

The "tell and sell" methods calls for salesmanship and patience on the part of the appraiser. The employee is assumed to respond to positive or negative incentives extrinsic to the job itself and the appraising task is to make those connections clear. Patience is called for in managing conflicts that will develop. The flow of communication here is top down and thus such appraisal interviews tend to perpetuate existing values. The "tell and listen" method calls for skill in listening and reflecting feelings as well as summarizing the responses of the appraisee. The appraiser plays the role of counsellor, and motivation lies largely in breaking down resistance to change. Also, the supportive counselling climate in itself is a motivating factor. In addition to these extrinsic motivations, if the interview results in solving a problem in the nature of the job itself this encourages intrinsic motivation. Some upward communication is possible here as the employee responds to the employer's comments. In a third interviewing method, "problem solving," the interviewer should be skilled not only in listening to and reflecting on the employee's feelings but also in posing exploratory questions that will yield new ideas about the job and the organization. Sensitively reflecting these new thoughts back to the employee individually and in the context of summarizing is a critical appraisal skill in this method. While some extrinsic motivations are always present, an intrinsic motivation is assumed in inviting the employee to discuss his/her job, how it might be restructured for greater productivity, and how the manager can contribute to the improved productivity effort. Motivation in this model flows from increased employee freedom and responsibility. Two-way communication, with the stress on bottom up flow, aims at mutual learning, free growth, and nurturing conditions for change. Here the active listening skills discussed in the communications chapter are particularly helpful.

Communications theory recognizes that two messages are communicated in any interpersonal exchange, a content message and a relationship message. The content has to do with what the manager and employee say, while the relationship message concerns the feelings involved in the exchange. Cohen has argued for special attention to process in performance discussions. (Cohen, 1979.) In the "tell and sell" method of appraising, the manager dominates the discussion and may be satisfied if she or he communicates main points. The subordinate listens passively, may feign acceptance of supervisor's assessment, but may privately harbor anger toward the critic and resentment at the exclusion of discussion. Because of traditional role expectations, this may happen even if the communications climate between the two individuals is relatively good. Cohen proposes using "process", or stopping the conversation wherever either party feels to need to make an observation that would strengthen the relationship, as a mechanism for improving performance discussion. Process intervention involves "expressing feelings about the way the discussion is being handled and ultimately needs for a hidden agenda that an individual has or perceives that the other has" (Cohen, 1979). Special conditions calling for the use of a process comment include the following:

1. When the purposes of the meeting seem not to be clear enough.
2. When there is inadequate opportunity to express ideas or share information.
3. When there is a feeling that one is not influencing the meeting as much as one wants to.
4. When the meeting tends to be dominated by one person.
5. When there appears to be not enough trust.
6. When individual needs and purposes start not being met.
7. When the discussion starts to get off target and becomes less concrete.
8. When differences in viewpoints tend to be handled, not in an adult manner through discussion and rational problem solving, but by either avoidance or imposition. (Cohen, 1979.)

The appraiser then has two issues to attend to: first, what method of conducting an appraisal interview is appropriate in a particular situation, and second, what attending skills are needed. Research on the content and process of appraisal interviews provides some general guidance in making this choice.

There are conflicting views on the impact of providing performance feedback in the appraisal interview. Meyer, Kay, and French (1965) report that negative feedback, or the discussion of performance weaknesses, depresses goal achievement while positive feedback has little effect. In contrast, Cummings (1973) reports that feedback results in a more positive view of appraisal and Beveridge (1974) qualifies this point by specifying that criticism needs to be directed towards performance, not the individual employee. There is substantial evidence to suggest that in balance stressing strengths and weaknesses is the most supportive strategy for future performance (Fletcher and Williams, 1975; Stone, 1973; Fletcher, 1973). And in the main a participative approach in appraisal interview has been found most successful. (Bassett and Meyer, 1968; Fletcher, 1973; Beveridge, 1974.)

CONCLUSION

Performance appraisal is a management control tool historically used to measure individual performance. With a trend toward increased employee participation in organizational decision making and the heightened awareness of employees as a valuable resource, performance appraisal is now asked to measure employee potential and to create the context for heightened employee involvement in the overall planning process. While these new duties assumed by performance appraisal are important and fitting, they do lead to at least two problems: 1) confusion over what performance appraisal is supposed to do and 2) placing expectations on a single performance appraisal system that may be conflicting or contradictory. It may be that managers ask too much of performance appraisal, asking more of it than it can accomplish well.

Effective public sector managers should know what they want from a performance appraisal, and opt for systems capable of producing that end while remaining aware of the contextual features limiting the capacity of any system and the interpersonal skills necessary to deliver the chosen system.

REFERENCES

Allan, Peter and Stephen Rosenberg. (1978). Formulating Usable Objectives for Manager Performance Appraisal. *Personnel Journal*. (November):pp. 626-629, 640.

Bassett, G. A. and H. H. Meyer. (1968). Performance Appraisal Based on Self-Review. *Personnel Psychology*. 21:pp. 421-430.

Beacham, S. T. (1979). Managing Compensation and Performance Appraisal Under the Age Act. *Management Review*. pp. 51-57.

Beatty, Richard W. and Craig E. Schneier (1977). *Personnel Administration*. Reading, Mass.: Addison-Wesley Publishing Co.

Beveridge, W. E. (1974). Attitudes in Three Work Organizations. *Management Education Review*. 5(2):pp. 68-74.

Brown, Robert, W. (1982). Performance Appraisal: A Policy Implementation Analysis. *Review of Public Personnel Administration*. 2 (Spring):pp. 69-85.

Brukenhoff, Derick W. and Rosabeth Moss Kanter. (1980). Appraising the Performance of Performance Appraisal. *Sloan Management Review*. (Spring):pp. 3-14.

Burke, Ronald J. (1970). Characteristics of Effective Performance Appraisal Interviews. *Training and Development Journal*. (March):pp. 9-12.

Calhoun, Richard and Thomas H. Jerdee. (1976). *Coaching In Supervision*. Chapel Hill, N.C.: Institute of Government.

Campbell, J. P., M. D. Dunnette, R. D. Arvey, and L. V. Hellervik. (1973). The Development and Evaluation of Behaviorally Based Rating Scales. *Journal of Applied Psychology*. pp. 15-22.

Cohen, Arthur M. (1979). Using Process in Performance Discussion. *Supervisory Management*. (March):pp. 33-36.

Cummings, L. L. (1973). A Field Experimental Study of the Effects of Two Performance Appraisal Systems. *Personnel Psychology*. 26:pp. 409-502.

Dornbusch, Sanford M. and W. Richard Scott. (1975). *Evaluation and the Exercise of Authority*. San Francisco: Jossey-Bass:p. 145.

Fletcher, Clive. (1973). Interview Style and the Effectiveness of Appraisal. *Occupational Psychology*. 47:pp. 225-230.

Fletcher, Clive and Richard Williams. (1976). The Influence of Performance Feedback in Appraisal Interviews. *Journal of Occupational Psychology*. (June): pp. 75-85.

French, J. R. P., E. Kay and H. H. Meyer. (1966). Participation and the Appraisal System. *Human Relations*. 19:pp. 3-20.

Goodale, James G. (1977). Behaviorally-Based Rating Scales: Toward an Integrated Approach to Performance Appraisal, in W. Clay Hamner and Fred L. Schmidt (Eds.) *Contemporary Problems in Personnel*. Chicago: St. Clair Press.

Greiner, John M., Harry P. Hatry, Margo P. Kass, Annie P. Millar, and Jane P. Woodward. (1981). *Productivity and Motivation*. Washington, D.C.: The Urban Institute Press.

Haberstroh, C. J. (1965). Organizational Design and Systems Analysis, in J. G. March (Ed.) *Handbook of Organizations*. Chicago: Rand McNally.

Holley, William H. Jr. (1978). Performance Appraisal in Public Sector Arbitration. *Public Personnel Management*. 7(January-February):pp. 1-5.

Kay, E., H. H. Mayer, J. R. French. (1965). Effects of Threat in a Performance Appraisal Interview. *Journal of Applied Psychology*. 49:pp. 311-317.

Kearney, William J. (1978). Improving Work Performance Through Appraisal. *Human Resource Management*. (Summer):pp. 15-23.

Lacho, Kenneth J., G. Kent Stearns, Maurice F. Villere. (1979). A Study of Employee Appraisal Systems of Major Cities in the United States. *Public Personnel Management*. (March/April):pp. 111-125.

Lazer, Robert and Walter S. Wikstrom. (1977). *Appraising Managerial Performance*. New York: The Conference Board.

Levinson, Priscilla. (1980). *A Guide for Improving Performance Appraisal*. U.S. Office of Personnel Management: Government Printing Office.

Maier, W. R. F. (1958). *The Appraisal Interview: Objectives, Methods and Skills*. New York: John Wiley.

Mayfield, H. (1960). In Defense of Performance Appraisal. *Harvard Business Review*. March-April.

McGuire, Peter J. (1980). Why Performance Appraisals Fail. *Personnel Journal*. (September):pp. 744-746, 762.

Meyer, H. H., E. Kay, J. R. P. French, Jr. (1965). Split Roles in Performance Appraisal. *Harvard Business Review*. (January-February) 43:pp. 123-129.

Oberg, Winston. (1972). Make Performance Appraisal Relevant. *Harvard Business Review*. (January-February):pp. 61-67.

Schneier, Craig E. and Richard W. Beatty. (1979). Combining BARS and MBO: Using an Appraisal System to Diagnose Performance Problems. *The Personnel Administrator*. (September):pp. 51-60.

Schneier, Dena B. (1978). The Impact of EEO Legislation on Performance Appraisals. *Personnel*. (July-August). pp. 24-35.

Stone, T. H. (1973). An Examination of Six Prevalent Assumptions Concerning
    Performance Appraisal. *Public Personnel Management*. (November-December):
    pp. 408-414.
Thompson, Paul H. and Gene W. Dalton. (1970). Performance Appraisal: Man-
    agers Beware. *Harvard Business Review*. (February):pp. 60-68.

MANAGING EQUAL EMPLOYMENT OPPORTUNITY

The two management application topics considered in chapters 9 and 10 deal with dynamics largely internal to organizations. While effective managers pay attention to management systems and performance appraisal, attention is not required by public policy and the sanction for ignoring such issues is rarely immediate. The topic of this chapter, managing Equal Employment Opportunity [EEO] is different. EEO typically gains impetus from forces outside the organization which press for significant and specific organizational changes. Organizational change, as we noted earlier (chapter 8) refers to any significant alteration of the behavior of the large part of individuals who constitute our organizations. The specific redistributive nature of EEO policies and programs means that this change will inevitably generate opposition and conflict. This chapter points out what the manager must know to deal creatively and productively with this management challenge.

Organizations are systems which interact with their environment. From an EEO perspective regulatory policy, as reflected in statutory, administrative and case law, is the critical force in that environment. Public sector management needs to know both the public policy requirements and the essential elements of EEO program design and implementation to fulfill those requirements. As well, the manager needs to bring to EEO implementation a sensitivity to the legal status of voluntary affirmative action programming including the issue of "reverse discrimination." Finally, the effective executive must be aware of the capacity of organizational structures and individual attitudes to shape achievement of EEO goals. The following sections address each of the issues in turn.

THE PUBLIC POLICY ENVIRONMENT[1]

Among the major laws and regulations covering EEO today are Title VII of the Civil Rights Act of 1964 as amended by the Equal Employment Opportunity Act of 1972, the Equal Pay Act of 1963, Executive Order 11246, the Age Discrimination in Employment Act, and the Rehabilitation Act of 1973. Also, significant implementation regulations, in the form of Equal Employment Opportunity Commission (EEOC) and Office of Federal Contract Compliance Programs (OFCCP) guidelines have been issued and revised periodically through the 1960's and 1970's, and 1980's. The Uniform Guidelines for Employee Selection, issued in 1978, is one of the most significant of these documents. A description of the coverage, practices prohibited, specific judicial interpretations, and administrative enforcement of each enactment provides a picture ot the environment for managing EEO in the public sector.

Civil Rights Act of 1964

The Civil Rights Act of 1964 is the most comprehensive piece of civil rights legislation ever enacted in the United States. From the employer's perspective, Title VII of that Act is critical. Most employers, all unions, and all employment agencies dealing with employers must abide by the provisions of the Act. In 1973, when Title VII was amended by the Equal Employment Opportunity Act, state and local government employers, and private and public educational institutions also came under its jurisdiction.

The Civil Rights Act prohibits an employer from using race, color, religion, sex, or national origin as a reason for: 1) failing or refusing to hire any individual; 2) discriminating against any individual regarding compensation, work conditions or privileges, or employment; 3) limiting, segregating, or classifying employees or applicants in any way which would tend to deprive that person of employment opportunities or adversely affect his or her status in the workplace.

The Equal Employment Opportunity Commission was established to administer these Title VII provisions. As the enforcement agency, it investigates charges of discrimination and initially attempts to reach a voluntary settlement with the employer. It is also empowered to initiate its own investigations. However, the Act provides for deference to the principles of federalism by requiring that the proper complaint procedure must first be brought under any applicable state or local statute. When investigating a complaint against a state or local government employer, the EEOC follows a standard procedure, attempting to forge a voluntary settlement. However, when such efforts fail, the complaint, with the EEOC findings, is referred to the Department of Justice for litigation.

Since Title VII is a vital piece of Civil Rights legislation, the public manager must be well educated in the judicial interpretation of the discrimination it prohibits, the coverage it provides, and the legitimacy of its enforcement. Thus this chapter addresses the Title VII interpretation in some depth, treating other acts in briefer form.

Perhaps the most basic question put to the courts from the genesis of Title VII litigation is simply: what counts as discrimination? Three modes of judicial thinking emerge clearly from careful analysis of court decisions. In the early days of Title VII enforcement, discrimination was assumed to be a motivational or moral problem—a human relations difficulty. Congressional Oversight hearings in 1971 on the EEOC captured this phase well: "In 1964, employment discrimination tended to be view as a series of isolated and distinguishable events, for the most part due to ill will on the part of some identifiable individual or organization" (1971). This definition clearly informed the thrust of the various state and local human relations commissions dominating the EEO landscape in the 1960's.

A second mode of thinking regarding discrimination evolved in the 1960's around the notion of "unequal treatment" or "disparate treatment." Discrimination here occurs when an employer simply treats some people less favorably than others because of their race, sex, color, religion, or national origin. But the courts have noted that even with disparate treatment, proof of discriminatory motive is critical, "although it can, in some situations, be inferred from the mere act of differences in treatment." (Teamsters vs. U.S., 1977.) Significant in this shift from "intent" to "treatment" is the new focus on *behavior* rather than simply attitude.

The third mode in the evolving definition of discrimination came to be expressed in terms of "effects," "consequences," or "impacts." Often referred to by the courts as "disparate impact," discrimination under this rule involves employment practices that are neutral on their face in their treatment of different groups" . . .but that in fact fall more harshly on one group than another and cannot be justified by business necessity" (Teamsters vs. U.S., 1977). The third mode was first fully articulated by the Supreme Court in the case of *Griggs vs. Duke Power Company* (1971).

Perhaps the most important case ever decided under Title VII, *Griggs* significantly broadened the meaning of discrimination. Under disparate impact it was no longer necessary to prove a discriminatory motive, nor was it necessary to prove that employers were using different standards in evaluating employees. Discrimination could reside simply in the effect of an action. While each mode of defining discrimination noted above appears in some current judicial decisions, a full understanding of the meaning of discrimination under Title VII requires detailed discussion of the *Griggs* case. (Blumrose, 1972.)

The Griggs case involved the legality of two of Duke Power's employment selection instruments, a standardized general intelligence test and a high school diploma requirement. According to statistical evidence, significantly more blacks than whites failed the tests and thus were excluded from employment. The court found Duke Power guilty of discrimination because neither standard was shown to be significantly related to job performance, both requirements operated to disqualify blacks at a substantially higher rate than white applicants, and the job in question formerly had been filled by white employees as part of a long standing practice of giving preference to whites. From one perspective, *Griggs* was a testing case, but its impact has been broad, reaching well beyond the narrow issue of testing.

The departure from definitions of discrimination prevalent in the 1960's emerged clearly in the Supreme Court's reasoning. Moving beyond the motivation definition the court said "Congress directed the thrust of the act to the consequences of employment practices, not simply motivation." Similarly the justices set forth a standard higher than merely equal treatment. "The Act proscribes not only overt discrimination but also practices that are fair in form, but discriminatory in operation." While it is true that the Civil Rights Act describes the discriminator as one who is "intentionally engaged in unlawful employment practice," intentionality means simply "not by accident." Thus any employment practice is intentional since the employer presumably intends the natural consequences of his or her action. (EEO Compliance Manual, 1979a.) In other words, in the post-*Griggs* era, any employment practice yielding adverse impact on a group protected under Title VII may be unlawful even if the employer's intentions are not discriminatory, or even if the employer is mistaken as to what the impact of the action would be. (EEO Compliance Manual, 1979a.)

The extensive applicability of the *Griggs* rule beyond the testing issue needs stress. The effect of the decision was to broaden coverage to any employment practice that could be shown statistically to have an adverse impact on any group protected by Title VII. In the decade of the seventies, height and weight requirements, arrest records, credit checks, and educational requirements have all been struck down under the *Griggs* interpretation of Title VII. They have fallen because they "operate to exclude" protected group members. Much of the ensuing discussion around discrimination under Title VII revolves around the basis for measuring this exclusion. Thus our next question must be, what statistical data is relevant to proving discrimination?

In the *Griggs* case, the Supreme Court did not require that the plaintiff show that the high school diploma requirement has an exclusionary effect on the actual applicants at Duke Power. Rather it turned to the statistics of high school education for the entire state of North Carolina for evidence. In footnote 6 of the *Griggs* decision, the Supreme Court notes "in North Carolina, 1960 census statistics show that while 34 percent of the white males had completed high school, only 12 percent of Negro males had done so." In Griggs, the court was persuaded by the view that the existence of the requirement in and of itself may have discouraged non-high school applicants. Thus, to measure the real impact of the requirements, one has to look at broader census data than application statistics alone.

When evidence does show that a practice operates to exclude members of a protected group, the only defense the employer has is business necessity. In the words of the court in *Griggs*, "the touch stone is business necessity." Duke Power failed to show that either the high school diploma or the written test constituted a business necessity.

The Griggs decision marked a critical turning point in the understanding of discrimination as it was prohibited by the Civil Rights Act of 1964. In *Griggs* the court clearly defined discrimination in terms of impact or effect. When Congress passed the Equal Employment Opportunity Act of 1972, it resoundingly ratified the *Griggs* definition of employment discrimination. But by indicating that after *Griggs* courts could look to "impact" to find discrimination we don't mean to suggest that other considerations became obsolete. U.S. Supreme Court decisions on the seniority exemption under Title VII illustrate this point.

Section 703 (H) of the Civil Rights Act provides that it is lawful to offer different terms and conditions of employment "pursuant to a bonafide seniority system." Though the seniority rights of employees, for example, may have been built up when the employer didn't hire Blacks, still these seniority rights may be maintained. The intent of the employer in implementing the seniority system is critical. In one case, *Franks vs. Bowman Transportation Company*, (1976), the Supreme Court granted retroactive seniority to Black applicants who proved they had been turned down for jobs *because of* race at an earlier point in time. In another case, *American Tobacco vs. Patterson* (1982), the Court ruled that a seniority system adopted after Title VII took effect didn't violate the law, even if it had a discriminatory impact, unless an *intent* to discriminate could be shown.

Beyond the *Griggs* decision, the courts have continued to work toward clarifying the conditions which trigger Title VII applicability. Included among the particularly important issues are the relevance of statistical data and the appropriateness of Bona fide Occupational Qualifications (BFOQ). With the emphasis in *Griggs* on discrimination as impact, the question of which statistical data are most relevant surfaced as important. In *Hazelwood School District vs. the U.S.* (1977), the Supreme Court spoke to this point. The high court found that if an employer can show that any statistical disparity between groups was caused by discrimination which occurred before the Civil Rights Act took effect, and that no discrimination has occurred since that time, the statistical evidence could not be used to indicate a violation of the law. Since state and local governments were not covered before 1972, statistics generated by action before that time would probably fail as evidence.

Another set of issues revolves around how Bonafide Occupational Qualification should be interpreted. Title VII provides that it is lawful to discriminate on the basis of religion, sex, or national origin when a BFOQ is involved: "A bona fide occupational qualification reasonably necessary to the normal operation of that particular business or enterprise." The more difficult and controversial cases have arisen over claims of sex as a BFOQ. The EEOC guidelines have taken a very narrow view of BFOQ sex based exemptions. Specifically ruled out as establishing a sex BFOQ are: 1) assumptions about employment characteristics of women in general (*Weeks vs. Southern Bell Telephone and Telegraphy Company, 1969*); 2) stereotyped opinions about the sexes; 3) preference of employer, employee, clients, or customers (*Diaz vs. Pan American World Airways, 1971*). Nor is it permissible under Title VII to escape the narrow BFOQ interpretation by using sex and another factor as a basis for excluding women from some employment opportunities, e.g., hiring fathers with preschool children while refusing to hire mothers in the same circumstance (*Phillips vs. Martin Marietta Corporation*, 1971). In general, the BFOQ exception is very narrowly drawn.

Throughout the litigation on the issues of the meaning of discrimination and the coverage of certain types of cases, the legitimacy of the EEOC judgment in these matters had itself been an issue. But, by the late 1970's, the legitimacy of the EEOC to flesh out the skeleton of Title VII law seemed firmly established. This fact was acknowledged by the 7th Circuit Court of Appeals: "The U.S. Supreme Court has stated that the Guidelines are entitled to considerable deference as the administrative interpretation of Title VII by the agency whose task it is to enforce it. . .This court has stated that compliance with these Guidelines is generally required absent some showing that a cogent reason exists for noncompliance." (*U.S. vs. City of Chicago*, 1977). However in a few significant cases the Supreme Courts majority failed to bow to EEOC interpretations. For example, the EEOC's interpretation of Title VII would have struck down the seniority system that the U.S. Supreme Court upheld in the *American Tobacco Company* (1982) case noted above.

Equal Pay Act

The Equal Pay Act, enacted in 1963 as an amendment to the Fair Labor Standards Act, required employers to pay equal wages regardless of sex for work that is equal in skill, effort, and responsibility. More narrowly drawn than Title VII, the Equal Pay Act (EPA) prohibits discrimination in wages only, but its coverage is comprehensive, applying to all employers with employees subject to the minimum wage provision of the Fair Labor Standards Act. While the U.S. Supreme Court has held that minimum wage provisions do not apply to state and local government, most of the court decisions on the Equal Pay law have uphelp its applicability to state and local jurisdictions. The Equal Pay Act has not required the extensive administrative interpretation given to Title VII, due largely to the relative narrowness of EPA's proscribed actions. But a significant amount of litigation on the EPA has given increased precision to the act. A few of EPA cases serve to illustrate these important refinements.

A number of EPA cases have dealt with the matter of how wages should be defined. Clearly under the act wages include all payments made as remuneration for employment. This includes commissions, bonuses, attendance payments, or any compensation for hazardous or disagreeable working conditions. The courts have also interpreted wages under the Equal Pay Act to include provision of board, room and some other services to employees. For example, in the case *Laffey vs. North West Airlines, Inc.* (1976) a federal court found it unlawful for North West Airlines to provide more expensive layover accommodations for male pursers than for female stewardesses, and to provide the pursers but not the stewardesses with a cleaning allowance.

A second active area for EPA litigation centers on what should be considered "equal" skill, effort, and responsibility. The standard that evolved in that jobs need not be identical, but only substantially similar, to evoke coverage under the Equal Pay Act. For example, the Supreme Court refused to review a decision by the Third Circuit Court of Appeals holding that performance of certain physical duties by males doesn't make a job unequal to similar jobs filled by females (*Schultz vs. Wheaton Glass Company, 1970*). Sometimes the courts seem to balance responsibility with physical tasks in trying to reach an interpretation of equal work, as in the case of *Hodgson vs. Daisy Manufacturing Company (1970)*. Here the court found that although male employees exerted greater physical effort than female employees, female employees performed a variety of tasks requiring greater mental alertness and responsibility. Thus, paying men more was unlawful.

A third area for EPA litigation in the last few years concerns one of the permissible grounds for discrimination written into the act. Explicit pay differentials are permitted under the Equal Pay Act if the wage rates are based on: a seniority system, a merit system, a system which measures earnings by quality or quantity of production, or any factor other than sex. The most controversial of these is the "factor other than sex." In one recent case, *Pearce vs. Witchita County (1979)* the plaintiff established that her male successor was paid substantially more than she had been although he assumed no additional duties. The court found no difference in "effort," "skill," and "responsibility" between the plaintiff and her successor. Since the plaintiff met the initial burden of proof, it was the burden of the employer to show that unequal pay was due to one of the four exceptions. The employer argued that the difference was due to "a factor other than sex," namely, the greater economic benefit of the successor's work. The court rejected this as an explanation of the difference between the plaintiff's final salary and her successor's starting salary. However, in a second case, *Horner vs. Mary Institute (1980)*, the 8th Circuit Court of Appeals said that a school was justified in paying a male gym teacher more than a female because he was the best person available and the higher salary was necessary to get him to take the job. Defining "market conditions" as a legitimate "factor other than sex" exception, the court said, "an employer may consider the marketplace value of the skills of a particular individual when determining his or her salary."

A fourth related area of pay litigation centers on the issue of "comparable worth" or "equal pay for work of equal value." The issue is best described by an example. Assume secretaries in a particular county are paid considerably less than liquor store clerks, who are also county employees. The comparable worth question is: Are they paid less because most secretaries are women, or because their job is of lesser value and requires less than that of the liquor store clerk? If the lower salary is because of sex, discrimination exists. Though we discuss comparable worth under the Equal Pay Act heading the practice described in our example is actually a violation of Title VII of the Civil Rights Act. An employment practice, such as paying female workers less than male workers for dissimilar work that is of comparable difficulty and responsibility would be legal under the Equal Pay Act but possibly illegal under Title VII. In the *Gunther vs. County of Washington* Case (1981) the U.S. Supreme Court established comparable worth as a valid Title VII claim.

In predicting the future direction of EPA litigation, it is important to note that, as a result of the late 1970's reorganization, enforcement and administration of the EPA shifted from the Wage and Hour Division of the Department of Labor to the EEOC. In the 1980's the substance and legitimacy of Equal Pay Act enforcement will be closely tied to that of Title VII enforcement.

Age Discrimination in Employment Act of 1967

The Age Discrimination in Employment Act of 1967 (ADEA) aims both to promote the hiring of workers over 40 and to prohibit discrimination against older workers. Its protection against discrimination extends to those in the 40-70 age bracket and applies to all action elements covered in Title VII: hiring, firing, wages, terms, conditions, or privileges of employment. State, local, and federal government agencies are all covered under the ADEA. However, to avoid setting policies which would work at cross purposes with other EEO legislation, all activities and programs designed especially to provide employment opportunity for people with employment problems are explicitly excluded or exempt.

In design and rationale, the Age Discrimination in Employment Act was based on parallels between race discrimination and age discrimination. However, the judicial interpretation of the ADEA has begun to suggest a possible breakdown in that comparison. (Schuck, 1979.) We know from the history of Title VII enforcement that race discrimination is not acceptable judicially even if it is deemed reasonable, unless that discrimination is favorable to race minorities. The courts, however, are willing to accept age differentials between groups of people. For example, the court upheld a statute mandating that state police retire at age 50 (*Mass. Board of Retirement vs. Murgia, 1976*).

We must note that some courts have accepted an analogy between age and other protected groups. For example, in *Marshall vs. the Board of Education of Salt Lake City (1977)*, the court said that a school system may not refuse to promote an employee to a principal's position just because he is 64 years old and only one year from retirement. Nor would one court allow an employer to fire an employee because of his age, even if there were other factors involved (*Laugesen vs. Anaconda Company, 1975*). Nonetheless, many of the administrative regulations and some important court decisions suggest that age discrimination legislation elicits a set of conditions unique to the age factor. More detailed examples will illustrate this point.

The Age Discrimination in Employment Act has been interpreted by administrative officials to mean that you cannot discriminate between two workers within a protected age bracket solely on age grounds. In other words, if one applicant is 42 and the other 52, it is unlawful to hire the 42-year-old because he or she is younger. This excludes bona fide apprenticeship programs, since usually the purpose of such programs is to train young people for future careers. In January of 1981 the EEOC also gave its blessing to this exemption. A third area where some important differences between race and age as factors have emerged in the BFOQ exception. As noted above in the Title VII discussion, the BFOQ grounds for race in particular are virtually nonexistent. But age has been upheld as a legitimate BFOQ, particularly in the public safety area. For example, one court upheld a bus company's rule against hiring drivers over age 35 (*Hodgson vs. Greyhound Lines, 1975*). A similar rule establishing 40 as an age ceiling by another bus company was upheld by another court (*Usery vs. Tamiami Trail Tours, Inc., 1976*). Admittedly, this exemption is somewhat muddled by a 1977 court ruling which held that a test pilot over 50 could not be grounded because of evidence about the general physical condition of people over 50. The court said that this general information could not be applied to a particular individual (*Haughton vs. McDonnel Douglas Corporation, 1977*). The courts have been less willing to interpret the Age Discrimination in Employment Act as strictly parallel to prohibitions against race discrimination. However, in at least one instance the courts' restrictiveness has been counteracted by legislative action. In *United Airlines vs. McMann (1977)*, the Supreme Court ruled that compulsory early retirement was lawful because of the special clause in the law safeguarding any terms of a bonafide employee benefit or retirement plan. To counteract this decision, the Congress, in 1978, amended the Age Discrimination in Employment Act, to prohibit compulsory retirement of employees between 40 and 70, even if an existing pension plan calls for retirement.

The ADEA was enforced by the U.S. Department of Labor from its passage in 1967 until July 1, 1979. On that date, as part of the Carter reorganization of the Civil Rights establishment, the EEOC took over enforcement responsibility.

Under the new legislation, the EEOC is authorized to review and evaluate all agency programs designed to carry out the law, and to obtain progress reports on covered agencies, to issue rules and regulations for enforcing the law, to consult with interested persons and groups regarding nondiscrimination on account of age, and to provide for processing complaints of age discrimination in the Federal government. As noted in our discussion about the relocation of the Equal Pay Act enforcement within the EEOC, the future of the ADEA rests largely with the legitimacy granted to EEOC actions in this area.

A common thread weaving together the Civil Rights Act of 1964, the Equal Pay Act of 1963, and the Age Discrimination in Employment Act of 1967 is their uniform endorsement of nondiscrimination. Under each, the employer may be ordered by the conciliation agency or by a court to provide some remedy only after a finding of discrimination. The remedies may vary. In one Title VII case, an injunction was granted against an employer forbidding further discriminatory practices and ordering affirmative action. Under the Equal Pay Act or Age Discrimination in Employment Act the payment of back wages plus liquidated damages or even criminal penalties may be ordered. But whatever the remedy, the objective in each case is to set right a specific documented discriminatory act or pattern of discrimination. Additionally, Executive Order 11246 and the Rehabilitation Act of 1973, by way of contrast, require affirmative action irrespective of a specific judicial or administrative finding of discrimination.

Executive Order 11246

Presidential Executive Order 11246, as amended by Executive Order 11375 (1967), prohibits discrimination by federal contractors and subcontractors. "Contract" is defined very broadly to cover virtually all government contracts. In some instances grants are also considered as contracts under the Executive Order. Contractors with grants amounting to $10,000 or more are obliged under the Executive Order to implement affirmative action to assure nondiscrimination. Additionally, a contractor with 50 or more employees and a contract of $50,000 or more, must submit a written affirmative action plan. The specific affirmative action proposal developed must be based on a comprehensive analysis of the use of minorities and women in the work force compared to their availability in the labor force. Numerical goals and timetables must be established for correcting any deficiencies revealed in this analysis. The program must be publicized and its implementation carefully monitored.

Most of the litigation surrounding Executive Order 11246 has concerned the legality of "quota" programs that have been established under the order's requirements but are alleged to violate Title VII's nondiscrimination provisions. The compatibility of Title VII and Executive Order 11246 is the central issue in most preferential treatment cases and will be discussed later in the chapter.

Since the Carter reorganization of the civil rights establishment, the Office of Federal Contract Compliance Programs (OFCCP) of the Department of Labor has been directly responsible for enforcement of Executive Order 11246. If, in response to a complaint, a violation is found and reconciliation efforts fail, it is possible for OFCCP to order penalties and sanctions after a formal hearing. Included among the penalties are cancelling or suspending contracts in whole or in part, blacklisting the contractors, recommending to the attorney general that legal action be taken to enforce the EEO clause of a contract, and recommending to EEOC or Department of Justice that action be taken under Title VII.

The Reagan administration supports a major revamping of Executive Order 11246 requirements. The principal modifications proposed are:

- to require affirmative action plans only from larger contractors with million dollar contracts
- to restrict the conditions under which goals and time tables are required
- to reduce the amount of reporting required.

Some modification along these lines is likely, but the impact will be felt more in the private than in the public sector, since the lions share of contracts are held by private employers.

The Rehabilitation Act of 1973

The Rehabilitation Act of 1973 (Section 503) prohibits employers with federal contracts over $2500 from discriminating against handicapped people in all employment policies including: employment, upgrading, demotion or transfer, recruiting, advertising, layoff, rate of pay, or other forms of compensation. As well, the act requires that employers take affirmative action for such handicapped employees. Under the legislation, a handicapped person is defined as anyone who has: 1) a physical or mental impairment substantially limiting that person's life activities; 2) has a record of such impairment; or 3) is regarded as having such impairment. "Life activities" are defined as those which affect employability and "substantially limits" refers to the extent to which the handicap limits employability for a particular person.

The law requires that reasonable accommodation must be made by the employer to facilitate employment for the handicapped individual. "Reasonable accommodation" means making necessary adaptations to enable a qualified handicapped person to work. According to the legislation this may include making facilities used by all employees accessible to handicapped people (ramps, restroom adaptations, wide aisles, etc.), or making modifications in jobs, work schedules, equipment or work area, (such as simplifying a job so that a retarded person can fill it or changing working hours so a paraplegic person doesn't have to fight traffic).

Under this legislation, a federal contractor or subcontractor with 50 or more employees and a contract of $50,000 or more is obligated to prepare a written affirmative action program which may or may not be integrated into the affirmative action program required under the Executive Order. While neither utilization analysis nor goals and timetables are required under this act, the recruitment and policy dissemination requirements are the same as those required under Executive Order 11246. The program itself must be available for inspection by government officials on demand. However, employers are not required to submit these programs to federal officials.

A unique feature of this act as compared to the Executive Order 11246 is that employers are obligated to "invite employees or applicants who think they are covered by the act and who want the benefits of the affirmative action program to identify themselves." However, an employer is not required to search employee files in order to discover a handicap.

The Rehabilitation Act is administered and enforced by the OFCCP of the Department of Labor. Complaints are filed with the Department of Labor. After the employer has reviewed the complaint through existing internal procedures (or after 60 days), the Department of Labor will investigate. As with Executive Order 11246, disputes are settled by informal means when possible, but penalties and sanctions can be invoked when all else fails.

One issue as yet unresolved in Rehabilitation Act enforcement concerns the individual handicapped person's right to sue for job bias. One federal district court in California ruled that an individual handicapped person could sue under the act (*Hart vs. County of Alameda, 1979*). Another federal district court in New York agreed (*Chaplin vs. Consolidated Edison Co. of New York, 1980*). But recently the 4th Circuit Court of Appeals has ruled that handicapped persons have no right to sue under the Rehabilitation Act (*Rogers vs. Frito-Lay, Inc.* and *Moon vs. Roadway Express, Inc., 1980*). Under the Carter administration the OFCCP insisted that the right of handicapped individuals to sue was intended by Congress. Such a right was viewed as central to the agency's enforcement efforts and as helpful in reducing the agency's large backlog of complaints. From the individual plaintiff's perspective, they argued the right to private suit is critical. While administrative procedures are always available, the only remedy for enforcement otherwise open to the OFCCP is termination of funding. Such a drastic remedy is politically difficult and counterproductive, because it would not further a handicapped person's employment prospects. The position of the Reagan administration is that a private right to sue does not exist in the law. Further litigation and possibly legislation will resolve this issue.

Uniform Guidelines on Employee Selection Procedures

Prior to the Fall of 1978, all of the various agencies with EEO authority at the federal level were not operating under the same guidelines for employee selection. Needless to say, this created substantial confusion. In September 1978, the four agencies involved, including the Equal Employment Opportunity Commission, the Civil Service Commission, the Department of Labor, and the Department of Justice, did come to accept and adopt "Uniform Guidelines on Employee Selection Procedures" (UGESP). The UGESP are currently under scrutiny by the Reagan Taskforce on Regulation Review, possibly leading to a relaxation of the related paperwork requirements but the procedure detailed in the Guidelines has proven a helpful process for managers to adopt in monitoring the EEO impact of selection practices. The critical areas affected by the uniform guidelines on employment selection procedures include hiring, promotion, and eligibility for additional training.

The rule to be followed under the guidelines is: if the selection procedure used for making employment decisions has an adverse impact on members of any racial, ethnic, or sex group, the procedure must be brought into conformity with the UGESP. It is important to note that the effect of the total selection process for a job category triggers the requirement. If a selection process does not have adverse impact, the employer is not required to look at individual procedures. However, if it does have adverse impact, the procedures must be examined to ensure that they are valid. Currently, the employer is also obliged to keep records detailing the impact of his selection procedures.

The critical issue here is what *adverse impact* means. Under the guidelines adverse impact is defined as the lower selection rate of protected racial, ethnic, or sex group members compared to members of other groups. Generally a selection rate for any racial, ethnic, or sex group which is less than 4/5 (80 percent) of the group with the higher selection rate will be regarded as evidence of adverse impact. The rate of selection for each group is determined by dividing the number of applicants selected from that group by the total number of applicants and by comparing the results with the result derived in the same way for the group with highest selection rate. For example, if over a six-month period there are 120 applicants (80 white and 40 black) of whom 60 were hired (48 white and 12 blacks), the selection rate for the white group would be 48/80 or 60 percent, while the selection rate for blacks would be 12/40 or 30 percent. Here the selection process adversely affected the blacks. Their selection rate was only half that of whites (30 percent as compared to 60 percent). But if the selection rate for blacks had been within the 4/5's or 80 percent of the rate for the group with the highest rate the impact would not be considered adverse. A second example will illustrate this point. If there were 120 applicants, 80 white and 40 black, and 42 whites were selected while 18 blacks were selected, the selection rate for whites would be 42/80 or 52.5 percent and the selection rate for blacks would be 18/40 or 45 percent. The comparative selection rate would be calculated by taking 45 percent/ 52.5 percent and would produce a comparative selection rate of 85.7 percent. This would be above the 80 percent or 4/5 "rule of thumb" and therefore, the difference in impact is not seen as substantial.

Managers should recognize that the 4/5 "rule of thumb" does not, however, mean that the guidelines will tolerate up to 20 percent discrimination. Rather its purpose is merely to establish a numerical basis for drawing inferences and for requiring additional information. Regardless of the amount of difference in selection rates, unlawful discrimination may be present and may be demonstrated through appropriate evidence. Managers may still be held accountable.

Of course part of the strength of adverse impact data depends upon the magnitude of the numbers on which the percentage calculations are based. For example, if an employer selected three men and one woman from an applicant pool of 20 men and 10 women, the 4/5 rule would indicate adverse impact (selection rate for women is 10 percent; selection rate for men is 15 percent; 10/15 percent or 66.6 percent is less than 80 percent). Yet the numbers are so small that a difference in one person hired could show a difference the other way. In such circumstances the enforcement agency would not require validity evidence in the absence of additional information.

DESIGNING AND IMPLEMENTING AFFIRMATIVE ACTION

The first step in developing an Affirmative Action program is drafting an EEO policy statement. This statement should serve four objectives: 1) to inform the employee of what the EEO policy is; 2) to explain briefly what steps the agency will take to implement the policy; 3) to motivate employees to comply by assigning responsibility for enforcement; 4) to comply with all legal requirements designed by an agency.

Using these objectives as guidelines, a statement conforming to the "personality" of the particular agency should be developed. While remaining sensitive to the unique characteristics of an agency, most EEO policy statements should include reference to the following:

- that the agency is committed to equal employment opportunity for all employees, regardless of race, color, sex, or national origin
- that providing equal employment opportunity will require special affirmative action throughout the agency

- that equal employment opportunity will touch all employment practices including recruiting, hiring, promotions, and training
- that responsibility for affirmative action is assigned to a high level agency executive
- that all managers are responsible for affirmative action and will be assigned specific tasks to ensure that compliance is achieved
- that managerial performance in implementing the affirmative action plan will be evaluated in the same way as performance on other agency goals and objectives
- that successful attainment of affirmative action goals will benefit the entire agency by a more productive use of human resources

The EEO policy statement should include a reference to what department of an agency is responsible for administering affirmative action. However, there are definite differences in opinion among EEO/AA experts on where affirmative action responsibilities should rest. If the chief personnel officer shows a commitment to EEO and enjoys the confidence of the chief executive officer, he or she is the logical choice for assignment of affirmative action responsibilities. In some organizations, however, the personnel office itself contributes to the problem of institutional discrimination. When this condition holds, authority for the EEO program must reside outside personnel. Still, in the long run, it is most reasonable to develop an EEO commitment within the personnel office. Motivational approaches (Chapter 2) and participatory strategies (Chapter 7) discussed earlier should guide top managers in eliciting this commitment.

A policy statement once drafted needs to be communicated. Everyone in the organization should be made aware of its content. Immediate strategies for communicating the organization's EEO commitment would include: issuing an official bulletin from the agency head endorsing the policy statement; printing the EEO policy statement in a departmental newsletter; revising personnel manuals to include the EEO policy statement; and posting the EEO policy statement on bulletin boards and other prominent spots throughout the organization. When the statement is issued, work sessions should be held with managers and supervisors to explain the intent of the policy and their role in its implementation. Finally, broad organizational support for the affirmative action program can be enhanced by holding discussion sessions with groups of employees so they will understand it, what the agency plans to do, how it may affect them as individuals, and how they can help implement it.

Wherever the formal focus of responsibility rests, affirmation action must be bound ultimately to performance appraisal in order to function. The surest way to guarantee success in affirmative action is to build accomplishment of EEO objectives into the annual evaluation of performance. If some type of management by objectives system is already in place, this element of affirmative action implementation can be easily introduced. In some settings the need for EEO evaluation may serve as a catalyst for the rethinking of the performance appraisal system in use.

There is no "one best way" to develop an affirmative action program. However, critical to affirmative action planning is that each action be specified, that the person responsible for implementation of that action be named, and that a target date for accomplishment be set. Activities typically included in the development of an affirmative action program include:

1. Appoint an Affirmative Action Director.
2. Establish an Affirmative Action Committee to include representation from protected groups.
3. Develop an Affirmative Action Plan for the Organization.
4. Develop a grievance system whereby personnel who feel they have received unjust treatment may appeal to the Grievance Committee and/or the Affirmative Action Director.
5. Initiate action programs in major administrative units to increase the number of protected group members in all categories of employment.
6. Ensure that EEO policy and information concerning the Affirmative Action Program appears on all recruitment literature, pamphlets and publications of the organization.
7. Establish an action plan in each department which will outline goals and timetable for increasing the number of protected members.
8. Develop a system to analyze data and publish reports to include EEO-4 form.
9. Initiate and maintain a records system for all grievances and actions concerning the Affirmative Action Program.
10. Notify all suppliers and contractors of the anti-discrimination policy of the organization.
11. Place the EEO statement on all contract documents of the organization.
12. Publish the Affirmative Action Plan and make it available to all employees.
13. Post EEO posters prominently in appropriate facilities of the organization.
14. Establish an annual meeting to review Affirmative Action policies with appropriate division, department and office heads.
15. Develop an improved in-service education program for support staff personnel.
16. Complete a study of salaries and promotions of protected employees.
17. Complete a study of terminations.
18. Update plan as subsequent studies indicate needs.

Managers need to pay special attention to certain organization routines in implementing their organization's affirmative action plan. Always single-loop and sometimes double-loop learning efforts (Chapter 8) are required to realize affirmative action purposes. Areas of human resource management which often have sheltered discriminatory action in the past include the following:

- *Recruitment* You must ensure that protected group members know about vacancies in your organization. They *may* believe from past experiences that your policy statement claiming an organizational commitment to EEO is not sincere.
- *Selection* You must ensure the selection system is free of bias. Check to see if the interviewing officials are sensitive to behaviors which alienate protected group members.
- *Place Assignment* Review each applicant's employment history and examination scores to ensure that he or she is placed in a job with potential for growth. Don't assume that people will shun responsibility. Be sure that in work assignments you are giving individuals a chance to succeed or fail based on their own abilities.
- *Promotion* Often at promotion time, a bright young man who shows promise will be noticed while the clearly competent woman who trained him will be overlooked. Be sure to guard against exploiting the talents of women or other protected group members as "trainers," while ignoring them at promotion time.
- *Transfer-reassignment* Be sure that all openings are posted so that everyone is eligible to apply for transfers to better jobs. When transfers occur be sure that all protected group members know about the career development potential inherent in new positions.
- *Wage and Salary* A salary analysis should be undertaken at an early stage in EEO program. Not only should initial hiring salary be examined, but merit and other adjustments must also be examined to ensure that any disparities lingering from original hiring decisions are eliminated.
- *Training* As a good manager you should prepare your staff for more responsibility. Make sure that training assignments do not reflect traditional societal role assignments.
- *Separation/Termination* Look carefully at your turnover rate. If you are spending a lot of time training new employees, this signals trouble. Determine whether protected group members are leaving your organization at a higher rate than white males. It

is a good idea to use the exit interview to determine if people are leaving because of an unwelcome climate or culture (Chapter 8). In the case of involuntary separation be sure that the same rules apply for protected and non-protected group members.

LEGAL STATUS OF VOLUNTARY AFFIRMATIVE ACTION

Some have argued, from a practical managerial perspective, that affirmative action as it evolved throughout the 1970's and as described above created an organizational environment catch-22 for the well-intentioned employer. Employees were urged to develop affirmative action programs, or if they were federal contractors, they were obligated to do so. Yet acting aggressively in this regard simply invited reverse discrimination suits, with only those employers found guilty of discrimination in the past able to defend affirmative action measures such as numerical objectives.

The Supreme Court in the case of *Regents of the University of California vs. Bakke (1978)* simply heightened concern among employers about the legality of engaging in certain kinds of voluntary affirmative action. In that case, the court struck down a voluntary affirmative action plan in place at the University of California-David Medical School on the grounds that the type of quota system used violated both Title VI of the Civil Rights Act and the equal protection clause of the 14th Amendment. While this case dealt with educational opportunity, rather than employment opportunity, its message was nonetheless clear; remedies fashioned for injuries unproven is a risky affair.

In this environment of uncertainty the landmark Weber decision (*United Steel Workers of America vs. Weber, 1979*) held a welcome message for employers. The case spoke to the issue of voluntary affirmative action in employment. The facts in the case outline the classic reverse discrimination dilemma triggered by voluntary affirmative action.

Before 1974, only 2 percent of the craft workers at the Kaiser Aluminum's Gramercy, Louisiana plant were black—a condition produced by a longstanding policy of hiring only experienced workers. As part of an affirmative action program at Kaiser, the union agreed to establish a training program in which one-half of the trainees assigned would be black. Two lists were established and the most senior were selected from each of the lists. Brian Weber, a white employee, applied for the program and was denied admission, while blacks with lesser seniority were accepted under the two-list arrangement. Weber brought suit claiming reverse discrimination—a violation under Title VII of the Civil Rights Act. A federal district court ruled in favor of Weber, but the Supreme Court reversed the lower court's decision and supported the voluntary affirmative action under which Weber had been denied admission to the training program. The court reasoned that the plan in question furthered the objectives of Title VII—to open job opportunities to blacks, and it did not "unnecessarily trammel the interests of white employees," i.e., no whites lost their jobs in the process. The court carefully considered the section in Title VII which says that no employer is required "to grant preferential treatment to any individual or to any group because of race. . .." But it concluded that a proper reading interprets this phrase to mean that employers are not *required* to make preferential decisions, rather than that employers are forbidden to utilize preferential criteria in voluntary affirmative action plans.

From a public sector perspective, the distinction between the Bakke and the Weber cases is important. Some commentators have concluded simply that the courts will tolerate more preferential treatment in employment than in education. However, others stress that the Weber case differed from Bakke because in Bakke the action of a state institution, University of California-Davis, was involved. The 14th Amendment prohibits states from treating citizens differently based upon their placement in state established categories, except where the category can be justified by a judicially acceptable state purpose. Racial classifications typically fall under judicial scrutiny. Under this reasoning public sector voluntary preferential treatment strategies, even in employment, may be open to question. (Rosenbloom, 1979.) However, at least two recent lower court decisions signal that the Weber rule will apply to governmental as well as private employers.

In March of 1980, the California Supreme Court issued a decision in a Weber type case, supporting voluntary affirmative action taken by a public employer (*Price vs. Civil Service Commission, 1980*). In this case, the County of Sacramento had adopted a race-conscious affirmative action plan. Under it, the Civil Service Commission issued a rule that two blacks should be hired for every one white in the district attorney's office. The district attorney went to court challenging the legality of the practice. He argued that under the Bakke precedent such a strategy would be illegal. However, the court ruled that both Bakke and Weber would permit such race-conscious plans.

Also, the 8th Circuit Court of Appeals decided in a reverse discrimination case that public employers may lawfully bypass white applicants if they do so in accord with a bona fide affirmative action plan implemented to remedy past discrimination. In *Valentine v. Smith, et al.* (1981), the court concluded that neither Title VII nor the 14th Amendment was violated when the Arkansas State University failed to hire a candidate deemed "most qualified" in favor of a black applicant. The Court of Appeals said that the university had been "substantially motivated by a race-conscious choice" in order to implement its affirmative action plan. The court sanctioned this action. While to be sure all of the evidence is not in, the U.S. Supreme Court has not spoken on the issue, it appears that public managers may enjoy the same protection from reverse discrimination suits that the Weber decision provides for their private sector counterparts.

THE MANAGER'S ROLE IN EEO: DIAGNOSING ORGANIZATIONAL PROBLEMS

The public manager today faces a difficult and challenging task in implementing EEO/AA policy. The managerial role calls for awareness of the role of management and organization in the overall task of working toward EEO objectives. While the broad environment of the organization is important to the implementation of Equal Employment Opportunity, the organization itself is also a critical element in the implementation process (Stewart, 1980). Equal Employment Opportunity can break down because of attitudes of either managers or protected group members. Managers can contribute to this breakdown by holding low expectations for members of protected groups. Some managers maintain a sense of personal uneasiness in interpersonal interaction with protected group members. Other managers may hold on to conventional stereotypes, such as "women crack under pressures," or "blacks are unreliable workers." Members of protected groups might also contribute to the breakdown of EEO implementation by maintaining low confidence levels, by holding limited visions of possibilities for movement, or by failure to recognize their own strengths.

Sometimes equal employment opportunity breaks down because of features of the organization itself. Organizational structures can militate against effective equal employment opportunity when the upper levels of the hierarchy leave little room for delegation of work. As well, organizations with highly specialized requirements within job classifications allow little possibility for horizontal movement. Finally, when there is no meaningful performance appraisal and career development program in an organization, protected group members may suffer. Organizational procedures can also frustrate equal employment opportunity. Such is the case when no conscious effort is made to include in the recruiting process schools or community groups representing protected group members, or when organizational communications materials include sexist language or people in race/sex stereotyped roles. Protected group members are also hurt when no procedure exists for regular open posting of job opportunities. Of course, this discussion is not comprehensive, but only suggestive of the kind of elements in organizational life that act against meaningful EEO enforcement.

An affirmative action program should be based on a careful diagnosis of the barriers to equal opportunity in the organization. Once the problem areas are diagnosed a specific intervention tailored to that problem should be implemented. Typical interventions under each category would include strategies found in Table 9.

TABLE 9. Strategies for Achieving Affirmative Action Objectives Intervention

Attitudinal Intervention		Organizational Intervention	
Managers	Protected Group Members	Structure/Process/ Procedure	Affirmative Action Specific
Sensitize to issues of discrimination	Individual career counseling	Open posting of job opportunities	Program to upgrade skills targeting protected group members
Train in how to provide informal support to protected group	Disseminate information on successful protected group members	Maintain comprehensive recruiting system	Regular review or organizational practices to identify disparate effect on protected group members
Identify managers with attitude problems and counsel individually	Target protected group persons for career development workshops	Employ a routine method for validation of selection criteria	Establish quantitative objectives for protected group members in all jobs/levels/functions
Program of positive reinforcement for managers successful in EEO	Encourage protected group employees to take educational leave	Maintain an explicit performance appraisal system oriented to career development	Institute negative reinforcement for managers failing to meet their goals or bringing legal action by their behavior
Survey feedback of EEO progress to managers	Offer assertiveness training	Maintain clear criteria for termination	Require protected group members to be among those interviewed for any opening
Provide full information to managers about A/A program and plan	Establish formal sponsorship systems	Routinely reexamine job classifications	Develop internal and external reporting systems monitoring EEO progress
			Develop A/A-directed recruiting system
			Program of spot checks in divisions for AA/EEO compliance

CONCLUSION

In organizational change normatively committed organizational leaders are the key variable. (Chapter 8). This chapter is premised on the thesis that assuring equal opportunity in the organization turns on qualities of organizational management. EEO progress is forwarded by public managers knowledgeable about EEO policy and mechanisms for enforcement, capable of designing rigorous EEO programs, sensitive to the equity issues involved and cognizant of the constraints and opportunities inherent in the managerial role. As we see the 1980's the regulatory environment has become placid. We can increasingly expect changes in EEO policy to occur less at the center and more at the margins of public policy as it is now defined. To the measure that this forecast is on target, the strategic factors in assuring success are management knowledge of, and commitment to equal employment opportunity as public policy and management skill in applying principles of individual and group behavior to produce organizational change.

ENDNOTE

1. This discussion of the Public Policy Environment is drawn from Debra W. Stewart, Assuring Equal Employment Opportunity in the Organization, *Handbook on Public Personnel Administration and Labor Relations* (ed.) Jack Rabin, *et al*, New York: Marcel Dekker, 1983.

REFERENCES

Aguilera vs. Cooke County Police and Corrections Merit Board (1976). MD. Ill., 11-26-76, No. 77 C 3452.

Albemarle Paper Company vs. Moody (1975). 422 U. S. 405.

Allen vs. City of Mobile (1978). 331 FSupp 1134, Affiliated 122, Cert. Den. 412 U. S. 909.

American Tobacco Company vs. Patterson (1982) U.S. Supreme Ct., 4-5-82, No. 80-1199.

Blumrose, A. W. (1972). Strangers in Paradise: Griggs vs. Duke Power Company and the Concept of Discrimination. *Michigan Law Review* 59.

Bridgeport Guardians, Inc. vs. Civil Service Commission (1973). 482 F.2d 1333.

Carter vs. Gallangher (1971). 452 F.2d 315.

Chaplin vs. Consolidated Edison Co. of New York (1980) FSupp.

Communication Workers of America vs. EEOC (1978). 556 F.2d. 167, Cert. Den. 438 U. S. 915.

Contractors Association of Eastern Pennsylvania vs. Secretary of Labor (1971). 442 F.2d 1959, Cert. Den. 404 U. S. 954.

Diaz vs. Pan American World Airways (1971). 404 U. S. 950.

EEO Compliance Manual (1979a). Paragraph 70,053. Englewood Cliffs, New Jersey: Prentice Hall Publishers.

Franks vs. Bowman Transportation Company (1976). 424 U. S. 747.

Geduldig vs. Aiello (1974). 417 U. S. 484.

General Electric Company vs. Gilbert (1976). 429 U. S. 125.

Griggs vs. Duke Power Company, (1971). 401 U. S. 424.

Gunther vs. the County of Washington (1981) 452 U.S. 161.

Hart vs. County of Alameda (1979). N. D. Calif, 9-6-79, No. C-79-009.

Haughton, vs. McDonnell Douglas Corporation (1977). 553 F.2d 561, Cert. Den, 434 U. S. 966.

Hazelwood School District vs. United States (1977). 433 U. S. 299.

Hodgson vs. Daisy Manufacturing Company (1970). 445 F.2d 823.

Hodgson vs. Greyhound Lines (1975). 499 F.2d 859, Cert. Den. U. S. S. CT.

Horner vs. Mary Institute (1980). - F.2d -.

Joyce vs. McCraine (1970). 320 F.Supp. 1284.

Laugesen vs. Anaconda (1975). 510 F.2d 307.

Laffey vs. North West Airlines, Inc. (1976). 567 F.2d 429.

Leach, D. E. (1979). An Emerging Concept: Equal Pay for Work of Equal Value. *EEO Compliance Manual*, par. 219. Englewood Cliffs: New Jersey: Prentice-Hall.

Marshall vs. Board of Education of Salt Lake City (1977). D. Utah, 5-24-77.

Mass Board of Retirement vs. Murgia (1976). 427 U. S. 307, 312.

McDonald vs. Santa Fe Trail Transportation Company (1976). 427 U. S. 273, 281.

Monell vs. Department of Social Services (1978). 436 U. S. 658.

Moon vs. Roadway Express, Inc. (1980). - F.2d -.

Owen vs. the City of Independence, Missouri (1980). - U. S. -.

Paxman, et al. vs. Campbell et al. (1980). - F.2d -.

Pearce vs. Witchita County (1979). 590 F.2d 128.

Personnel Administrator of Mass. vs. Feeney (1979). 442 U. S. 256.

Phillips vs. Martin Marietta Corporation (1971). 400 U. S. 592.

Price vs. Civil Service Commission (1980). 1-25-80, 80 Daily Journal, D. A. R. 273.

Regents of the University of California vs. Bakke (1978). 483 U. S. 265.

Rogers vs. Frito-Lay, Inc. (1980). - F.2d -.

Rosenbloom, D. H. (1979). Kaiser vs. Weber: Perspectives from the Public Sector. *Public Personnel Management*. 8:392-397.

Rosette Contractor Co. vs. Brennan (1975). 408 F.2d, 1039, 1041.

Sears, Roebuck and Company vs. Attorney General (1979). - F.Supp -.

Senate Committee on Labor and Public Welfare (1971). Senate Report. 92-415, October 28, 1971.

Shuck, P. H. (1979). The Graying of the Civil Rights Law. *Yale Law Journal*. 89: pp. 23-93.

Schultz vs. Wheaton Glass Company (1970). 421 F.2d 257.

Stewart, D. W. (1980). Organizational Variables and Policy Impact: Equal Employment Opportunity. *Policy Studies Journal*. 8:pp. 870-878.

Teamsters vs. United States (1977). 431 U. S. 324.

Thompson, J. J. (1973). Preferential Hiring. *Philosophy and Public Affairs*. 2: pp. 364-384.

Townsend vs. Nassau County Medical Center (1978). 538 F.2d 314, Cert. Den. 98 S.Ct. 732.

United Airlines vs. McMann (1977). 434 U. S. 192.

U. S. vs. City of Chicago (1977). 549 F.2d 415, 430.

United Steel Workers of America vs. Weber (1978). 443 U. S. 193.

Usery vs. Tamiami Trail Tours, Inc. (1976). 531 F.2d 224.

Valentine vs. Smith (1981). 8th Cir., 7-21-81, No. 80 - 1460.

Weeks vs. Southern Bell Telephone and Telegraph Company (1969). 408 F.2d 228.

White vs. Dallas Independent School District (1978). 581 F.2d 556.

MANAGEMENT ETHICS

The application of management ethics is one of the most challenging facets of good management. It requires action based on a firm grasp of organization concepts and theory. Unlike decision making in the areas of performance appraisal, management systems, and equal employment opportunity—where research has provided a smorgasbord of well-described and tested techniques and strategies—applying management ethics to everyday situations presses the innovative capabilities of the public manager. Public managers must create the ethical understanding which will guide them.

Though morality is an important regulator of human action, standard treatments of organizational behavior seldom address ethics.* In one of the few texts devoting a chapter to ethics, Bradley and Wilkie explain the apparent aversion of most scholars to exploring ethics to audience discomfort with the issue. (Bradley and Wilkie, 1964.) In the public sector this has not always been so. The literature surrounding the Pendleton Act of 1883, which enacted the basic framework for modernization of the public sector, is replete with ethical overtones. But in the 1920's, as scientific management brought a businesslike orientation to government and an engineering mentality to administration, ethical reflection became passé. New thinking focused on work flow and physical layout analyses as private sector management contributions worthy of adoption by public managers. (Simmons and Dvorin, 1977.)

Through much of the twentieth century students of organizational behavior in the public sector have been playing catch-up with their private sector counter-

---

*This chapter adapts Waldo's distinction between "moral" and "ethical." *Moral* signifies right behavior in an immediate and customary sense; *ethical* signifies right behavior as examined and reflected upon. (Waldo, 1980.)

parts striving to describe the public sector organization by making adjustments to theories and concepts generated for analysis of private sector organizations. This approach to defining research questions and seeking usable theories has had significant implications for the range of subjects considered. Models of organizational behavior in the private sector are founded on the assumption of one overriding principle which precludes most ethical debate: the principle of maximization of profit. This means that organizational behaviors are judged as "good" or "bad" depending on how they contribute to making a profit.

Though the public sector setting always encouraged ethical discourse, public organizations relied on managers who emulated the private sector, discouraging ethical considerations. But the events of the 1970's changed all that. Briefly, two factors led to renewed concern with public management ethics: the dramatic drop in public confidence in social institutions, and the Watergate affair. The first the public ascribed to the failure of leaders to act ethically (Bowman, 1981), the second confirmed their feelings by revealing corruption and betrayal of public trust at the pinacle of democratic government.

For whatever reason, students and managers of public organizations are again discussing the ethical dimensions of organizational behavior. But where the ethically sensitive "reformer" of a century ago found a fairly straightforward remedy to the "morality" problem in government organizations, today's observer confronts complexity and ambiguity. In most areas of management, we try to provide managers with answers. Treatment of ethics requires a different approach, stimulating managers to ask the right questions. This chapter discusses material relevant to this questioning process.

First we compare the disparate definitions of public management ethics to the apparent consensus on "the ethical question" a century ago. Next we describe three major avenues managers may take in thinking about ethics. Finally we advance a matrix capturing the major dimensions of variation and fit a strategy to each intersection.

ETHICS DEFINED

When governmental reformers argued for passage of the Civil Service Reform Act of 1883 (the Pendleton Act) their argument was moral. A striking unity of perspective prevailed on the character of the moral challenge occasioned by the spoils system. The reformers were persons deeply concerned with liberty who saw "spoils" as enslaving the body politic. (Van Riper, 1958.) Civil service reform was held forth as the instrument for elevating the moral tone of political life. (Van Riper, 1958.) Quite simply, civil service reformers of the Guilded Age defined ethics in government as synonymous with civil service reform. A century later ethics in public service again commands considerable attention. But in the 1980's attention and discussion belies the consensus of our ethically-confident Victorian forefathers.

Even a casual reading of contemporary public management ethics literature reveals competing definitions. Often ethics is defined for the practicing manager as a "set of standards by which human actions are determined to be right or wrong." (Bowman, 1981.) Some definitions stress the subjective nature of managerial ethics: "An ethical problem is one where at least some of the actors actually perceive a dilemma of competing ethical criteria (or ethical criteria competing with pragmatic considerations) being raised by some action." (Godfrey and Zashin, 1981.) Other definitions shift the focus of ethics to impact: "[ethics] is concerned primarily with the impact of decisions on people within and without organizations, individually and collectively. Any action which has a present or potential impact on human beings involves ethics." (Evans, 1981.) One recent contribution tries to invade ethics territory by turning to the concept of administrative discretion and sees the exercise of individual power at the root of ethics for the public manager. (Worthley, 1981.) The common thread which runs through most definitions of ethics is some notion of obligation.(Waldo, 1981.) Taking the concept of obligation as a common theme, it is possible to identify three distinct approaches to analyzing public management ethics today. Each approach yields a dichotomous variable. The first approach focuses on the agent bearing the obligation, the individual or the organization. The second approach considers the negative or affirmative nature of the obligation incurred. The third approach analyzes loci of response to the obligation, or whether the source of the regulation is internal or external. While this way of partitioning the ethics field does not deny obvious interdependencies across approaches, it is a mechanism for sorting through current analyses.

APPROACHES TO ETHICAL ANALYSIS[1]

The Moral Agent: Individual or Organization

It has been nearly a decade since Harlan Cleveland observed that "The first line of defense against antipublic actions by Public Executives is to develop their own moral sensitivities." (Loucks, 1981.) Lodging responsibility for ethical judgment with individual administrators underpins the popular press admonitions to public officials. Fitting with this perspective, the postmortem on the Watergate experience in the mid-1970's diagnosed the "Watergate Affair" as a problem of character failure.

However, managers on the front line rarely encounter issues that present themselves as involving a choice between "doing the right thing" or "doing the wrong thing." On the contrary, managers typically report that the first question confronting them when they believe they are facing a moral dilemma is whether or not they have any right to self-consciously treat their decision as an ethical one. Before even getting to "what is good" or "what is moral," most managers ask: "What right do I personally have to exercise moral judgment in this case?" (Powers and Toffler, 1980.) Does this dilemma call for responsible action from me or from the organization? Thus, the first conceptual distinction managers must make in facing moral judgment is identification of the moral agent.

Personal ethics determines right or wrong individual behavior in interaction with others in the organization. Organizational ethics serves to set the parameters and specify the obligations for the organization itself, and defines the context within which personal ethical decisions are forged. Probing the natures of personal ethics and organizational ethics in a public agency setting provides a firm basis for considering critical areas of interaction.

On the personal or individual level available evidence suggests that ". . .managers are interested in ethical issues and can identify them as being associated with rules and standards, morals, right and wrong, and values of honesty." (Bowman, 1981.) The source of the ethical dimension for the individual public manager is his/her authority to take action affecting persons inside and outside the organization. (Worthley, 1981.) Given that authority, Stephen Bailey describes the mind set needed for ethical behavior in the public service as a blend of moral qualities and mental attitudes. The requisite mental attitudes include awareness of moral ambiguity inherent in the public service, appreciation of contextual forces that play in decision situations and sensitivity to the "paradoxes of procedures" which might lead to rules frustrating reponsible action. Qualities supporting ethical attitudes are optimism, courage, and charity, or a willingness to lose oneself in public service. (Bailey, 1965.) While such a mind set may well equip a public manager for ethical decision making, the real world of practicing administration often challenges these qualities to their limits. The public employee is expected to behave competently, efficiently, honestly, loyally, responsively, fairly, and accountably with no clear directions on priorities. Worthley describes in rich detail the competing claims placed on the individual moral actor in the public agency today:

> "At the micro level, the level of the individual employee, this is no smooth environment in which to work. The tax auditor reviewing a tax return is faced with supporting efficiency (reviewing the most returns possible), fairness (taking time to inform me of what he is doing and giving me an appeal), accountability (responding to his appointed superior who says to take it easy on middle income returns), and the rule of law (doing precisely what the regulations stipulate). The caseworker faces the rule of law (which specifies eligibility), responsiveness (listening to all applicants), honesty (reporting the exact income figures), expertise (judging whether an applicant is truly in need), and efficiency (processing the most cases possible). And the supervisor is expected to be responsive (understanding and sympathetic to subordinates), fair (treating all subordinates with the same standard), legal (enforcing the rules and conforming to civil service regulations), and expert (handling each subordinate with managerially sound methods). What does one do?" (Worthley, 1981.)

It is in this context that the organization emerges as the institution capable of either guiding individual members through this series of ethical tug-of-wars or compounding and rigidifying ethical dilemmas. Bowman reports that when faced with ethical dilemmas people turn first to the immediate organization itself for help. (Bowman, 1981.) But with the growth of organizations in both size and complexity has come a diffusion of responsibility and accountability so that there are no specific persons charged with setting standards. (Bowman, 1981.) When individual judgment reflects group norms, the organization becomes the moral community, the referent for determining right from wrong. (Bowman, 1981.) With the organization as the moral community the supervisory role incorporates some elements of the moral advisor; public managers become normsetters. (Rizzo and Patka, 1981.)

It is in the interaction between individual and organizational ethics that some of the most difficult issues and greatest opportunities arise. From the vantage point of the organization, the atmosphere cultivated can foster either integrity or baseness among employees. An organization which presses individuals to achieve results while disregarding means fosters unethical behavior. (Bowman, 1981.) The individual who challenges the agency must weigh his or her own assessment of right against that of the organization. In cases of irresolvable conflict it may be necessary for the individual to leave the organization. But typically conflicts between individual and organizational judgment of "good" center on a competing claims issue. For example, one public manager reported the following dilemma.

> Recently I encountered a problem involving my interpretation of the law as opposed to the division director's interpretation of the law. Based on my experience in another program, I am certain that case law in this area supports my interpretation. While it was my desire to request an "opinion" from the office of the state attorney general in an attempt to receive the favorable ruling for a client, the director vetoed this and ruled the case closed. My dilemma was this: Should I have informed the client to request an opinion from the AG's office, thereby going over the head of the director, or should I honor the order of the director and close the case?

Viewed from the perspective of the organization as a whole, broad program interests might be served by the director's decision to close the case. Perhaps the division director wanted to delay a premature ruling in the hopes that a ruling at a later point would benefit a larger proportion of the program clientele. The competing claims at stake in this case would be those of the individual client versus those of the entire program clientele. After weighing the interests involved, the administrator recounting this dilemma must still consider his or her own ethical burden: What powers does the individual administrator have? What obligations go with these powers? What are the limits of one's authority and responsibility?

George Graham advises the administrator to be guided by the following rules when such dilemma arise:

> Recognize that the rules of the game permit him to contest a decision made by his own organization, but not yet final, by going over his superior's head, or by going to other organizations within the government. . .only when he can honestly ensure himself 1) that a mistake is being made on an

*issue of major public importance; 2) that his judgment is unbiased by per-
sonal or partisan, as opposed to public interest, considerations; 3) that the
risk he runs of being forced out of government is justified by the importance of the issue; and 4) that what will be lost by the decision outweighs
the value of his probably future usefulness to the government if he continues in government. . .*

*[Finally] resign if he cannot accept valid interpretations of the law
by higher administrative authorities which would control his action. . .
(Graham, 1974.)*

The literature focusing on the nature of the moral agent touts a prescriptive
theme. It sees the organization as capable of encouraging or discouraging ethically
appropriate behavior. The manager is held accountable for setting the atmosphere
for the unit or agency. Managers determined to cultivate an ethically sensitive
climate in an agency could provide mechanisms for making ethical concerns a
matter of normal consideration, such as introducing ethics into training programs.
These managers would promote or reward those employees who welcome an open
and ethically sensitive atmosphere. (Godfrey and Zashin, 1981.)

Nature of Obligation: Negative or Affirmative

A second question designed to sharpen the ethical skills of public managers asks:
what is the nature of the obligation of administrators to act? When does the situation give rise to negative responsibilities; when are affirmative responsibilities engaged? The guideline presented here suggests that negative responsibilities are
more stringent than affirmative responsibilities; or the responsibility to avoid harm
to others is a more stringent obligation than the responsibility to help others. In
an essay on corporate ethics, Mike Rion uses a personal example to illustrate this
point:

*Suppose you encounter a beggar soliciting donations as you walked
down the street of a large city. Should you make a contribution? Should
you aid her to find shelter or even take a continuing interest in her welfare
. . . ? The answers are not obvious, for they depend upon your understanding of why persons must beg, your charitable commitments and priorities,
and your financial means. Judging affirmative responsibilities to do good to
others can easily lead to disagreements about values and appropriate roles
but if asked whether you should intentionally push the beggar off her chair
into the rain puddle, surely all moral agents would say that you should not.
Morally, we agree that we should not harm others. (Rion, 1980.)*

Traditionally ethics in public administration has meant the negative obligation
to do no harm, to avoid injury. The admonition to avoid waste, public deception,
and other abuses of power, is directed toward abstaining from doing injury to one's
managerial role. No one disputes that the administrator bears a negative obligation
to avoid injuring others in the execution of public service. But the nature of injury
requires careful analysis. Rion offers, as a core definition of harm, the following:

1. physical injury, including direct assault, impairment of health, deprivation of food, clothing, and shelter;
2. deprivation of freedom, including political rights and personal choices;
3. violation of certain moral principles such as promise keeping, truth telling, and justice." (Rion, 1980.)

The manager's challenge is to understand the nature of harm involved in a particular action and then to balance that action against another potential harm inflicted by non-action or by an alternative action. Take the following case related to us by one administrator:

> Client discharge from a teenage drug abuse rehabilitation program is a primary treatment goal of my agency. Discharge is considered only when a client's treatment team reaches consensus about the client's readiness. Recently a treatment team's decision to discharge a young woman from the program was strongly objected to by her parents. Adamant about continuing program treatment for the girl, the parents used influence with a legislator on the appropriations committee to put pressure on the agency head. I am the intermediary between the agency head and the treatment teams. The agency head asked me to intervene and halt discharge plans. He believes there may be some chance the treatment team was wrong in its discharge decision. He also suggests that the level of funding for the entire program and therefore the capacity to meet client's needs in general may be jeopardized by this discharge decision.

Clearly, this case presents potential for injury on a number of fronts. In order to analyze the nature and extent of injury, the manager first asks who the principal "stakeholders" are in this dilemma. Stakeholders are the parties affected by a decision. They might include individuals, groups, and/or organizations. Next managers ask what rights or interests does each party have. Finally the manager considers the nature of all the conflicting values among the stakeholders and rates the relative importance of each value. Doing harm to the interest of some stakeholders might derive from avoiding injury to other stakeholders. In the ethical dilemma reported above the stakeholders would include at least the following:

- the teenage girl;
- the parents;
- the treatment team;
- the legislator;
- the agency head;
- the other clients of the program;
- the administrator reporting the dilemma.

Each of these parties has a potential to be injured by the administrator's response. Avoiding injury to some party is not possible in this case. Often this kind of ambiguity dominates the decision making in the public sector. But the task of the administrator is to sort out these potential injuries, and within his or her authority to select the least injurious decision from the value rankings derived from thoughtful analysis. Viewed from this perspective, though the most stringent obligation of the administrator is to avoid doing harm, defining this obligation in particular context is difficult.

This negative notion of avoiding injury is reflected in the public ethics literature in John Rohr's discussion of the "low road" approach to management ethics. The "low road" emphasizes adherence to formal rules and regulations, the thrust of which are to keep government managers "out of trouble." (Rohr, 1978.) It finds empirical expression in ethical codes, financial disclosure regulations, and broader conflict of interest statutes. While often the first response of an agency newly sensitized to the ethical dimension of organizational life, this negative stress can lead to channeling all ethical reflection into "avoiding infractions." Ultimately, some argue, it can trivialize ethics in management.

The Kew Gardens Principle: Between Avoiding Injury and Doing Good

Conventionally an ethical distinction is made between the obligation to avoid doing harm to others (negative responsibilities), sometimes called the "low road," and doing good (affirmative responsibilities), referred to by Rohr (1978) as the "high road." But before turning to a discussion of this high road, we need to consider those instances falling in between, where a manager may have an opportunity to correct harm caused by others. Some ethicists have argued that managers have an obligation not only to avoid inflicting injury but also to correct injury caused by others. Referred to as the "Kew Gardens Principle," a label borrowed from the widely publicized murder in the Kew Gardens section of New York City, witnessed by 30-40 silent bystanders, the principle tries to highlight conditions triggering obligatory action. The analysis from the Kew Gardens perspective suggests action is obligatory to the extent that the following conditions prevail:

1. *Need*—There is a clear need for aid.
2. *Proximity*—The agent is "close" to the situation, not necessarily in space but certainly in terms of notice.
3. *Capability*—The agent has some means by which to aid the one in need without undue risk to the agent.
4. *Last Resort*—No one else is likely to help. (Rion, 1980.)

The Kew Gardens Principle is offered as a tool to guide managerial decision-making. As Rion suggests: "When claims are pressed on managers by various stakeholders, the four considerations outlined may be useful in sorting through whether the managers are obliged to act. . ." (Rion, 1980.) Take as an example the following dilemma reported to us by a state government executive.

> *A major part of my responsibility requires making decisions affecting*
> *private property. I have to make these decisions as fairly uniformly as pos-*
> *sible. Recently, a property owner used his influence with my superiors in*

*the organization to gain a reversal on a property decision I had made. I can
accept this reversal of my decision as "how things are." The problem is
such actions make it difficult to justify denying reconsideration to other
property owners. This week I received a call from a reporter who had
caught wind of an allegation of unequal treatment and favoritism in the
handling of private property decisions by our office. He wants to know
why some property owners receive favorable consideration and others are
refused. He indicates knowledge of the recent reversal of my decision. I
can easily avoid lying by a no comment. Only my superior and I have the
true information about what happened.*

The question is: does this manager have a more stringent obligation to respond
than that imposed by the affirmative obligation to do good? The Kew Gardens
Principle suggests that a more stringent negative obligation might exist. The public has been injured by favoritism toward a single property owner (need). The
manager in this case is close enough to the situation to have the vital information
(proximity). Whether or not he/she could act without jeopardizing his or her job or
future effectiveness in the organization is uncertain (capability). It does appear
that the manager in this case may be the only one who can come to the aid of
citizens at large (last resort).

To summarize this discussion of the nature of moral obligation for the manager up to this point, the basic moral principle admonishes managers to avoid
doing injury to others. Careful ethical reflection is required to actually define an
injury in terms of all stakeholders involved and to weigh injuries caused by others,
according to the Kew Gardens Principle. This principle identifies an area where
there is a less stringent obligation than in the requirement to avoid injury, but a
more stringent obligation than the affirmative obligation to do good. In the world
of public administration this principle might be the thrust behind institutionalizing
protections for whistle-blowers in organizations.

Affirmative Obligation: Doing Good

The negative responsibilities are discussed above as the most stringent because
"they are minimal; without adherence to these obligations, our generous deeds
would be to no avail. . . In contrast, affirmative responsibilities extend to all human needs and open up a range of actions beyond the resources and capacities of
the individual agent." (Rion, 1980.) The range of affirmative responsibilities is set
by the resources and distinctive roles managers and agencies represent. Since the
"good to be done" in the world is boundless, efficiency and effectiveness regarding primary tasks requires parameters on administrative action in this sphere. Evans
reports that in the last decade the traditional notion of government ethics has
notably expanded to suggest that administrators actively undertake socially-just
acts. (Evans, 1981.) Rohr describes this new thrust as the "high road" approach
to management ethics (Rohr, 1978). It requires public managers to actively work
for social equity, for only then can a public agency be ethical and just. (Evans,

1981.) The proactive drive for social equity can be channeled outside the organization by public policy making and within the organization through personnel practices. Its adherents criticize the older negative tradition for merely proscribing unethical acts. Clark and McInturff indict the negative approach because it constructs a value system which does not encourage positive behavior. (Clark, and McInturff, 1981.) Those who advocate the affirmative notion of ethics call for the development of the moral administrators of the future. They campaign for ethics training for managers which stresses the achievement of social equity.

While this affirmative obligation concept has received considerable treatment in the literature (Dvoren and Simmons, 1972; Frederickson, 1974) many observers question whether practicing administrators typically subscribe to such an expansive obligation. Research on this question is limited, but one study by Evans of 790 public administrators in California does suggest that age is a significant variable shaping adherence to the affirmative obligation stance. Both older and younger administrators support a negative obligation concept; they feel people should not be manipulated and that administration behavior should be honest, efficient, and nonabusive. (Evans, 1981.) But significant age differences emerge on the issue of affirmative responsibilities: ". . .younger respondents believe that an organization should proactively advocate social equity and allocate its resources accordingly." Older respondents by contrast believe government should refrain from this proactive stance. (Evans, 1981.)

Source of the Regulation: Internal or External

The distinction between internal and external regulation composes a third facet of management ethics. Our analysis asks whether the effort to shape ethical decision-making comes from within or without the moral agent, which can be either a person or an organization. If agents are controlled externally, this means their behaviors are chosen by whether they are rewarded or not. (Foster, 1981.) If agents are controlled internally, theoretically, ethics in government will not rely on implementation of often sporadic external controls that can be circumvented.

In a now classic exchange on this issue published in the 1940's, Carl Friedrich and Herbert Finer staked out polar positions. Friedrich (1940) took the position that a public lacking professional and technical expertise could not effectively oversee administrative action. He argued that trust should be placed in professional managers' internal values as a guarantee against abuse of administrative discretion. In contrast, Finer (1941) argued for strengthening political institutions to curb bureaucratic power. In current literature this tension is reflected in Fox's analysis of multilateral accountability versus unilateral accountability in public service. Fox asks the questions: "Where's the proper locus of ethical agency? Where's the authority to interpret the public interest and to act to advance it?" The unilateral (Finer) view sees public administrators as accountable through their political bosses who must stand for elections. Hence external control, exercised through investigating commissions, auditing agencies, and oversight committees, is the proper instrument for ethical monitoring. The multilateral view argues all public servants, elected and nonelected, are accountable to the public. (Fox, 1981.) Logically, widely-spread ethical responsibility will result in more ethical action. (Fox, 1981.) In agreement with Friedrich, Fox also sees professional norms and standards as a meaningful source of ethical behavior.

The empirical world of public management reflects both perspectives on ethical agency. Herbert Simon's discussion of professionalism and neutrality among public servants explains internal regulation in its classic form. Simon argues against an ethically neutral public service in favor of one highly committed to goals dictated by professional standards and values. He sees corruption as more likely to occur in a neutral value-free professional corps than in a heavily value-ladened one. Accordingly, professional codes rooted in positive, goal-oriented values are the best regulating mechanisms for ethical action in public organizations. (Simon, 1967.) But, as Gunn points out, the public at large is no longer willing to trust professional norms: "confused by conflicting evidence over the risks of exposure to a range of hazardous substances, shocked by revelations of such occurrences as the Tuskegee Syphilis experiments. . . , and overwhelmed by disclosures of pay-offs, bribery, immoral conduct, etc. of public officials, the public has demonstrated its desire for more control over the decision-making process." (Gunn, 1981.)

Advocates of financial disclosure laws and regulations anchor the "external" end of the continuum. Aimed at detecting and determining conflicts of interest, financial disclosure laws are at the substantive core of most state ethics codes. (Hays and Gleissner, 1981.) Though financial disclosure regulations vary regarding who and what they cover and how they are enforced, their more epansive versions have come under attack in recent years. One line of criticism is rooted in fears that: 1) excessive severity of financial disclosure laws will weaken the capacity to recruit public servants; 2) the cavalier treatment of privacy inherent in financial disclosure laws might make public servants insensitive to the privacy of citizens they serve; and, 3) financial disclosure laws may treat public officials unjustly by confusing a condition of a "conflict of interest" with actually committing an offense. (Rohr, 1981.)

On the other hand, financial disclosure requirements serve many jurisdictions as the sole mechanism for warding off conflict of interest. Public opinion polls confirm a dramatic drop in the public's confidence in social institutions during the 1970's. (Bowman, 1981.) The argument for financial disclosure regulation is that public confidence can only be bolstered and sustained by an external mechanism clearly in place. It provides a real and symbolic obstacle to private exploitation of public goods.

MATRIX SUMMARIZING DIMENSIONS OF VARIATION AND THEIR INTERACTION

The preceding discussion poses ethical questions designed to stimulate managerial thinking on the ethical dimension of life in the public sector organization. The

TABLE 12.1. Strategies for Ethics Intervention in a Contemporary Ethical
Analysis Matrix

	Individual		Organization	
	Internal Regulation	External Regulation	Internal Regulation	External Regulation
Affirmative Obligation	Establish as performance measures "proactive" behaviors/part of performance appraisal	Establish rewards for excellence external to the organization, eg, bonuses as in the Senior Executive Service	Modify organizational culture to affirm the proactive role	Appoint and empower Advocacy Boards for government programs
Negative Obligation	Select and promote employees exhibiting traditional virtues, eg. honesty, promise keeping	Enact financial disclosure laws, conflict of interest statutes, governmental codes of ethics	Institutionalize protections for whistle-blowers	Appoint and empower legislative oversight committees

matrix presented in Table 12.1 uses each of the analytical divisions as axes which
provide a conceptual framework for locating the range of ethical intervention
strategies in use today.

The strategies appearing in the matrix are simply suggestive of the kinds of
interventions occasioned by the juxtaposition of these three perspectives on
ethical decision-making. This summary does not claim to be comprehensive, but
rather it highlights areas for ethical reflection.

CONCLUSION

Few managers are highly skilled in articulating ethical issues. Still, behavior in
organizations is determined largely by someone's consideration of appropriate or
"right" action. Today public managers need to acquire skills in ethical reasoning
in order to understand behavior within the organization and to find their own
way through the moral ambiguity pervading many administrative decisions. The
starting point for both understanding and steering one's own course is asking the
right questions. (Bradley and Wilkie, 1974.)

The model adopted here is one which urges managers to ask the right questions. To advocate managers asking questions at all is to reject the view that public administrative behavior can be described as either "administrative Darwinism"
(where managers pursue self-interests) or Weberian idealism (where dutiful civil

servants move in obedience to bureaucratic superiors). Rather we stand with those who see administrative discretion as both legitimate and unavoidable (Warwick, 1981). On that basis we conclude that administrative "choice" must inform and be informed by organizational behavior theory and concepts. We end our text with *Management Ethics* to stress this point. As we focus on issues of motivation, leadership and roles, or on the group dynamics accompanying communication, decision making and participation, or on facilitating organizational change, we engage in a process fraught with choices. Applying organizational behavior knowledge to management ethics means using theory and concepts to enlighten those choices.

We began this book by defining management as simply the organization and direction of resources to achieve a desired result. We conclude by noting that in the public sector in particular managers are obliged to manage with self-conscious reflection on the public interest involved. We see public managers of the future as moving beyond the naive morality of the founders of the American Civil Service System (Stewart, 1982) to become ethically mature administrators, sensitive to the responsibility incurred in managing public organizations and willing to ask questions about right and wrong.

ENDNOTE

1. This discussion of "Approaches to Ethical Analysis" is drawn from, Debra W. Stewart, From Expunging Evil to Moral Judgment: The Pendleton Concept of Ethics in a Contempory Ethics Matrix, in *Centenary Issues of the Pendleton Act of 1883*, ED. David H. Rosenbloom. New York: Marcel Dekker, 1982.

REFERENCES

Bailey, Stephen K. (1965). Ethics and the Public Service. *Public Administration and Democracy*. Roscoe C. Martin (ed.), (Syracuse: Syracuse University Press).

Bradley, David and Roy Wilkie. (1974). *The Concept of Organization* (Glasgow: Blackie).

Bowman, James S. (1981). The Management of Ethics: Codes of Conduct in Organizations. *Public Personnel Management*. 10:pp. 59-66.

Clarke, Michael and McInturff, Patrick. (1981). Public Personnel In An Age of Scientificism. *Public Personnel Management*. 10:pp. 83-86.

Dvoren, Eugene P. and Robert H. Simmons. (1972). *From A Moral to Humane Bureaucracy*. (San Francisco: Caufield Press).

_____. (1977) *Public Administration*. (Port Washington, N.Y.: Alfred).

Evans, James W. (1981). A New Administrative Ethic?: Attitudes of Public Managers and Students. *Public Personnel Management*. 10:pp. 132-139.

Finer, Herman. (1941). Administrative Responsibility in Democratic Government. *Public Administrative Review*. 1: (Summer), pp. 335-350.

Foster, Gregory D. (1981). Legalism, Moralism and the Bureaucratic Mentality. *Public Personnel Management*. 10:pp. 93-97.

Fox, Charles J. (1981). Civil Service Reform and Ethical Accountability *Public Personnel Management*. 10:pp. 98-102.

Fredrickson, H. George, ed. (1974). Symposium on Social Equity and Public Administration. *Public Administration Review*. 1: (January/February), pp. 1-51.

Friedrich, Carl J. (1940). Public Policy and the Nature of Administrative Responsibility. *Public Policy*. 1:pp. 3-24.

Godfrey, E. Drexel and Zashin, Elliot. (1981). Integrity in Work and Interpersonal Relations. *Public Personnel Management*. 10:pp. 110-118.

Graham, George A. (1974) Ethical Guidelines for Public Administrators. *Public Administration Review*. 1: (January/February), pp. 90-92.

Gunn, Elizabeth M. (1981). Ethics and the Public Service: An Annotated Bibliography and Overview Essay. *Public Personnel Management*. 10:pp. 172-178.

Hays, Steven W. and Gleissner, Richard R. (1981). Codes of Ethics in State Government: A Nationwide Survey. *Public Personnel Management*. 10:pp. 48-58.

Loucks, Edward A. (1981). Bureaucratic Ethics from Washington to Carter. *Public Personnel Management*. 10:pp. 77-82.

Powers, Charles and Toffler, Barbara. (1980). Overview of Reading Materials for the 1980 Institute of Ethics in Management. (Catalina, Ca. Institute on Ethics in Management).

Rion, Michael. (1980). Ethical Principles. (Columbus, Indiana) (mimeographed).

Rizzo, Ann-Marie and Patka, Thomas J. (1981). The Organizational Imperative and Supervisory Control. *Public Personnel Management*. 10:pp. 103-109.

Rohr, John A. (1978). *Ethics for Bureaucrats*. (New York: Marcel Dekker, Inc.)

Rohr, John A. (1981). Financial Disclosure: Power in Search of Policy. *Public Personnel Management*. 10:pp. 29-40.

Simon, Herbert. (1967). The Changing Theory and Changing Practice of Public Administration. in Ithiel de Sola Pool (ed.), *Contemporary Political Science*. (New York: McGraw-Hill).

Stewart, Debra W. (1982). From Expunging Evil To Moral Judgment, in David H. Rosenbloom (ed.) *Centenary Issues of the Pendleton Act of 1883* (New York: Marcel Dekker).

Van Riper, Paul P. (1958). *History of the United States Civil Service*. (Evanston: Row, Peterson and Company).

Waldo, Dwight. (1980). *The Enterprise of Public Administration*. (Novato: Ca.: Chandler and Sharp).

Warwick, Donald P. (1981) The Ethics of Administrative Discretion., in Joel Fleishman, *et. al.* (eds.) *Public Duties: The Moral Obligation of Government Officials* (Cambridge, Mass: Harvard University Press) pp. 93-127.

Worthley, John A. (1981). Ethics and Public Management: Education and Training. *Public Personnel Management*. 10:pp.41-47.

AUTHOR INDEX

SUBJECT INDEX